# GOVERNMENT REGULATION

## OF THE

# ELIZABETHAN DRAMA

# GOVERNMENT REGULATION

## OF THE

# ELIZABETHAN DRAMA

BY

VIRGINIA CROCHERON GILDERSLEEVE

## GREENWOOD PRESS, PUBLISHERS
### WESTPORT, CONNECTICUT

**Library of Congress Cataloging in Publication Data**

Gildersleeve, Virginia Crocheron, 1877-
   Government regulation of the Elizabethan drama.

   Reprint of the 1961 ed. published by B. Franklin,
New York, as no. 23 of Burt Franklin research and source
works series.
   Bibliography: p.
   Includes index.
   1.  Theater--Great Britain--Laws and regulations--
History.  I.  Title.
PN2044.G6G5  1975      354'.42'00854      75-7238
ISBN 0-8371-8097-X

Originally published in 1908 by the Columbia University Press

Reprinted with the permission of Columbia University Press

Reprinted in 1975 by Greenwood Press,
a division of Williamhouse-Regency Inc.

Library of Congress Catalog Card Number 75-7238

ISBN 0-8371-8097-X

Printed in the United States of America

# PREFACE

In preparing this essay I have, of course, obtained many suggestions from the well-known works of Collier, Fleay, and Ordish,
and especially from Mr. Chambers' admirable *Mediæval Stage*
and *Tudor Revels*, which, in the portion of my field that they
cover, have been of great use to me. So far as possible, I have
based my work on the official documents of the time, in the form
in which they appear in the authoritative governmental collections, such as the *Statutes of the Realm* and the *Acts of the Privy
Council*. But in many instances, of course, I have had to use
transcripts and excerpts made by independent scholars.

In the case of quotations of any considerable length, I have
endeavored, so far as I could, to reproduce the spelling used in
my source. I cannot pretend, however, that there is the slightest consistency in the usage found in my various documents; for
the methods of transcribers vary greatly, — ranging from Mr.
Kelly's apparently exact reproductions of the Leicester Records,
showing every curl and abbreviation, to such forms as some of
Collier's, which are quite modern in spelling save for the
interjection of an occasional final *e*, and to the entirely modern-
ized versions, such as Birch's *Charters*. From the point of view
of my subject, fortunately, this matter is of small importance.

All dates I have expressed in the new style, except in the case
of direct quotations. In these few instances the reader should
bear in mind that according to the old style the year began on
March 25.

I desire to acknowledge my indebtedness to Professor William
Allan Neilson, of Harvard University, who first suggested to me
an investigation into some of the social conditions surrounding
the theaters of Shakspere's day, and to the inspiration of whose
teaching I owe much. My thanks are due also to Professor
William W. Lawrence, of Columbia University, for suggestions,

v

and to Professor John W. Cunliffe, of the University of Wisconsin, for his kindness in assisting me to procure some material. I am chiefly indebted, however, to Professor Ashley H. Thorndike, of Columbia University, who has aided me with constant advice and kindly encouragement, and, from his wide and minute knowledge of the Elizabethan drama, has contributed to my essay many valuable suggestions.

COLUMBIA UNIVERSITY,

# CONTENTS

# GOVERNMENT REGULATION OF THE ELIZABETHAN DRAMA

## INTRODUCTION

THE following study has grown out of an investigation into the conditions surrounding the Elizabethan theaters and the characteristics of the people who attended them. In endeavoring to secure some light on Shakspere's audience, I was led to investigate the standing of players and playhouses in the eyes of the law. Since the facts concerning the government regulation of the drama under the Tudors and the early Stuarts have apparently never been collected in complete and orderly form, — though they have been incidentally treated in various books, — it seemed to me worth while to attempt an account of the laws and regulations, national and local, which affected the drama during this important period of its history.

The results of such an investigation have considerable historical and sociological interest. They illustrate the political and religious controversies following the Reformation, when the still primitive drama was a dangerous controversial weapon. They bring us into touch with the economic and social unrest in the days when multitudes of "rogues, vagabonds, and sturdy beggars" roamed through the country, and the memorable Poor Laws of Elizabeth made the first serious attempt to grapple with this problem, — laws which mentioned strolling "players in their interludes" among many other varieties of "masterless" vagabonds. We see, too, the economic system of monopolies, so widespread under Elizabeth and James, applied to the stage, in the granting to certain favored companies of players royal patents which gave them practically the exclusive right to perform. From the point of view of constitutional history it is interesting to note the development of the Tudor and Stuart despotism, — the gradual extension of royal power and the overriding of the rights of local self-government; so that finally, instead of regulation of plays by municipal and shire authorities, we find an officer of the King's household, the Master of the King's Revels, endowed with absolute licensing power over plays, players, and playhouses throughout the kingdom.

Of more concrete interest is the long controversy over plays in London, with edicts and counter-edicts from the royal Council and the municipal government. In miniature we see here the same conflict as in the civil war which was soon to come, — a spirit of Puritanism and love of civil liberty encountering the increasingly autocratic power of the royal government. This long controversy over the stage is supposed to have helped inflame the Puritans with hatred of the Court and of royal despotism. They were forced to subside for a time, to submit to royal encroachment upon their liberties; but in 1642 and the years that followed they obtained their revenge upon players and Court alike.

In the course of the controversy we gain also an interesting glimpse of the illogical irregularities of the English governmental system, the complicated and confused organization which the government of London had gradually developed, with its uncertain jurisdiction, its privileged persons and places, its laws which might or might not be enforced, its strange relics of guild rights and ecclesiastical exemptions.

From the literary point of view such a study of laws and ordinances is of course valuable only in so far as it throws light on the history of the stage during this golden age. Patents and laws regulating the licensing of plays may be dull reading in themselves, but it is interesting to watch the pen of the censor rigorously expurgating pages of the plays submitted to him, and to speculate on the different lines the drama might have followed had it been free to treat all subjects at will. By far the most striking aspect of the study, however, is the acquaintance it gives us with the actual conditions surrounding the theaters of Shakspere's day, when the Lord Mayor endeavored to suppress them as resorts where the "basest sort of people" rioted and plotted "most ungodly conspiracies," and as abominations which drew down upon the city the wrath of God. Through the maze of conflicting regulations and protesting letters one can catch vivid glimpses of that strange audience for whom Shakspere wrote, — ranging from the noblemen of the Essex conspiracy, who met at the Globe, including the brilliant figure of the young Earl of Southampton, a daily frequenter of the playhouses, down to the rabble of apprentices, vagabonds, and cutpurses who rioted in the pit, to the scandal of all peaceful citizens.

In the essay which follows I have partially abandoned the usual chronological plan, in order to obtain a clearer and more unified view of the development of the different aspects of legislation and regulation. I shall deal first with the general regulation of the drama by the central government, through parliamentary statutes, royal proclamations, council orders, and patents, applying to the country at large. This includes the laws and patents concerning the status of players and the licensing of them, the licensing of playhouses, and, in general outline, the development of the power of censorship. The succeeding section traces the rise of the Master of the Revels from mere manager of court entertainments to regulator of the drama throughout the kingdom, the growth and exercise of his very extensive powers of licensing players, playhouses, and plays. Following this is a fairly minute study of the nature of that censorship of which the Master was the official administrator, as it appears in the expurgations he made, and in the cases when players or playwrights were disciplined for indiscretions. The next two chapters give a somewhat detailed account of the local regulations in London, especially of the long and bitter strife between a municipal government trying to keep plays out of the city and royal authority endeavoring to have them admitted. With details of dramatic regulation in other parts of England I have not attempted to deal. The period is finally and definitely closed by the victory of the Puritan movement. This had caused bitter attacks on the stage during most of the Elizabethan era, and it culminated at last in the Ordinances of the Long Parliament in 1642, 1647, and 1648, prohibiting all theatrical performances whatsoever.

# CHAPTER I

## NATIONAL REGULATION

BEFORE investigating the more interesting details of administrative history in London during the golden years of the Elizabethan age, it is essential to survey the general regulation of the drama by the national government throughout our period, until 1642; that is, to consider such statutes, orders, proclamations, and patents as emanated from royal and parliamentary authority and applied to the kingdom at large. It is convenient to consider such legislation under three general heads, as it concerned itself with the licensing of plays, the licensing of players, or the licensing of playing places. The licensing of plays was the first to receive serious consideration from the government, and may conveniently be treated first.

The licensing of plays evidently involved two questions, — *when* they should be allowed, and *what* they should contain. Sometimes they were suppressed altogether; sometimes merely their content was restricted, — they were censored. The exercise of the censorship in London under Elizabeth and the early Stuarts will be treated in detail in a later chapter. We have here to consider the general history of the censoring power from the beginning of the Tudor period until the Civil War.

When Henry VII ascended the throne in 1485, the drama was already flourishing in England. Mysteries were being performed in many towns and parishes, and moralities were common. Noblemen kept among their retainers companies of professional players, and the King himself had a company in his household.[1] But in spite of all this dramatic activity, apparently no necessity for governmental censorship was yet felt. The regulation of plays seems to have been attended to

---

[1] See below, pp. 22-23.

4

satisfactorily enough by the local civil and ecclesiastical authorities. Not until the troubles of the Reformation and the policies
of Henry VIII began to arouse a spirit of revolt among the
people, did the royal government feel that there was anything to
fear from the content of plays. Then it became evident that
the religious nature of the drama at this time, coupled with
the religious nature of the questions in dispute, made the stage
a peculiarly dangerous weapon.

According to most stage historians, a proclamation in 1533
attempted to regulate the content of plays. It forbade, we are
told, all evil-disposed persons to preach, either in public or private, "after their own brains, and by playing of interludes and
printing of false, fond books, ballads, rhymes, and other lewd
treatises in the English tongue, concerning doctrines in matters
now in question and controversy." Were this authentic, it
would be the earliest formal pronouncement concerning censorship. But no such edict was issued in 1533. This proclamation, as may be seen by a comparison of the phrasing, was that
promulgated by Queen Mary on August 18, 1553.[1] Warton,
in his *History of English Poetry*,[2] by a slip, mentioned the
document as having been issued in 1533, describing it as I have
quoted above and citing Foxe's *Martyrologie* as his authority.
But Foxe mentions no such edict in 1533. He does, however,
on the page referred to by Warton,[3] give at length Mary's proclamation of 1553. Historians of the stage, following Warton's
statement, have continued this error.[4]

Though no formal censoring regulation of this sort was made
at this early date, the drama was already being used for controversial purposes. Even in 1526 Wolsey had felt obliged to
defend himself against the political attacks of a play at Gray's
Inn, John Roo's morality of *Lord Governaunce and Lady
Publike-Wele*.[5] In the religious controversy it is interesting to
note how, under royal sanction, the stage was being employed
as a weapon on both sides, as the policy of the Crown changed.

---

[1] See below, p. 10.
[2] 1824 edition, III, 428.
[3] *Martyrologie* (1576 edition), 1339.
[4] Collier, *English Dramatic Poetry*, I, 119; Chambers, *Mediæval Stage*, II, 220.
[5] Chambers, *op. cit.*, II, 192, 219.

The royal Defender of the Faith smiled at first on dramas in support of the Papacy. In 1527 there is record of a play by the St. Paul's boys before ambassadors from France, on the captivity of the Pope, in which the "herretyke Lewtar" was a character; and in 1528 comedies were acted before Wolsey on the release of the Pope, — also orthodox, no doubt.[1] But in 1533, the year of Henry's marriage to Anne Boleyn, we note a change. A comedy was acted at Court in that year "to the no little defamation of certain cardinals";[2] and in 1537 much offense was given to Bishop Gardiner, the Chancellor of Cambridge University, by the performance at Christ's College of a "tragedie," part of which was "soo pestiferous as were intolerable" — no less a play than the famous anti-papal *Pammachius* itself.[3] The high officials of church and state now seem to have encouraged the use of interludes to spread the Protestant doctrine. There is evidence that Cromwell, especially, found the stage a convenient weapon in the Protestant cause;[4] and Cranmer was apparently in sympathy with this policy, for in 1539 there was an interlude at his house which a Protestant described as "one of the best matiers that ever he sawe touching King John," and which may have been John Bale's famous play.[5]

When thus used to support views favored by the Crown, the controversial drama was graciously approved. But as the spirit of revolt spread through the country, the government discovered that plays could be used also as a weapon of attack by the opponents of the royal policy. In 1537 it was found necessary to prohibit games and unlawful assemblies in Suffolk, on account of a "seditious May-game," which was "of a king, how he should rule his realm," and in which "one played Husbandry, and said many things against gentlemen more than was in the book of the play."[6] A more serious case of seditious use of the drama occurred in York about the same time (the exact date is unknown). We learn of it from a letter written by Henry VIII to some Justice of the Peace in York,[7] regarding the "late evil and seditious

---

[1] Chambers, *Mediæval Stage*, II, 219–220.    [2] *Ibid.*, II, 220.    [3] *Ibid.*
[4] *Ibid.*    [5] *Ibid.*, 221.    [6] *Letters and Papers of Henry VIII*, XII, 557, 585.
[7] Printed in a translation from the original Latin in Halliwell-Phillipps, *Letters of the Kings of England*, I, 354.

rising" in that city at the performance of a "religious interlude of St. Thomas the Apostle." The King has been informed that the disorder was due to the seditious conduct of certain papists who took part in preparing for the interlude, and he exhorts the Justice to prevent any such commotion in future, and gives him authority to arrest and imprison "any papists who shall, in performing interludes which are founded on any portions of the Old or New Testament, say or make use of any language which may tend to excite those who are beholding the same to any breach of the peace."

The passage, in 1539, of the *Act abolishing Diversity in Opinions*, which reasserted the doctrine of transubstantiation, communion in one kind, the celibacy of the clergy, monastic vows, private masses, and auricular confession, marked Henry's reaction against Protestantism, and was followed by persecution of the unorthodox. One Spencer, an ex-priest who had become an interlude-player, was burned at Salisbury for "matter concerning the sacrament of the altar"; [1] and in London a man was "presented for procuring an interlude to be openly played, wherein priests were railed on and called knaves." [2]

Such cases as these led to the first legislation concerning the content of plays, — an important step in the history of governmental censorship. This was the Statute 34 and 35 Henry VIII, cap. 1, passed in 1543, and entitled "An act for the advancement of true religion and for the abolishment of the contrary." [3] With the drama it deals only incidentally. It condemns Tyndale's translation of the Bible and other unorthodox writings, and orders the suppression of anything conflicting with the doctrines authorized by the King. Seditious people, the act states, have tried to subvert the true doctrine not only by sermons, "but allso by prynted bokes, prynted balades, playes, rymes, songes, and other fantasies." Any of these conflicting with the authorized religion are to be "abolished, extinguished, and forbidden." But the act shows no trace of the later Puritan disapproval of plays as such; seditious matter in them it condemns, but their use for proper ends it expressly approves. It provides

---

[1] Chambers, *Mediæval Stage*, II, 221.  [2] *Ibid.*
[3] *Statutes of the Realm*, III, 894.

that "it shalbe lawfull to all and everye prsone and prsones, to
sette foorth songes, plaies and enterludes, to be used and exercysed within this Realme and other the kinges Domynions, for
the rebuking and reproching of vices and the setting foorth of
vertue: so allwaies the saide songes, playes or enterludes meddle not with interpretacions of Scripture, contrarye to the doctryne set foorth or to be sett foorth by the Kinges Majestie."

Any one accused of spreading unorthodox views in such ways
is to be tried before any two of the King's Council or the Ordinary of the diocese (*i.e.* the bishop sitting in ecclesiastical court),
and two Justices of the Peace of the same shire where the Ordinary sits, or before any other person especially appointed for
the purpose. Such censorship as there was, was therefore in
the hands of these officials.

With the accession of Edward VI, in 1547, royal approval
turned again to extreme Protestantism. But during this reign
there was, nevertheless, much difficulty in keeping plays within
proper bounds. We find at the very outset that the actors were
not held in good discipline. On February 5, 1547, the Bishop
of Winchester wrote to the Lord Protector, requesting his interference to thwart the Southwark players' project for a "solemn
play" during his memorial services for the late King, "to trye
who shall have most resorte, they in game, or I in ernest." [1]
Protestant dramas were now written and encouraged by those
high in authority. Edward VI, according to Bale, wrote a
comedy *De Meretrice Babylonica*, John Foxe, the martyrologist,
a *Christus Triumphans*, and Bale himself was of course the
chief Protestant writer of controversial plays.[2] In 1551 the
English comedies "in demonstration of contempt for the Pope"
were reported by the Venetian Ambassador to his government.[3]

It was now the Catholic interludes which needed suppression;
and so serious was the danger of sedition from this source, that
on August 6, 1549, there was issued a royal proclamation prohibiting English plays altogether for the next three months.
"For asmuche as a greate number of those that be common

[1] *State Papers, Dom.*, 1547–1580, 1.
[2] For details, see Chambers, *op. cit.*, II, 217–218, 223–224.
[3] *Ibid.*, II, 222–223.

Plaiers of Enterludes and Plaies," the edict recites, "as well within the citie of London, as els where within the realme, do for the moste part plaie suche Interludes as contain matter tendyng to sedicion and contempnyng of sundery good orders and lawes, where upon are growen, and daily are like to growe and ensue, muche disquiet, division, tumultes, and uproares in this realme; the Kynges Maiestie . . . straightly chargeth and commaundeth al and every his Maiesties subjectes . . . that from the ix day of this present moneth of August untill the feast of all Sainctes nexte comming, thei ne any of them, openly or secretly plaie in the English tongue any kynde of Interlude, Plaie, Dialogue or other matter set furthe in forme of Plaie in any place publique or private within this realme, upon pain that whosoever shall plaie in Englishe any such Play, Interlude, or other matter, shall suffre imprisonment, and further punishment at the pleasure of his Maiestie." [1]

The Act of Uniformity, passed by Parliament in the same year, 1549 (2 and 3 Edward VI, cap. 1), forbade interludes containing anything "depraving and despising" the Book of Common Prayer.[2]

Serious trouble with the drama evidently continued, for on April 28, 1551, another royal proclamation dealt with plays, and made the first attempt to establish a definite system of censorship. The avowed purpose of the edict is the "reformacion of Vagabondes, tellers of newes, sowers of seditious rumours, players, and printers without license & divers other disordred persons." It inveighs at length against sedition, unfaithfulness to the true religion, and lawbreaking, and commands magistrates to enforce the statutes. Devisers of rumors and tales touching his Majesty are to be punished. No one is to print, sell, or distribute anything in English without the written permission of the King or the Privy Council, on pain of imprisonment and fine. Finally, a regulation similar to this one concerning the licensing of printing, is made concerning the censoring of plays: "Nor that any common players or other persons, vpon like paines, to play in thenglish tong, any maner Enterlude, play or mattre, without they have special licence to shew

---

[1] Hazlitt, *English Drama*, 8.    [2] *Statutes of the Realm*, IV, pt. i, 38.

for the same in writing vnder his maiesties signe, or signed by
.vi. of his highnes priuie counsaill." [1]

It was impossible, of course, for the Privy Council to exercise
this censorship with any thoroughness throughout the kingdom;
but in some cases they certainly acted. In June, 1551, for example, the Council apparently considered that even noblemen's
players should not perform before their masters without special
leave, for they granted the Marquis of Dorset permission to
have his players play "only in his lordship's presence." [2] And
in June, 1552, it appears that they had ordered a "cowper"
shut up in the Tower "for the making of plays." [3]

With Mary's accession, in 1553, the pendulum swung again.
At the very commencement of her reign a morality called *Res-
publica* was represented at Court, which was bitterly anti-Protes-
tant in sentiment, and introduced the Queen herself in the character of Nemesis. [4] On the occasion, also, of her marriage with
Philip, there were Catholic interludes and pageants. [5] Her
realization of the danger from the use of the same weapon by
her enemies to stir up Protestant revolt is shown in the long and
interesting proclamation of August 18, 1553. [6] This declares
that the Queen favors the Roman Catholic doctrine, but that
she will not at present compel her subjects to accept it. She
commands them, however, not to stir up any sedition or any
disputes about these matters. Among methods of arousing
revolt printing and playing again appear prominently.

"And furthermore, forasmuche also as it is well knowen, that sedition and false rumours haue bene nouryshed and maynteyned in this
realme, by the subteltye and malyce of some euell disposed persons, whiche
take vpon them withoute sufficient auctoritie, to preache, and to interprete the worde of God, after theyr owne brayne, in churches and other
places, both publique and pryuate. And also by playinge of Interludes and pryntynge false fonde bookes, ballettes, rymes, and other lewde
treatises in the englyshe tonge, concernynge doctryne in matters now in
question and controuersye, touchinge the hyghe poyntes and misteries

---

[1] Hazlitt, *English Drama*, 9–14.
[2] *Acts of the Privy Council*, III, 307.    [3] *Ibid.*, IV, 73.
[4] Printed in Brandl, *Quellen des weltlichen Dramas in England*.
[5] Chambers, *Mediæval Stage*, II, 223.
[6] Printed in full in Hazlitt, *English Drama*, 15–18.

of christen religion. . . . Her highnes therfore strayghtly chargeth and commaundeth all and every her sayde subiectes . . . that none of them presume from henceforth to preache . . . or to interprete or teache any scriptures, or any maner poyntes of doctryne concernynge religion. Neyther also to prynte any bookes, matter, ballet, ryme, interlude, processe or treatyse, nor to playe any interlude, except they haue her graces speciall licence in writynge for the same, vpon payne to incurre her highnesse indignation and displeasure."

In this provision for royal license and censorship no express mention is made, as in Edward's proclamation of 1551, of the license by six of the Privy Council as alternative to the royal permission. But it was evidently through the Council that the royal authority was exercised. In spite of the proclamation, troubles with plays were frequent, and we find the Council vigilantly interfering in various parts of the country. In 1556 and 1557 the difficulties seem to have grown acute. On February 14, 1556, the Privy Council ordered Lord Rich, the Lord Lieutenant of Essex, to stop and investigate a play about to be given in that county, and report to the Council.[1] In the following April they directed the Lord President of the North to suppress a company of players who had "wandered abowt the North partes, and represented certaine playes and enterludes, conteyning very naughty and seditious matter touching the King and Quene's Ma^{ts} and the state of the realme, and to the slaunder of Christe's true and Catholik religion, contrary to all good ordre, and to the manifest contempt of Allmighty God, and daungerous example of others." The Council directed the Lord President of the North to give orders to all the Justices of the Peace within his rule that "they doo in no wyse suffer any playes, enterludes, songues, or any suche lyke pastymes whereby the people may any wayes be steryd to disordre, to be used by any manner p'sonnes, or under any coulour or pretence."[2] It is evident from this that, in spite of the proclamation limiting the licensing power to the Crown, the actual exercise of censorship, the responsibility of determining whether any play contained seditious

[1] *Acts of the Privy Council*, V, 234, 237.
[2] Letter printed in Lodge, *Illustrations*, I, 212–213.

or heretical matter, rested with the Justices of the Peace and other local officials.

In May there is another mention of an order "against players and pipers strolling through the kingdom, disseminating sedition and heresies."[1] In June of the following year, 1557, the Council ordered the Mayor of London to arrest players who had been giving "naughty plays," and to permit no play henceforth within the City "except the same be first seen and allowed"[2] — presumably by the municipal officials. In the same month the Mayor of Canterbury arrested some actors and sent their "lewd play-book" to the Council for its consideration.[3] The boldness of the players apparently became so great that the Council decided to forbid all plays during the summer. Orders to this effect were sent to the Justices of the Peace of every shire,[4] but the enforcement of the rule was difficult. The Council reprimanded the Justices of Essex, because of their laxness in this duty;[5] in September it directed the Mayor of London to prevent the performance of another "lewd play," called a "Sacke full of Newes," at the Boar's Head without Aldgate, to arrest the players, and to send their playbook to the Council.[6] On due consideration the Lords evidently decided that the "Sacke full of Newes" was harmless, for the next day they bade the Mayor release the players.[7]

At the same time they directed him to charge the actors throughout the city "not to play any plays, but between the feasts of All Saints[8] and Shrovetide, and then only such as are seen and allowed by the Ordinary,"[9] —that is, by the Bishop of London sitting in ecclesiastical court. This appears to be the first formal delegation by the Crown and Privy Council of the power of licensing plays, though, as we have seen, in practice such power had been exercised before by local officials. In view of the religious nature of the plays and of the matters in dispute, it was natural that the Bishop should be chosen for this duty in London. As we have found, the Ordinary had before

[1] State Papers, Dom., 1547–1580, 82.
[2] Acts, VI, 102.
[3] Ibid., 110, 148.
[4] Ibid., 118–119.
[5] Ibid., 119.
[6] Ibid., 168.
[7] Ibid., 169.
[8] November 1.
[9] Acts, VI, 169.

this possessed a somewhat similar jurisdiction.[1]  Concerning the Bishop of London's administration of this power, we have no definite information.  In later years, as we shall see, he and the Archbishop of Canterbury sometimes interfered again in dramatic affairs in London.

In tracing the history of the censorship we have now reached the opening of Elizabeth's reign.  Hitherto, as we have seen, such scanty and vague legislation as there was concerning the licensing of plays had reserved this power to the Crown and the Privy Council, except for some authority granted to the Ordinary.  In practice, however, it is evident that the Council did not expect this rule to be followed.  It was obviously impossible for them to overlook beforehand and license plays throughout the kingdom.  There was no definite system of licensing, but they apparently expected the local officials, — the Lord Lieutenants and the Justices of the Peace in the shires, and in the towns the Mayors. — to exercise supervision.  The Council reserved, of course, supreme authority, and in cases of flagrant impropriety they interfered, through the local officials, and sometimes called for the book of the play, to see how serious the matter was.  We shall find that during the early years of Elizabeth's reign practically the same system was in force, though it was now formulated more definitely.

In summing up this early period we should notice also that the censorship and licensing apparently applied to both public and private performances; that it sometimes, however, dealt only with those in English, not with Latin plays; and that the censoring was concerned with suppressing sedition and heresy, — anything likely to stir up political revolt, — and not with matters of decency and morality.

The opening of Elizabeth's reign reveals a situation in the dramatic world not unlike that which confronted her predecessors.  Moderate Protestantism was now again in the ascendant, and steps were taken to prevent danger of sedition from Catholic or other unorthodox plays.  The Act of Uniformity, in 1559 (1 Elizabeth, cap. 2), reënacted the provision of 2 and 3 Edward VI, cap. 1, against "depraving or despising" the Book

---

[1] See above, p. 8.

of Common Prayer in interludes.[1]  In April, 1559, Elizabeth
found it necessary to adopt the precaution used at times by her
predecessors, — that of prohibiting plays altogether for a season.
As in the past, it was felt that summer was the time of greatest
danger from the controversial drama.  This first proclamation
of Elizabeth therefore inhibited all plays and interludes until
the following November.  So, at least, Holinshed informs us,
and he refers to this proclamation as having been issued "at the
same time" as another which he has just been telling us was
made on April 7.[2]  As we find no other reference to this April
proclamation on the drama, and as Holinshed does not mention
Elizabeth's second edict on the subject, in the following month,
it may be that he is here referring rather inaccurately to this
edict of May 16, generally called by stage historians Elizabeth's
second proclamation concerning plays.

It is certain, at all events, that on May 16, 1559, the Queen
issued an important proclamation [3] which explicitly established
a more definite system of licensing plays than had previously
existed, though it was really little more than a codification of
the practice hitherto in use, — supervision by the municipal
officers in towns and by Lord Lieutenants and Justices of the
Peace in shires.  "Forasmuche as the tyme wherein common
Interludes in the Englishe tongue are wont vsually to be played,
is now past vntyll All Halloutyde," the proclamation recites,
"and that also some that haue ben of late vsed, are not conuen-
ient in any good ordred Christian Common weale to be suffred.
The Quenes Maiestie doth straightly forbyd al maner Interludes
to be playde, eyther openly or priuately, except the same be
noticed before hande, and licenced within any citie or towne
corporate by the Maior or other chiefe officers of the same, and
within any shyre, by suche as shalbe Lieuetenaunts for the
Queenes Maiestie in the same shyre, or by two of the Justices
of peax inhabyting within that part of the shire where any shalbe
played."

Then follow instructions to guide the officials in their censoring,

---

[1] *Statutes*, IV, pt. i, 356.  And see above, p. 9.
[2] Holinshed, *Chronicles* (1586–1587 edition), III, 1184.
[3] Printed in full in Hazlitt, *English Drama*, 19–20.

and these show in an interesting way the establishment of the conciliatory policy followed, in the main, during all of Elizabeth's reign, — that of removing the drama altogether from the field of political and religious controversy. "And for instruction to euery of the sayde officers, her maiestie doth likewise charge euery of them as they will aunswere: that they permyt none to be played, wherin either matters of religion or of the governance of the estate of the commõ weale shalbe handled, or treated; beyng no meete matters to be wrytten or treated vpon, but by menne of aucthoritie, learning, and wisedome, nor to be handled before any audience but of graue and discreete persons."

If any shall attempt to disobey this edict, the officials are ordered to arrest and imprison the persons so offending for fourteen days or more, as the case shall warrant, and until they give surety that they will be of good behavior in the future.

This system of censorship by local authorities continued in force undisputed for some fifteen years, nor was it, indeed, ever entirely superseded. We should not imagine, however, that it was ever very rigorously carried out, and that every play was carefully "seen and allowed" before presentation. There must have been great laxness in the administration. Royal authority was still, of course, supreme, and, directly or through the Privy Council, it intervened at will to permit favored plays or to suppress and punish peculiarly flagrant impropriety in dramatic handling of political affairs.

An example of the working of the system is to be seen in a letter of June, 1559, to the Earl of Shrewsbury, Lord President of the North, from Sir Robert Dudley, afterwards Earl of Leicester, on behalf of his servants, players of interludes. They have received, he says, license for their interludes in various shires from the Lord Lieutenants, and he begs that they may be similarly favored for Yorkshire by Lord Shrewsbury. They are "honest men," he assures the Earl, "and suche as shall plaie none other matters, I trust, but tollerable and convenient." [1]

The administration of the system in towns is strikingly exemplified in the Order of the London Common Council, of

[1] Lodge, *Illustrations*, I, 307.

December 6, 1574,[1] which we shall consider at length in a later chapter. In the matter of censorship this provides that, before presentation, plays must be perused and permitted by the persons appointed for that purpose by the Lord Mayor and Aldermen; and the utterance of unchastity or sedition at performances is to be punished by a fine and the fourteen days' imprisonment specified by the proclamation of 1559. Very striking is the emphasis laid upon the necessity of censoring "unchaste, uncomely, and unshamefaced speeches," — a Puritan care for morality in contrast with the purely political attitude of the governmental declarations which we have hitherto considered, concerned, as they were, solely with the suppression of matter tending to sedition.

A few months before this order of the London authorities, the first definite step had been taken towards the establishment of a licensing power which was eventually to supersede that of town and shire officials. The Master of the Revels will be treated in detail in the following chapter; it is here necessary only to survey very briefly his place in the general history of the censorship. An official of the King's household, subordinate to the Lord Chamberlain, he was originally concerned only with the management of court entertainments. In the performance of this duty he naturally overlooked beforehand and expurgated, if need be, plays which were to be performed at Court. The first sign of the extension of this power to outside performances is found in the royal patent to Leicester's players issued on May 7, 1574,[2] which granted them the privilege of performing throughout the kingdom, provided that their plays "be by the Master of our Revels (for the time being) before seen and allowed." The authority here given over one company was immensely extended by a patent to the Master in 1581,[3] which, among other powers, authorized him to "warne, comaunde and appointe in all places within this our Realme of England, as well within Francheses and Liberties as without, all and ev'ry plaier or plaiers, with their playmakers, either belonginge to any Noble Man or other-

[1] Hazlitt, *English Drama*, 27–31. See below, pp. 156 ff.
[2] *Ibid.*, 25–26. See below, pp. 33–34.
[3] *Shakspere Society Papers*, III, 1 ff. See below, p. 51.

wise bearinge the Name or Names or usinge the Facultie of Playmakers or Plaiers of Comedies, Trajedies, Enterludes, or what other Showes soever, from tyme to tyme and at all tymes to appeare before him, with all suche Plaies, Tragedies, Comedies or Showes as they shall have in readiness, or meane to set forth, and them to presente and recite before our said Servant or his sufficient Deputie, whom we ordeyne, appointe and authorise by these presentes of all suche Showes, Plaies, Plaiers and Play-makers, together with their playinge places, to order and reforme, auctorise and put downe, as shalbe thought meete or unmeete unto himself or his said Deputie in that behalfe."

The first part of this passage may refer merely to his selection of plays for court performance, but it could be stretched to other purposes. The latter part certainly confers on him very ex-tensive, if rather vague, powers over all the drama. Since the licensing of plays was a profitable business, it was to the interest of the Master to develop this authority as extensively as possible. This he began straightway to do; but it would be folly to sup-pose that this patent created at once any revolution in the censor-ing of the drama. It was years before the Master's licensing authority was thoroughly established in and about London. It could never have been thoroughly established throughout the rest of the kingdom. But it grew steadily during all our period.

The London officials continued for some time to exercise censoring power; but the system outlined in the Common Council Order of 1574 was apparently not carried out very con-sistently. In 1582, when the Privy Council was requesting that plays be allowed in London, it suggested that the City should "appoint some proper person to consider and allow such plays only as were fitted to yield honest recreation and no ex-ample of evil." [1] The Mayor replied that this suggestion would be carried out, and that "some grave and discreet person" would be appointed to peruse the plays. [2]

When the Martin Marprelate Controversy was raging in 1589, some of the players ridiculed the Martinists on the stage. Though the persons attacked were the adversaries of the Estab-lished Church, the government, in pursuance of its policy of al-

[1] *Acts*, XIII, 404.     [2] *Remembrancia*, 351.

c

lowing no matters of "divinity and state" to be agitated upon the stage, took rigorous steps to suppress all offensive plays. For more effective censorship in this emergency, the Privy Council devised a commission representing the three powers which had been recognized as possessing authority over the drama, — the Church, the City, and the Crown. The Council requested the Archbishop of Canterbury to appoint "some fit person well learned in Divinity," and the Mayor to choose "a sufficient person learned and of judgment." These two were to act with the Master of the Revels, the representative of the Crown, in examining all plays to be publicly presented in and about London, and striking out and reforming "such parts and matters as they shall find unfit and undecent to be handled in plays, both for Divinity and State." [1]

There is no further record of this commission. Whether it was ever appointed and ever acted, we do not know. The episode is interesting and illuminating, however, as showing the conception of the power of censorship in 1589, and the gradual progress of the Master of the Revels towards exclusive licensing power. In 1592, the city authorities refer to his supreme power of licensing plays in and about London,[2] but he does not seem to have established this firmly and permanently until the beginning of the seventeenth century. He appears but dimly in the agitation of the years 1600–1601, when the Privy Council was trying to restrain "the immoderate use and company of Playhouses and Players" in and about London, and sent urgent orders to the Lord Mayor and to the Justices of the Peace of Middlesex and Surrey.[3] In May, 1601, when the Council was displeased by the content of a play at the Curtain, it wrote to the Justices of Middlesex as those having power of censorship, and directed them in the exercise of this.[4]

But by the accession of James I the Master was fairly well established as censor of plays in and about London. As we shall see, he performed this duty rigorously and profitably under

[1] *Acts*, XVIII, 214–216; Collier, *English Dramatic Poetry*, I, 268–269, note.
[2] *Remembrancia*, 352–353.
[3] See below, pp. 190 ff.      [4] See below, p. 100.

the Stuart rule. A slight invasion of his prerogatives is found
in January, 1604, when the royal patent to the Children of the
Queen's Revels provided that Samuel Daniel should approve
and allow all plays to be performed, before the Queen or publicly, by this company.[1]  The city authorities seem to have made
no further claim to licensing plays. The church only occasionally interfered. In 1619, for example, the Bishop of London exercised the right once granted him, by forbidding the
production of *Barnevelt*.[2]  The Crown and the Privy Council,—
still reserving supreme power, of course, — frequently intervened, as we shall see, through the Master or over his head, to
protest against unfit matter in plays or to suppress them altogether at times, as during the plague, in Lent, or on Sundays.
The Lord Chamberlain, as the immediate superior of the Master,
also claimed especial authority over the drama, and towards the
end of the period he frequently acted directly in cases of trouble.
Thus the hierarchy of dramatic rulers ran, — King, Privy
Council, Lord Chamberlain, Master of the Revels; and all the
higher powers interfered at will, though for the most part they
left the exercise of authority to the Master, the servant of the
Crown.

There remains to be considered in this connection some general legislation affecting the licensing of plays, — their content
or their entire suppression at times. The Puritans had a majority in James' first Parliament, and this domination continued.
Its influence now appears in legislation. In May, 1606, an
act was passed "for the preventing and avoiding of the great
abuse of the Holy Name of God in Stage playes, Interludes,
Maygames, Shows and such like." If any person shall, in such
performances, "jestingly or prophanely speak or use the Holy
Name of God or of Christ Jesus, or of the Holy Ghost or of the
Trinity, which are not to be spoken but with fear and reverence,"

---

[1] Patent in Hazlitt, *English Drama*, 40–41.

[2] *State Papers, Dom.*, 1619–1623, 71. Mr. Fleay (*London Stage*, 266), considering the intervention of the Bishop a "remarkable innovation in stage history," thinks the mention of him a mistake, the Lord Mayor being the person
really meant. But, as we have seen, the Bishop had previously possessed such
authority, and the Mayor would not have been likely to interfere at this late
date. See below, p. 114.

he shall, the act provides, be fined ten pounds for each offense.[1]  As we shall see, the Master of the Revels conscientiously endeavored to put this into effect.

The Puritan objection to any sports on the Sabbath also appears in general legislation.  On his accession James issued a proclamation forbidding all "Bearbaiting, Bullbaiting, Enterludes, Common plays, or other like disordered or unlawful Exercises or pastimes" on the Sabbath.[2]  But the extremes to which the Puritans went in their suppression of "lawful recreations and honest exercises" on Sunday annoyed James.  Such exercises were beneficial to the people, he declared, and besides, this prohibition of them would militate against the conversion of papists, who would think our religion allowed "no honest mirth or recreation."  In 1618 the King therefore issued the order known as the "Book of Sports,"[3] and to the indignation of the Puritans commanded that it be published in all parish churches.  This allowed, after evening prayers, on Sundays and holy days, dancing, archery, leaping, vaulting, May-games, Whitsun Ales, and Morris Dances.  But plays were still prohibited, along with bear and bull baitings and bowling.

Apparently these unlawful pastimes still continued, for the first statute of the first Parliament of Charles I was one for "punishing of divers abuses committed on the Lord's day, called Sunday."[4]  The phrasing of this act is strongly Puritan in tone.  Under penalty of a fine, all persons are forbidden to produce or attend the condemned shows, — bear baitings, bull baitings, interludes, etc.  "Lawful sports" are still permitted. The Puritans complained that this prohibition of Sunday plays was not enforced;[5] but to Charles it seemed that the Puritan extremists were again prevailing.  In 1633, accordingly, he ratified and republished his father's order of 1618, declaring that no one was to be molested when engaging in "lawful sports"

[1] 3 James I, cap. 21.  *Statutes*, IV, pt. ii, 1097.  *Journals of the House of Commons*, I, 270, 286, 294, 300.  *Journals of the House of Lords*, II, 416, 419, 422, 436.
[2] Collier, *English Dramatic Poetry*, I, 341.
[3] Printed in Lang, *Social England Illustrated*, 311–314.
[4] *Statutes*, V, 1.  Continued by 3 Charles I, cap. 5. *Statutes*, V, 30.
[5] Prynne, *Histrio-Mastix*, 645, 717; *1821 Variorum*, III, 148, note.

on Sunday. The prohibition of plays on the Sabbath remained as before.[1] Such was the course of general legislation on this subject until 1642, when the Puritans prevailed and prohibited all plays whatsoever at all times and seasons. The details of the London regulations will be considered in a later chapter.

We have followed, in general outline, the history of the power of licensing plays, of determining what might be played, and when plays must be stopped altogether. The next point to consider is the licensing of players. Who might play? How were they licensed? There has been some misunderstanding on these points. The mention in the statutes of unlicensed players as "rogues and vagabonds," liable to brutal punishment, and the frequency with which Puritan writers reproached the profession with this degrading fact, have led people to believe that according to the English law all players were outcasts. It is true that the Roman law regarded the actor as without civic standing, incapable of citizenship, and the early church legislation continued this policy, compelling him to give up his profession before he could be baptized.[2] Though the class of actors against whom these laws were made died out, the medieval church preserved in its legislation much the same attitude towards their successors, the minstrels, regarding them as beyond the pale. But until the growth of extreme Puritanism revived the early church policy on the subject, this attitude towards players does not appear in English law.

No explicit provision for the licensing of actors was made until the statute of 1572; but, as we found in the case of the censorship, when the law came it was little more than a codification of the practices which had already grown up. Our first step is to try to discover what the status of players was during the preceding century or more, when feudal England was passing over to modern.

It is important to bear in mind that, according to the feudal conception of society, every man must have a definite place in

---

[1] Lang, *Social England Illustrated*, 316.
[2] See Chambers, *Mediæval Stage*, I, chap. I, and Thompson, *Puritans and Stage*, 20-21.

the social hierarchy; some personage or organization must be responsible for him; he must owe allegiance to some suzerain, lay or ecclesiastical, or to some guild or town corporation. The unattached person, "the masterless man," was an object of suspicion, an outcast; feudal society had no hold upon him. How, then, did the players fit into this social system? The predecessors of the professional actors, the minstrels, had solved the problem in various ways: they had been retainers of nobles and other powerful personages; they had imitated the trades in organizing guilds with power to license and regulate the profession.[1] By the time the professional players developed, however, it was too late for a guild system to be the natural method of regulation. It was rather the protection of a powerful lord given to his retainers that grew into a licensing system.

As we view the state of affairs in the latter part of the fifteenth century, we find various sorts of companies performing. There were, as every one knows, many plays given in towns, especially the great cycles of mysteries presented by the trades guilds. The actors in these were members of the guilds, in good civic standing, and the performance was generally regarded as a worthy religious act. There were parish plays somewhat similar in character. There were — rather later, perhaps — plays given by pupils in schools, by students in universities, by the young lawyers of the Inns of Court. All these were more or less amateur performances, approved by public opinion; the actors were persons of definite standing in the community; there was, of course, no suspicion of their being "rogues and vagabonds."

Of a somewhat different type were the companies kept by noblemen for their own amusement, — the strictly professional players, descendants, apparently, of the minstrel class. By the opening of the Tudor period these were fairly well established. The earliest of which we have definite record are those of Henry Bourchier, Earl of Essex, and Richard, Duke of Gloucester, afterwards Richard III, both mentioned in 1482.[2] Before the end of the century the Earls of Northumberland, Oxford, Derby,

---

[1] Chambers, *op. cit.*, I, 55.
[2] Collier, in *Shakspere Society Papers*, II, 87–88.

and Shrewsbury, and Lord Arundel, all had their players,[1] and
later the practice became widespread. Royal patronage was
not lacking. Henry VII had four players of interludes in his
household; his son Arthur, Prince of Wales, had a company
of his own by 1498, and Prince Henry, afterwards Henry VIII,
one by 1506.[2] All the Tudor rulers continued to have a royal
company in their household.

As personal retainers of such noble and royal personages,
these players had, of course, adequate protection and a definite
place in the social system. No explicit recognition of their
rights by the law was necessary. The earliest mention of them
in the statutes, in 1463, though merely incidental, indicates a
rather favorable attitude towards them. Together with hench-
men, heralds, pursuivants, swordbearers to mayors, messengers,
and minstrels, "players in their enterludes" are exempted from
the sumptuary law regulating the apparel to be worn by different classes of society.[3] This exemption was continued by later
statutes.[4]

While such town, parish, and household players performed
in their own homes, they were obviously safe from arrest as
vagabonds. It was the players who "wandered abroad" who
needed some definite license to protect them. And they began
to travel very early. The guild and parish players frequently
left their homes. In the towns of Lydd and New Romney, for
instance, we find, as Mr. Chambers tells us, records of the visits
of players, between 1399 and 1508, from no less than fourteen
neighboring places in Kent and Sussex.[5] When their services
were not required in the households of their masters, royal and
noblemen's companies also traveled,[6] playing wherever most
profit might be gained. Court performances by outside companies also began early. Under Henry VII there are records of
payments to players of noblemen and corporate towns, and to
"French players." [7]

[1] Chambers, *Mediæval Stage*, II, 186.      [2] *Ibid.*, 188, note.
[3] 3 Edward IV, cap. 5. *Statutes*, II, 402.
[4] 1 Henry VIII, cap. 14; 6 Henry VIII, cap. 1; 7 Henry VIII, cap. 6; 24
Henry VIII, cap. 13. *Statutes*, III, 9, 122, 181, 432.
[6] *Mediæval Stage*, II, 121. See also *ibid.*, 184–185.      [6] *Ibid.*, 187.
[7] *1821 Variorum*, III, 42–43; Kelly, *Drama in Leicester*, 75, note.

While he could show his connection with some guild or town corporation, or some royal or noble personage, and claim such protection, the traveling player was safe from molestation by the authorities, except in cases of flagrant misbehavior. But the player who wandered without any such connection was obviously a "masterless man," without place in the social system, and if he attracted the notice of the local officials, he was liable — not as player, but as masterless man — to the penalties imposed upon all vagabonds. And these penalties were severe. For centuries England had suffered from the disorders caused by multitudes of such unattached and irresponsible persons. With the Statutes of Laborers, in the middle of the fourteenth century, began a long course of legislation endeavoring to suppress such "vagabonds and valiant beggars." As the feudal households broke up after the Wars of the Roses, as soldiers found no lord to follow to battle, as the monasteries were dissolved, and the monks and the beggars they had fed were thrown upon the world, the necessity grew for rigorous action against the hordes of tramps and rogues who infested and made dangerous the highways. The laws became extremely severe; but severity alone could accomplish little. Under Elizabeth, however, a great series of statutes grappled seriously with the problem, and established what remains to this day the basis of the English Poor Law.[1] It was one of this series which first laid down, in 1572, a definite system of licensing players. But before taking up these provisions in detail, it is well to consider a few incidents of government action showing the situation of players during the period just before the passage of the statute.

The notable act of 1543, already mentioned as the first to suggest censorship, indicates that at this time no license for players was required, at least for mysteries and moralities, for it provides that "it shalbe lawfull to all and everye prsone and prsones, to sette foorth songes, plaies and enterludes, to be used and exercysed within this Realme and other the kinges Domynions, for the rebuking and reproching of vices and the setting foorth of vertue." [2]

---

[1] For the history of this legislation, see Nicholls, *English Poor Law*, I.
[2] See above, p. 7.

There are signs that wandering players were beginning to become prominent among the crowd of other troublesome vagabonds. In 1545 Henry VIII issued a proclamation "for the punishment of Vagabonds, Ruffins, and Idle psons."[1] condemning the evils of vagabondage and declaring that for the reformation thereof the King had decided to employ on his galleys and other vessels, for service in his wars, "all such ruffyns, Vagabonds, Masterles men, Comon players, and euill disposed psons." It is probable from the context, as Mr. Chambers suggests,[2] that "Comon players" here refers to gamblers; or it may be the first appearance of actors in the ignoble classification of vagabonds. The protection of great names had evidently been wrongfully used by wanderers, for the proclamation requires that no one shall avow any man to be his servant unless he really and legally is.

An example of a company traveling under the protection of a nobleman's name is found in the incident already referred to, when, during the acutely troubled times of Queen Mary's reign, in April, 1556, the Privy Council wrote to the Earl of Shrewsbury, Lord President of the North, requiring him to suppress a company which had been presenting "naughty and seditious plays" in the north parts. These players, six or seven in number, had "named themsellfs to be servaunts unto S$^r$ Frauncis Leek," and had worn "his livery and badge on theyr sleves." Evidently Sir Francis was considered responsible for the conduct of his servants, for the Council ordered Lord Shrewsbury to write fo him, "willing him to cause the said players that name themsellfs his servaunts to be sought for, and sent forthw$^{th}$ unto you, to be farther examined, and ordred according to theyr deserts," and commanding also "that he suffer not any of his servaunts hereafter to goo abowte the countrie, and use any playes, songs, or enterludes, as he will aunswer for the contrary."[3]

The liability of unprotected traveling players to punishment as vagabonds is evident in the concluding portion of this letter.

---

[1] Printed in Hazlitt, *English Drama*, 6–7.
[2] *Mediæval Stage*, II, 222, note.
[3] Lodge, *Illustrations*, I, 212–213.

"And in caase any p'sonne shall attempt to sett forth these sorte
of games or pastymes at any tyme hereafter, contrary to this
ordre," — *i.e.* the order given earlier in the letter against seditious
plays, etc. — "and doo wander for that purpose, abrode in the
countrie; yo" L. shall do well to gyve the Justices of Peace in
charge to see them apprehendyd owt of hande, and punished as
vagabounds, by vertue of the statute made agaynst loytering
and idle p'sonnes."

Elizabeth's proclamation of 1559, though containing no
provision concerning the licensing of players, mentions the
companies of noblemen and gentlemen, and recognizes the responsibility of the patrons in seeing that their servants obey the
regulations concerning censorship. "And further her Maiestie
gyueth speciall charge to her nobilitie and gentilmen, as they
professe to obey and regarde her maiestie, to take good order in
thys behalfe wyth their servauntes being players, that this her
Maiesties commaundement may be dulye kepte and obeyed."[1]
We have seen how, in accordance with this order, Sir Robert
Dudley, in the following month, wrote a letter on behalf of his
players to the Lord President of the North.[2]

The operation of this system of licensing — if it may be called
a system — can be observed also in the records of the town of
Leicester, which Mr. Kelly has published. Many traveling
companies appeared in Leicester, and when the Mayor or other
municipal officers had approved of their right to play, they
were permitted to give a sort of official performance. It is
interesting to note the kind of license these companies had, —
that is, under the protection of what personage or corporation
they traveled.[3]   The first company so recorded is in 1530, —
a royal one, the Princess Mary's players. In the following year
the same company came again, and also the King's players.
In 1537 came the Earl of Derby's company and the Lord Secretary's.   Later on appear those of Sir Henry Parker, of the Lord

[1] Hazlitt, *English Drama*, 20.
[2] See above, p. 15.
[3] See the records in Kelly, *Drama in Leicester*, under the years mentioned.
Portions of similar records for other towns may be found in the *Historical MSS.
Commission Reports.*   See, for example, visits of companies to Cambridge from
1530 on, III, 322–323; and to Abingdon from 1559 on, II, 149–150.

Protector, of the Marquis of Northampton, of the Duke of Northumberland, and in 1555 and 1557 the Queen's players. After Elizabeth's accession the "Queen's players" appear frequently, and the number of noblemen's and gentlemen's companies increases. One appears under the name of "my Lady of Suffolk." Companies from other towns also come, — the "players of Coventry" in 1564, 1567, 1569, and 1571, the "players of Hull" in 1568. So runs the record up to the passage of the statute of 1572.

It is evident, then, that in this period, though no license was explicitly required, something like a licensing system had grown naturally out of existing social conditions. Players who wandered abroad needed to have their legal status certified to by connection with some town or some person of rank. Otherwise they were liable to be treated as vagabonds, like other masterless men. The determination of their standing was naturally left to the discretion of the local authorities, — Mayors and Justices of the Peace. In all cases, of course, they were supposed to obey such censorship regulations as there were, and the edicts stopping plays at times.

The famous Statute 14 Elizabeth, cap. 5 (1572),[1] was entitled "An Acte for the Punishement of Vacabondes, and for Relief of the Poore and Impotent." Besides many other provisions, it endeavored to regulate the throngs of wanderers on the highways, and it provided a system of licensing for such of them as were engaged in legitimate business, — proctors, fencers, bearwards, actors, minstrels, jugglers, peddlers, tinkers, chapmen, and scholars of the Universities of Oxford and Cambridge going about begging. Two forms of license were available for players who "wandered abroad." They might "belong to any baron of the realm or other honorable personage of greater degree." Mere gentlemen, who had previously authorized companies, as we saw in the proclamation of 1559,[2] were no longer allowed the licensing power. If players had not the protection of a noble personage, they were required to procure a license from "two Justices of the Peace at the least, whereof one to be of the Quorum, where and in what shire they shall happen to wander."

---

[1] *Statutes*, IV, pt. i, 590.    [2] See above, p. 26.

Subsequent Poor Laws altered this system, steadily limiting the number of those authorized to license traveling players, taking away power from local officials, and gradually concentrating it, theoretically at least, in the Crown. The 39 Elizabeth (1597–1598), cap. 4,[1] no longer permitted the license of two Justices of the Peace. Only barons or other personages of greater degree could license players who "wandered abroad," and the authorization must be in writing, "under the hand and seal of arms of such baron or personage." Finally, the Statute 1 James I, cap. 7 [2] (1604), limited the licensing power to the Crown alone. "Henceforth," it declared, "no authority to be given or made by any baron of this realm, or other honorable personage of greater degree, shall be available to free and discharge the said persons, or any of them, from the pains and punishments" inflicted on vagabonds. This left only the possibility of royal license.

It will be noticed that these laws applied only to players "wandering abroad." This was a vague and elastic term, never, so far as I know, explicitly defined. It might have been taken, one would suppose, to apply to any town actors performing away from their home town, and to any nobleman's or royal company acting in public away from the household and presence of their patron.

The penalties to which the unlicensed traveling player was liable were extremely severe. According to the 14 Elizabeth, cap. 5, if convicted of vagabondage, he was "grievously whipped, and burnt through the gristle of the right ear with a hot iron of the compass of an inch about . . . except some honest person take such offender into his service for one whole year next following." If he left this service, he was to suffer the punishment just described. On a second offense he was to be put to death as a felon, unless taken into service for two years, and if he deserted from this, he was to be executed. On a third conviction he was to suffer death and loss of land and goods as a felon, without allowance of benefit of clergy or sanctuary.[3] These punishments were altered somewhat by later laws. The 35 Elizabeth, cap. 7, substituted setting in the stocks for the burn-

---

[1] *Statutes*, IV, pt. ii, 899.    [2] *Ibid.*, 1024.    [3] *Ibid.*, pt. i, 590.

ing described above.[1]  According to the 39 Elizabeth, cap. 4, the vagabond was to be whipped and sent back to his birthplace or last residence; on repeated offenses to be imprisoned and banished; and if he returned, put to death.[2]  According to the 1 James I, cap. 7, incorrigible rogues, considered dangerous by Justices of the Peace, were to be branded with an "R" and sentenced to labor; on the second offense to be declared felons without benefit of clergy.[3]

When one considers these laws baldly, it certainly seems that players must have been a degraded and outcast class.  But this impression is hardly justified.  Of course the inclusion of any sort of players in such company was discreditable to the profession; and wandering actors must have made themselves obnoxious, to cause their specific mention among vagabonds. But in estimating the significance of the laws, we must remember that the rigor of these statutes was not directed primarily against players.  Their purpose and scope was vastly greater than any mere regulation of actors.  The severity of the penalties was supposed by a brutal age to be necessary for the suppression of the grave dangers of vagabondage.  The 14 Elizabeth, cap 5, recites in its preamble that "all the partes of this Realme of England and Wales be p'sentlye with Roges Vacabondes and Sturdy Beggers excedinglye pestred, by meanes wherof daylye happeneth in the same Realme Murders, Theftes and other greate Outrage."  The remedy of this grave social trouble was the object of the act.  The status of players it touched on only incidentally.

We must remember, too, that the term "vagabond" was applied only to players who "wandered abroad," and only to unlicensed players; and that it was similarly applied to many other classes of people, some of them pursuing occupations considered entirely legitimate, when carried on under the regulations laid down by law.  The significance of the mention of players in this connection can best be seen from a perusal of the very interesting definition of Rogues, Vagabonds, and Sturdy Beggars in the 14 Elizabeth, cap. 5, which gives a vivid picture of English wayfaring life in the days of the great Queen.

[1] *Statutes*, IV, pt. ii, 855.     [2] *Ibid.*, 899.     [3] *Ibid.*, 1024.

"All & every suche p'sone & p'sones that be or utter themselves
to be Proctours or Procuratours, going in or about any Countrey or
Countreys within this Realme, without sufficyent Aucthoritye de-
ryved from or under our Soveraigne Ladye the Queene, and all other
ydle p'sones goinge aboute in any Countrey of the said Realme,
using subtyll craftye and unlawfull Games or Playes, and some of
them fayninge themselves to have knowledge in Phisnomye, Palmes-
trye or other abused Scyences, whereby they beare the people in
Hand they can tell their Destinyes Deathes and Fortunes and suche
other lyke fantasticall Imaginacions; And all and every p'sone and
p'sones beynge whole and mightye in Body and able to labour,
havinge not Land or Maister, nor using any lawfull Marchaundize,
Crafte or Mysterye whereby hee or shee might get his or her Lyvinge,
and can gyve no reckninge how hee or shee dothe lawfully get his or
her Lyvinge; & all Fencers Bearewardes Comon Players in Enterludes, and Minstrels, not belonging to any Baron of this Realme or
towardes any other honorable Personage of greater Degree; all
Juglers Pedlars Tynkers and Petye Chapmen; whiche said Fencers
Bearewardes Comon Players in Enterludes Mynstrels Juglers Pedlers,
Tynkers and Petye Chapmen, shall wander abroade and have not
Lycense of two Justices of the Peace at the leaste, whereof one to be
of the quorum, wher and in what Shier they shall happen to wander.
And all Comon Labourers being persons able in Bodye using loytering, and refusinge to worke for suche reasonable Wages as ys taxed
and comonly gyven in suche partes where such persones do or shall
happen to dwell; and all counterfeytures of Lycenses Passeportes
and all users of the same, knowing the same to be counterfeyte; And
all Scollers of the Universityes of Oxford or Cambridge y$^t$ goe about
begginge, not beinge aucthorysed under the Seale of the said Univ'-
sities, by the Comyssarye Chauncelour or Vicechauncelour of the
same; And all Shipmen p'tendinge Losses by Sea, other then suche
as shalbe hereafter provided for; And all p'sones delivered out of
Gaoles that begge for their Fees or do travayle to their Countreys
or Freendes, not having Lycense from two Justices of the Peace of
the same Countye where he or shee was delyv'ed." [1]

Though they wandered in such company at times, players, as
players, were evidently *not* vagabonds in the eyes of the law.
Players who disobeyed the government regulations were liable

[1] *Statutes*, IV, pt. i, 591–592. Definitions in subsequent laws differ somewhat,
but follow this in the main. Hazlitt notes (*English Drama*, 37, note) that the
Statute 7 James I (1609–1610), cap. 4, directed against Rogues, Vagabonds, and
Sturdy Beggars, contains no mention of "Common Players." This is, however,
of no significance, since the act does not contain any definition or enumeration of
vagabonds, and so would not mention players.

to be considered such, as were other masterless and lawless men. Of course this argument is not intended to imply that actors were, on the whole, high in the social scale; that is a different matter. But to say, as does one of the most scholarly of stage historians, that "but for courtesy and a legal fiction, they were vagabonds and liable to a whipping," [1] seems inaccurate and unjust. As is the case to-day, there were players of all sorts, — some no better than tramps, some, like William Shakspere, high in prosperity and royal favor. The royal patents, which we shall consider later on, show the regard in which many actors were held and their assured legal status. And no player, while he obeyed the regulations laid down by the law, had need to fear punishment as a vagabond. Under Puritan domination, of course, the whole situation was radically altered.

It is interesting to investigate the practical effect of these laws, though it is naturally possible to consider here only a few examples of their operation. So far as we can see, the statute of 1572 made very little change from the conditions which we observed in the preceding period. The number of town players was diminishing; but companies still traveled under royal or noble protection; the validity of their license was still passed on by town and shire officials, who would, however, as in the past, rarely venture to refuse their approval for performances by a properly protected company. Somewhat more regularity and rigor was perhaps observed.

As time went on, and the relics of feudal ideas waned, the players seem to have had a less personal relation to their patron. They were no longer always servants of the household; their noble patron often conferred his name and license on them largely as a matter of form, in token of his approval of the drama, or perhaps sometimes in return for favors received.[2] We have noticed that Sir Francis Leek's company, in 1556, wore his livery and his badge on their sleeves,[3] in token of their connec-

---

[1] Chambers, *Mediæval Stage*, II, 226.

[2] It seems very likely that some of the traveling companies may have purchased from impecunious noblemen the right to use their name and license. Such a commission had a considerable cash value. Later on, royal licenses were sometimes bought and sold, even pawned. See below, pp. 41-42.

[3] See above, p. 25.

tion with him. Later on, as the relation became less personal, the system of a formal written license apparently became common, and this was required, as we have seen, by the statute of 1597–1598.[1] An example of such a license has come down to us, — that shown to the town officials of Leicester in 1583 by the Earl of Worcester's company. The following copy of it is given in the town records: —

"William Earle of Worcester &c. hathe by his wrytinge dated the 14 of Januarye A° 25° Eliz. R$^e$ licensed his s'unts v'z. Robt Browne, James Tunstall, Edward Allen, W$^m$ Henryson, Tho. Coke, Ryc' Johnes, Edward Browne, Ryc' Andrewes to playe & goe abrode, vsinge themselves orderly &c. (in theise words &c.) These are therefore to require all suche her Highnes offycers to whom these p'nts shall come, quietly & frendly w$^{th}$in yo$^r$ severall p'sincts & Corporac'ons to p'myt & suffer them to passe w$^{th}$ yo$^r$ furtherance usinge & demeanynge y$^{em}$selves honestly & to geve them (the rather for my sake) suche intertaynement as other noblemens players haue (In Wytnes &c.)"[2]

Companies still traveled, also, under royal authority. As we have seen, the players of interludes belonging to the royal household had gone on tour during the earlier Tudor reigns and the first years of Elizabeth's.[3] In March, 1583, a new company of the "Queen's servants" was organized, apparently on much the same basis as these earlier household players, but consisting of the most prominent members of the profession.[4] These actors traveled frequently. "The Queen's Majesty's players" are noted as visiting Leicester thirteen times within the years 1582–1602.[5] In 1591 came "the Queen's Majesty's players, being another company called the Children of the Chapel." This deserves further notice. From the time of Richard III it had been customary to issue orders for taking boys with good voices from the choirs of cathedrals and elsewhere in order that they might sing in the Chapel Royal or St. Paul's.[6] Various patents

---

[1] See above, p. 28.    [2] Kelly, *Drama in Leicester*, 212–213.    [3] See above, pp. 23, 26–27.

[4] For a more detailed account of this company, see below, pp. 166 ff.

[5] Kelly, *Drama in Leicester*, under the years cited. Probably this title does not always designate the same company.

[6] See Richard III's warrant in Collier, *English Dramatic Poetry*, I, 41–42, note.

conferring such authority were granted under Elizabeth.[1] These companies of children, as is well known, were used for dramatic as well as choral purposes. A striking case in connection with this same company which we find in Leicester in 1591, came up in 1600, when a complaint was made against Nathaniel Giles, Master of the Chapel Children, and others. Under her Majesty's patent, the complainant declares, Giles has wrongly and unjustly taken children away from schools and prentices from their masters, against the will of themselves, their parents, tutors, and guardians, — children not fitted for singing in the Chapel, but intended by Giles for acting in plays and interludes.[2] The case is an interesting one, and shows how royal patents were sometimes twisted to dramatic purposes.

The Crown also began to show favor to other companies besides those immediately in the royal service. The tendency towards greater formality in the licensing system and towards the concentration of licensing power in the Crown is shown strikingly in the royal patent to the Earl of Leicester's company in 1574, which is, so far as we know, the first explicit authorization of this kind to be made formally under the Great Seal. This document showing the high favor in which the Queen held the company which was afterwards Shakspere's, deserves to be quoted at length.

"Elizabeth by the grace of god Quene of England, France, and Ireland, defendo[r] of the faith &c. To all Justices, Mayors, Sheriefs, Bayliffs, heade Constables, under Constables, and all other our officers and ministers greeting. Knowe ye that we, of o[r] esp'iall grace, certen knowledge and mere moc'on, Have licensed and authorized, and by these p'sents do license and aucthorize, o[r] loving subjects James Burbadge, John Perkyn, John Lanham, William Johnson and Robert Wylson, servantes to o[r] trustie and welbeloved Cosyn and Counsello[r], the Earle of Leicestre, To use, exercise and occupie the art and faculty of playeng comedies, tragedies, Enter-ludes, Stage playes, and such other like as they have alredy used and studied, or hereafter shall use and studye, aswell for the recreac'on of o[r] loving subjects, as for o[r] solace and pleasure, when we shall

---

[1] See Lysons, *Environs*, I, 69, note; and such a patent printed in full in Hazlitt, *English Drama*, 33.

[2] See documents printed in Fleay, *London Stage*, 127 ff.

D

thinke good to se them.   As also to use and occupie all such Instrum$^{ts}$ as they have alredy practised, or herafter shall practise, for and during our ples$^r$: And the said Comedies, Tragedies, Enterludes and Stage playes, together w$^{th}$ there musick, to shewe, publishe, exercise and occupy to their best comoditie during all the terme afforesaid, as well w$^{th}$in o$^r$ Cyty of London and Libties of the same, as also w$^{th}$in the liberties and fredoms of any o$^r$ Cytyes, townes, Boroughes &c. whatsoever, as w$^{th}$out the same, thoroughout o$^r$ Realme of England: willing and comaunding yow and every of yow, as ye tender our pleasure, to p'mit and suffer them herin w$^{th}$out any yo$^r$ letts, hinderance, or molestac'on during the terme afforesaid, any act, statute, p'clamac'on, or com'aundm$^t$ hertofore made, or herafter to be made, to the contrary notw$^{th}$standing.   Provided that the saide Comedies, Tragadies, Enterludes and Stage-playes be by the M$^r$ of o$^r$ Revills (for the tyme being) before seen and allowed, and that the same be not published, or showen in the tyme of comen prayer, or in the tyme of greate and comen plague in o$^r$ said Cyty of London.   In witnes whereof, &c." [1]

It should be noted especially that this patent is explicitly declared to be supreme in all places over all other acts, statutes, proclamations, or orders whatsoever.   The authority which it bestowed would naturally prevail over all local regulations in London or elsewhere, and is an interesting example of the autocratic power exercised by the Crown.[2]

Less formal licenses were also granted indirectly by the royal authority.   On April 29, 1593, for example, the Privy Council gave an "open warrant" to the Earl of Sussex's players, authorizing them to "exercise their quality of playing comedies and tragedies in any county, city, town, or corporation, not being within seven miles of London, where the infection is not, and in places convenient and times fit." [3]   About a week later a similar license was issued to Lord Strange's company.[4]

Such royal authorization, even if not necessary under the law, was very valuable to any nobleman's players.   It brought them much greater consideration from local officials and higher pay, — for it was customary, as we see in the Leicester records, to pay a company in proportion to the rank and dignity of its protector.[5]

---

[1] From the text of the Privy Seal, printed in Hazlitt, *English Drama*, 25-26.
[2] See below, p. 155.         [3] *Acts*, XXIV, 209.         [4] *Ibid.*, 212.
[5] Kelly, *Drama in Leicester*, 94.

Another form of indirect royal authorization grew up within this period, — that by the Master of the Revels. By his patent of 1581, as we have seen, the Crown had delegated to him power "to order and reform, authorize and put down" all plays, players, and playmakers, together with their playing places, throughout the kingdom.[1] This appeared to confer power to license players everywhere. As we shall see, the Master succeeded in course of time in establishing his right to do so in the country at large, but his right to license actors within London remained somewhat doubtful. An example of a company traveling under his license appears in Leicester in 1583. Unfamiliar with this sort of authorization, the town officials entered the company on the records as the "servants of the Master of the Revels," — the form used in the case of noblemen's players. They entered also a copy of the license.[2]

The patent of 1574 and the other royal favors to certain companies mark a change which was taking place in stage conditions. A few more or less permanent companies were now becoming prominent, and as these gained in the newly erected theaters fixed playing places, they succeeded in establishing themselves more firmly and overshadowing the less important players. Certain prominent companies frequently performed at Court, and, as we shall see, the royal favor secured for them many privileges in London. The Privy Council occasionally requested the local officials in and about the city to permit performances by the favored players and no others, — thus giving them a sort of monopoly and foreshadowing the system which developed in the next reign.

The conditions under James and Charles differed to some extent from those under Elizabeth. As we have seen, the Statute 1 James I, cap. 7, took away from noblemen the power of licensing players.[3] There remained only the license from the Crown. Besides some desire for stricter regulation, the purpose of this

---

[1] See above, pp. 16–17.

[2] See below, p. 53. Some additional references for records of traveling companies during this period may be found in Halliwell-Phillipps, *Visits of Shakespeare's Company;* and J. T. Murray, *English Dramatic Companies in the Towns outside of London, 1550–1600,* in *Modern Philology,* II, no. 4 (April, 1905).

[3] See above, p. 28.

law appears to have been the granting of a monopoly to the
favored companies. The Puritan element in Parliament no
doubt desired restriction of the number of players and would,
indeed, probably have liked to abolish them utterly;[1] the King
was glad to have the power of licensing entirely in his own hands.
The system of royal patents, already begun, now developed extensively. This sort of authorization had, we have observed,
been available long before this, in one form or another: royal
companies had traveled abroad under the protection of the royal
name, probably under the earlier Tudor kings, and certainly
from Mary's time onward; the Chapel Children had used their
patent for a similar purpose; less formal authorizations, and in
1574 a patent under the Great Seal, had been issued to noblemen's companies.[2] The Crown now proceeded to extend this
system of formal patents, and to convert the prominent noblemen's companies into servants of the various members of the
royal family.

This policy James had begun immediately after his accession,
and before the passage of the statute. He arrived in London on
May 7, and on May 17 there was issued the Privy Seal, directing the
patent under the Great Seal to the Lord Chamberlain's company, Shakspere's, to be known henceforth as the King's Men.
This important document is here quoted as a type of such licenses. It is obviously modeled on Elizabeth's patent of 1574,
with some alterations. As permanent theaters were now in
existence, the company's London playing place is here specified.
The addition of the urgent royal request that courtesy and consideration be shown to the actors is also notable, and indicates
the high favor in which they were held.

"James, by the grace of God, King of England, Scotland, Fraunce
& Irland, defendo<sup>r</sup> of the faith, &c. To all Justices, Maio<sup>rs</sup>, Sheriffs,
Constables, Hedboroughes, and other o<sup>r</sup> officers and loving subjects
greeting. Know ye, y<sup>t</sup> we of o<sup>r</sup> speciall grace, certaine knowledge,
& meere motion have licenced and authorized, & by these prīnts doo
licence and authorize, these o<sup>r</sup> s'vants, Lawrence Fletcher, William
Shakespeare, Richard Burbage, Augustine Phillippes, John Hennings,
Henry Condell, William Sly, Rob't Armyn, Richard Cowlye, and the

---

[1] See below, p. 222.    [2] See above, pp. 32 ff.

rest of their associats, freely to use and exercise the Arte and facultie of playing Comedies, Tragedies, Histories, Enterludes, Moralls, Pastoralls, Stage plaies, & such other like, as they have already studied, or heerafter shall use or studie, aswell for the recreation of o[r] loving subjects, as for o[r] solace and pleasure, when we shall thinke good to see them, during o[r] pleasure. And the said Comedies, Tragedies, Histories, Enterlude, Morall, Pastoralls, Stage plaies, & such like, To shew and exercise publiquely to their best Commoditie, when the infection of the plague shall decrease, as well w[th]in theire now usuall howse called the Globe, w[th]in o[r] Countie of Surrey, as also w[th]in anie towne halls, or Mout halls, or other convenient places w[th]in the lib'ties and freedome of any other Cittie, Univ'sitie, Towne, or Borough whatsoev' w[th]in o[r] said Realmes and dominions. Willing and comaunding you, and ev'y of you, as you tender o[r] pleasure, not only to p'mitt and suffer them heerin, w[th]out any yo[r] letts, hinderances or molestac'ons, during o[r] said pleasure, but also to be ayding and assisting to them yf any wrong be to them offered. And to allowe them such former Courtesies, as hathe bene given to men of their place and qualitie: And also what further favo[r] you shall shew to these o[r] s'vants for o[r] sake, we shall take kindely at y[r] hands. In witness wherof &c." [1]

Within a short time after the date of this patent the Earl of Worcester's players must have been taken into the service of Queen Anne, and the Admiral's into Prince Henry's; for on February 19, 1604, there is a record of payments to the "Prince's players" and the "Queen's Majesty's players," [2] and in April, 1604, the three companies of the King, the Queen, and the Prince are mentioned in a letter from the Privy Council to the Lord Mayor.[3] The patent for the Queen's players exists only in a rough, undated draft, conjecturally dated in the Calendar of State Papers, July, 1603.[4] No patent for the Prince's company exists of earlier date than 1606.[4] Perhaps the first one granted has been lost; or the early authorization of the company may have been in some less formal shape. In January, 1604, a patent appointed the Chapel boys Children of the Revels to the

---

[1] From the text of the Privy Seal, printed in Hazlitt, *English Drama*, 38–40. See Appendix.

[2] Cunningham, *Revels Accounts*, xxxv.

[3] Printed in Halliwell-Phillipps, *Outlines*, 472, and in *Henslowe Papers*, 61–62.

[4] For particulars concerning dates and bibliography of patents, see the Appendix.

Queen.[1]  In the following June was passed the Statute I James
i, cap. 7, formally establishing this system by the abolition of
noblemen's licenses.[2]

The process of taking over the prominent London companies
to the service of members of the royal family continued.  The
Duke of York, afterwards Charles I, and the Lady Elizabeth,
afterwards Queen of Bohemia, were patrons of companies.  The
Elector Frederick, the King's son-in-law, took over to his service
the Prince's players on the death of Prince Henry in 1612.  In
1615 a provincial traveling company was granted a patent under
the name of "Her Majesty's Servants of her Royal Chamber at
Bristol."  All these patents are modeled, in the main, on that
of the King's Men, with some modifications.  For example,
more specific regulations are inserted concerning playing in time
of plague; in some later patents a proviso is introduced reserving all rights granted to the Master of the Revels; and various
theaters are of course specified as the authorized playing places.
A second patent was sometimes granted to a company for one
cause or another: the company was reorganized in some way,
or its patron changed, as when Charles I took over his father's
players, or the Elector, Prince Henry's; or it wished specific
authority to perform in some other theater, as in the case of the
new patent to the King's Men in 1619, confirming their right to
play at the Blackfriars theater as well as at the Globe.[3]

In running over even thus briefly the history of royal patents,
mention should be made of an interesting indication of the
growth of Puritan influence.  The warrant to Giles in 1626, for
taking up singing boys for service in the Royal Chapel, for the
first time expressly forbids their acting in plays, because "it is
not fit or decent that such as should sing the praises of God
Almighty should be trained or employed in such lascivious and
profane exercises." [4]

The result of the system of patents was a practical monopoly

[1] For particulars concerning dates and bibliography of patents, see the
Appendix.
[2] See *Journals of the House of Commons*, I, 193, 199, 207, 214, 240, 245;
*Journals of the House of Lords*, II, 301, 303, 304, 315, 319, 320, 321, 327.
[3] See below, pp. 201–202, and Appendix.
[4] Collier, *English Dramatic Poetry*, I, 446.

of playing in London for the group of favored companies in royal service. This was eminently in keeping with the customs of the time. Under Elizabeth, as the system of central control over industries supplanted local trade regulation, there had been royal patents of monopoly granted to favored persons, — one, for example, giving sole right to import, make, and sell playing-cards, which gave rise to a famous suit, and glass, salt, soap, and saltpeter monopolies. Under James and Charles the Crown sold such patents, with more or less profit to the royal treasury.[1]

In the case of the actors the monopoly of the patentees was not absolute. We find records of outside companies appearing occasionally in London. French players, for example, were granted permission to perform in 1629 and 1635, and a "company of strangers" appeared in 1623.[2]

There were other forms of license conferred on players besides the royal patents. The Lord Chamberlain, who, as we have seen, had special jurisdiction over the drama, issued various tickets of privilege to companies and to individual actors.[3] An interesting example is a "players' pass," issued in 1636 and signed by the Earl of Pembroke and Montgomery, Lord Chamberlain. It grants to certain members of the King's company who are to attend his Majesty on his progress, royal authority to travel and perform in all towns corporate, etc., while on this tour.[4] In the Leicester records we find in 1622 a note of a company of players traveling "under the Lord Chamberlain's authority"; and in 1625 and 1627 a company designated as "the Earl of Pembroke's servants," — a title which may indicate a similar authorization.[5]

The Lord Chamberlain's subordinate, the Master of the Revels, extended during this period the exercise of the large powers

[1] See Price, *English Patents of Monopoly.*

[2] *1821 Variorum,* III, 120, note, 121, note, 224; Chalmers, *Supplemental Apology,* 215, 216, note.

[3] Chalmers, *Apology,* 512, note.

[4] Printed in *1821 Variorum,* 166–167, note, from MS. in the Lord Chamberlain's Office.

[5] Kelly, *Drama in Leicester,* under the years cited. Pembroke was Lord Chamberlain from 1617 to 1630. He was succeeded in that office by his brother, the Earl of Pembroke and Montgomery.

delegated to him by the King. Though it is doubtful whether he ever actually licensed companies of players in London, he seems to have exercised this power freely in other parts of the kingdom. During the period several companies appeared at Leicester traveling under the Master's license, — one in 1623, one in 1626, three in 1630, and one in 1639.[1]

It seems that when a traveling company presented a proper license to town officials, it had by custom a right to perform. The royal patents, indeed, expressly granted this right, and later ones authorized the actors to play in any town halls, moot halls, or other convenient rooms within any town they visited. When such a performance in official buildings, or anywhere in the town, happened to be inconvenient or distasteful to the local authorities, they paid the players a lump sum of money for foregoing their right to perform.[2] From 1571 on, entries of such payments may be found in the Leicester records, varying in amount according to the dignity of the players' patron or license. As the Puritan feeling grew stronger these became more frequent, culminating in the year 1622, when seven such payments were made.[3] Similar entries are found in the records of other towns.[4]

Though the Statute 1 James I, cap. 7, limiting the licensing power to the Crown, was fairly well obeyed in London, it was apparently not consistently enforced in the kingdom at large. Noblemen had theoretically no longer the right to license wandering players; but their companies still traveled through the

---

[1] Kelly, *Drama in Leicester*, under the years cited.

[2] Thompson, in his *Puritans and Stage*, 131, quotes from the *Speech and Charge* of Justice Coke in 1606, as printed in a pamphlet published in 1607, a passage which seems to contradict this view of the players' right to perform. Referring to the abuses caused by actors throughout the country, the *Charge* asserts that they may be easily reformed. "They hauing no Commission to play in any place without leaue: And therefore, if by your willingnesse they be not entertained you may soone be rid of them." But Coke himself, in the Preface to the seventh part of his Reports, condemned this pamphlet as "erroneous" and "published without his privity." "Besides the omission of divers principal matters," he declared, "there is no on period therein expressed in that sort and sense that I delivered." (See a discussion of the matter in *Notes and Queries*, April 30, 1853.) We may therefore safely disregard the interpretation of the law contained in the printed *Charge*. See also below, p. 72.

[3] Kelly, *Drama in Leicester*, under the years cited.

[4] See *Historical MSS. Commission Reports*, X, pt. iv, 540; XI, pt. iii, 28.

country and were recognized by local officials as entitled to perform.[1] In the Leicester records of payments to players I have noted such companies after 1604, when the new law was passed. One appeared in 1605, two in 1606, 1608, 1610, 1614, and one in 1615. About this time some inkling of the new regulations seems to have reached Leicester. In 1616, for the first time, players are noted as having a "warrant under the King's hand and privy signet." Two such entries appear in this year and one in 1617; in 1618 is a notice of a company with a "commission under the Great Seal of England"; and during these three years no nobleman's company is mentioned. But if the town was consciously living up to the new law, it soon relapsed. In the following years, among the entries of royal companies, noblemen's appear again, — one in 1619, two in 1620, and one in 1624, 1625, 1627, and 1637. During the later years the name or authority of a company is often omitted, and the records of licenses are thus incomplete.[2]

One would not expect to find, of course, any rigorous or consistent enforcement of the law throughout the kingdom. Even if the local officials were familiar with the regulations and conscientiously tried to put them into effect, there were numerous possibilities of evasion. A pathetic protest has come down to us from the London Common Council, in 1584, complaining that when special privileges were granted to the Queen's Men, all the playing places in the city were filled with players calling themselves the Queen's Men.[3] Even when formal patents were in use, they could be handed from one company to another. We see the Mayor of Exeter in anxious uncertainty as to whether he had offended the Crown by refusing permission to a company of men, thirty, forty, and fifty years of age, with only five youths among them, to act on the authority of a royal patent for children.[4] The Mayor of Banbury, in 1633, arrested a company as rogues, because, though they had two licenses, one from the Mas-

---

[1] The company authorized by the Duke of Lennox in 1604 should perhaps be placed in this class. Or possibly his blood relationship to the King gave him some claim to licensing power. See his warrant in the *Henslowe Papers*, 62.

[2] Kelly, *op. cit.*, under the years cited.

[3] Document printed in Collier, *English Dramatic Poetry*, I, 216. See below, p. 174. [4] Fleay, *London Stage*, 310; *State Papers, Dom.*, 1611–1618, 549.

ter of the Revels and the other from the King, the date of the
first had been forged and the second had been purchased from
a pawnshop!<sup>1</sup>

There remains to be considered the national regulation of
playing places; but on this point there is comparatively little
to be said.  Apparently there was no definite system of licensing
playhouses, and no general legislation on the subject.  Such
regulations as there were, were chiefly matters of local administration, and, in the case of London, will be treated in detail in
a later chapter.  There are a few points, however, which may
fittingly be touched on here.

The earliest concern about playing places was an affair of the
church rather than of the state.  Growing out of the liturgical
origin of the English drama, the custom of giving plays in churches
survived sporadically until Stuart times, though many efforts
were made to suppress it.  In 1542 Bishop Bonner of London
issued a proclamation to the clergy of his diocese, prohibiting
"all manner of common plays, games, or interludes to be played,
set forth, or declared within their churches, chapels, etc."<sup>2</sup>
Similar orders were promulgated at later dates, and even in 1603
the abuse was noticed in one of the Canons of James I, given
soon after his accession.<sup>3</sup>  As late as 1602 players apparently
claimed at times a sort of prescriptive right to perform in churches,
for we find entered in the parish register of Syston, a village near
Leicester, a payment in that year by the churchwardens "to
Lord Morden's players because they should not play in the
church . . . xii d."<sup>4</sup>

As in the licensing of plays and players, the Crown and the
Privy Council exercised supreme power at will, and interfered
in local administration.  We shall find the Council frequently
asking or commanding the London authorities to permit performances in certain playing places; authorizing the erection of

---

<sup>1</sup> *State Papers, Dom.*, 1633–1634, 47–49.    <sup>2</sup> *1821 Variorum*, III, 45.
   <sup>3</sup> *Ibid.;* and see also Chambers, *Mediæval Stage*, II, 191, and Kelly, *Drama
in Leicester*, 15–16.
   <sup>4</sup> Kelly, *Drama in Leicester*, 16.  Probably the parish officials feared to offend
the players' noble patron by an unqualified refusal to allow their performance in
the church, and thus bought them off.

a new theater; or ordering that an old one be "plucked down" and abolished. The Master of the Revels also had power to license playing places, and, in one case at least, he granted permission for the erection of a new theater in London.[1]

The system of royal patents, moreover, extended to playing places. Those issued to certain companies, as we have seen, explicitly authorized performances in any "town halls, moot halls, guild halls, schoolhouses," or other convenient places in the towns they visited. And they also licensed the company specifically to perform in its permanent London theater, whether this was in the City or in the Liberties. Special royal patents, granting permission to erect new theaters in and about London, were issued, as we shall find, in 1615, 1620, 1635, and 1639. The last of these, to Sir William D'Avenant, is interesting as showing what is apparently a new feature in government regulation, — a restriction on the prices of admission. The patentee is authorized to charge only "such sum or sums as is or hereafter from time to time shall be accustomed to be given or taken in other playhouses and places for the like plays, scenes, presentments, and entertainments."[2]

---

[1] See below, pp. 73–74.      [2] See *1821 Variorum*, III, 93–95.

# CHAPTER II

## The Master of the Revels

THE various functions of the Master of the Revels were as characteristic of the age in which he served as was his picturesque title. He is therefore not altogether easy to understand unless one conceives him against a background of the customs of his time. His duties were of two sorts. The first and the more ancient, his original function as an officer of the King's household, was the devising and managing of court masques, disguisings, plays, and other entertainments for the amusement of the Sovereign and the celebration of festivals and great occasions. The second duty, that with which we are especially concerned, was the licensing and regulating of the drama outside the Court, throughout the kingdom, and was of much later growth. It is not possible to understand his exercise of this second function unless one bears in mind that it was of a twofold nature. The Master was a government official, whose duty it was to execute the laws and to regulate the stage in accordance with the best interests of the state. But his position was also frankly a money-making business. He sold licenses as profitably as he could; he devised new extensions of his power and new forms of commissions which would increase his income. By virtue of his royal patent he even exercised the right to sell permission to break certain laws, — as in the case of his dispensations for performances in Lent. Sometimes he purchased his office for a considerable sum, and then it was obviously necessary for him to recoup his outlay by the sale of all possible sorts of licenses and the securing of various payments from the players.

Though such an administration of a government office is not considered quite the proper thing to-day, it was usual enough and not especially frowned upon under Elizabeth and the

Stuarts. It is perhaps easier to understand the Master's exercise of the powers granted by his patents, when one compares other "dispensing patents" of a somewhat similar sort, common enough among the many grants of monopoly made during the period, which we touched on in considering the royal patents to players. These licensing or dispensing patents were awarded as favors or sold by the Crown. They authorized the patentees either to license others to do something, or to issue, upon receipt of composition, pardons for infractions of some penal law, or to grant dispensations from the penalties of a certain statute, in return for a fee.[1] This virtually enabled offenders to bargain, either periodically or once for all, for the right to break the law. Examples are numerous. An ordinary licensing patent was granted to Sir Walter Raleigh in 1588–1589, authorizing him "to make licenses for keeping of taverns and retailing of wines throughout England."[2] A striking case of a dispensing patent is that to Thomas Cornwallis in 1596–1597, empowering him "to make grants and licenses for keeping of gaming-houses, and using of unlawful games, contrary to the statute of 33 Henry VIII."[3] Laws were apparently sometimes passed in order to make possible profitable grants of the right to break them. Regulations were made, for example, concerning the tanning of leather, which could not possibly be followed; and then Sir Edward Dyer was authorized to pardon and dispense with penalties for the violation of this statute. In exercising this right he and his deputies gained an evil reputation for extortion.[4]

It was very natural that a similar practice should gradually grow up in the dramatic world, as the Master of the Revels strove to extend profitably the vague powers granted by his patents. As we have seen, the Statute 1 James I, cap. 7, finally took away from all other personages the right to license traveling players and the other wanderers on the highways who were engaged in legitimate business, and left only the license by the Crown.[5] By virtue of the royal patent delegating authority to him, the Master naturally granted licenses to traveling players, — "dis-

---

[1] Price, *English Patents of Monopoly*, 12.     [2] *Ibid.*, 146.
[3] *Ibid.*, 147.     [4] *Ibid.*, 13–14.
[5] See above, p. 28.

pensations" from the penalties of this statute. Similar power to license others of the wanderers was granted. There is a mention of a patent under James I for "the licensing of pedlars and petty chapmen," [1] and a much closer analogy to the Master's powers is found in the case of the royal patents to the "Master of the King's Games of Bears, Bulls and Dogs," which were apparently interpreted as granting power to license bear-baitings and bull-baitings in Paris Garden and by traveling showmen.[2]

It is scarcely probable that the original grant of authority outside the Court to the Master of the Revels was a conscious inauguration of a dispensing patent of this sort, or even that he himself, in extending his jurisdiction, consciously endeavored to make it such. The analogous cases which I have cited merely go to show how natural, how consistent with the customs of the time, was the growth of the Master's licensing power, — unconstitutional as it may appear at first sight. With them in mind it will perhaps be easier to understand the history of the development of his authority.

The loss of many important documents makes the tracing of this history a difficult task. Had we, for instance, the vanished office books of Tilney and Buc, the earlier Masters, we might find that their activity was as great as that of the busy Herbert, whose intermeddling in dramatic affairs shines out so vividly from the pages of his Register. If the Patent Rolls, moreover, and additional town records, are ever accessible in complete and orderly form, it will be possible to trace the Masters more clearly. As it is, much of their history must be conjectural.

In the Court of the early kings an important duty was that of managing the royal pastimes. The Lord Chamberlain, as head of the great branch of the royal household known as the Chamber, had charge of the Sovereign's amusements, — of his hunting by day and his revels and shows by night. As the Court grew more splendid and more complex, various subordinate officials gradually developed, to take charge of branches of this service. The Master of the Revels first appeared under Henry VII.

---

[1] Price, *op. cit.*, 167.
[2] Collier, *Alleyn Memoirs*, 70 ff., 99 ff.; *Alleyn Papers*, 26; *Henslowe's Diary*, 212; *Henslowe Papers*, 1, 4, 12, 97 ff.

Originally he seems to have been appointed temporarily, from among the officials already in attendance at Court, to devise and superintend the disguisings, masques, or other entertainments on special occasions. This practice continued in the reign of Henry VIII, until finally, as the office grew in importance under that splendor-loving king, a permanent Master was appointed in 1545, in the person of Sir Thomas Cawarden. The department continued, of course, to be under the general authority of the Lord Chamberlain.[1]

Sir Thomas Cawarden's patent is of importance and interest as the model on which the patents of appointment of all subsequent Masters were based. The date is March 11, 1545, but the appointment is to run from March 16 of the preceding year. Cawarden is named "Magister Jocorum, Revelorum et Mascorum omnium et singulorum nostrorum, vulgariter nuncupatorum Revells and Masks." The appointment is for life. Cawarden is granted all houses, mansions, rights, liberties, and advantages appertaining to the office, and a salary of £10 per year.[2] The phrasing of this patent was followed almost exactly in those of later Masters. The powers conferred are, it will be noticed, somewhat ill defined and capable of various interpretations. By extraordinary stretching of the phrase, Herbert later held that his very wide claims to licensing power over all sorts of shows throughout the kingdom were justified by the words "Jocorum, Revelorum et Mascorum."[3]

During the lifetime of Sir Thomas Cawarden, however, it occurred to no one to extend the Master's jurisdiction over plays outside the Court. He was busied only with the devising and presentation of masques and shows for the entertainment of the Sovereign.[4] He lived to superintend Elizabeth's coronation festivities, and died on August 29, 1559.[5] His successor, Sir

---

[1] On the origin of the Office of the Revels see Chalmers, *Apology*, 471–472; Chambers, *Mediæval Stage*, I, 404–405, and *Tudor Revels*, 1–5, 52.

[2] The patent is printed in Rymer, *Fœdera*, XV, 62–63, and noted in *Letters and Papers of Henry VIII*, XX, 213.

[3] Halliwell-Phillipps, *Dramatic Records*, 60.

[4] On the Office under Cawarden see Chambers, *Tudor Revels*, 9 ff.

[5] *Ibid.*, 13. Fleay's incorrect date for Cawarden's death leads him into serious error. (*London Stage*, 43.) He is followed by Schelling. (*Elizabethan Drama*, I, 101–102.)

Thomas Benger, was formally appointed by a patent of January 18, 1560, similar to Cawarden's, with the additional provision that it was to hold in the reigns of her Majesty's successors.[1] Benger was apparently a very inefficient Master. No patent appointing a successor was issued until after his death, which occurred in 1577; but, as we learn from the Revels Accounts, he gave up all active exercise of his functions by the summer of 1572. After this date he no longer signed the accounts. His duties were performed by the subordinate officers, especially by Thomas Blagrave, the Clerk of the Revels, who served as Acting Master from November, 1573, until Christmas, 1579, by special appointment of the Lord Chamberlain.[2] Under Benger's inefficient management the Office had apparently become disorganized, and in 1573 Lord Burghley took up the question of its reorganization. To this end, he seems to have called for reports or suggestions from the three officers then in charge, — the Clerk Comptroller, the Clerk, and the Yeoman. Their three reports survive in the Lansdowne MSS. and throw an interesting light on the organization and business of the Office at this time.[3] From our point of view they are especially noteworthy as showing that in 1573 it was busied solely with the preparation of court entertainments: the care of costumes, the purchasing of properties and supplies, — such were the chief concerns of the Revels. In the suggestion made by the three officers for the reformation of the department, there is no proposal that they should have jurisdiction or censorship over the drama in the outer world. Buggin, the Clerk Comptroller, suggests, it is true, that the power of the officers should be strengthened by a commission authorizing them to enforce service from the Queen's subjects,[4] — that is, to compel workmen to serve the Office in emergencies. This was apparently to be somewhat similar in nature to the commissions authorizing the Master of the Chapel to "take up" singing boys, and those empowering other departments of the

---

[1] Printed in Rymer, *Fœdera*, XV, 565.

[2] Cunningham, *Revels Accounts*, 48, 77; Chambers, *Tudor Revels*, 51–52.

[3] All three are printed at length in Chambers, *op. cit.*, 31 ff. The first is given in Halliwell-Phillipps, *Dramatic Records*, 68 ff. Mr. Chambers dates them all — rightly, I think — 1573.

[4] Chambers, *op. cit.*, 41–42.

household to command provisions and cartage.[1] Perhaps the Revels had already enjoyed such authority on special occasions. The suggestion bore fruit, as we shall see, in Tilney's commission of 1581, which granted him wide powers of this sort.

Though no proposal was yet made for the bestowal of the censorship on the Revels Office, the germ that was to develop into its extensive jurisdiction was already visible. The Master frequently called outside companies of actors before him, and had them rehearse plays which might be suitable for court presentation, in order that he might select the best.[2] He also looked over numerous plays in manuscript, to judge of their merits. Many needed alteration of some sort, in length or substance, before they were quite suitable for the Court. The responsibility of seeing that no offensive word reached her Majesty's ear rested, of course, on the Master, and he made many changes in the dramas to be produced. In 1571 we find in the Revels Accounts a list of six plays given at Court, ' all whiche vi playes being chosen owte of many, and founde to be the best that were to be had, the same also being often perused and necessarely corrected and amended by all thafforeseide officers." [3] In subsequent years "perusing and reforming of plays" appears frequently in the Accounts.[4]

In such summoning of outside companies before him to act plays for his approval, and in the expurgation of the manuscripts submitted, lay the germ of the Master's censoring and licensing power. His jurisdiction over performances outside the Court was formally begun in the patent granted by Queen Elizabeth to the Earl of Leicester's players in 1574.[5] These fortunate actors, servants of the Queen's favorite, were, as we have seen, given by patent under the Great Seal of England the right to perform in all cities and towns of the realm, even within London itself, without molestation from the authorities, any act, statute, proclamation or commandment to the contrary notwithstanding. Such an extraordinary favor had never been granted to any

---

[1] See above, pp. 32–33; and Chambers, *Tudor Revels*, 51.
[2] Cunningham, *Revels Accounts*, 39, 159. Plays were sometimes rehearsed before the Lord Chamberlain, for his approval. *Ibid.*, 120, 136.
[3] *Ibid.*, 13.      [4] See, for example, *ibid.*, 87, 92, 198.
[5] See above, pp. 33–34.

E

actors before, and it was but natural that the Crown should wish to have these players bound in some way not to abuse their privilege.  If the local officials were not to have jurisdiction over them, it was necessary that some Crown officer should see that they performed nothing harmful to the good order of the state. Obviously the Master of the Revels, already used to such supervision of plays, and already the director of these very players in their frequent appearances at Court, was the natural person to be intrusted with this function.  The actors were therefore permitted to perform only on condition that all their plays "be by the Master of our Revels, for the time being, before seen and allowed."

At the date of the granting of this first portion of licensing power, the Revels Office was, as we have seen, in a somewhat unsettled state.  Benger was not performing his duties, the Clerk, Blagrave, was serving as Acting Master, and the reorganization of the Office was under consideration.  In these circumstances it is not probable that any considerable effort was made to develop and extend this profitable jurisdiction.  But within a few years the situation was radically changed.  In 1577 Benger died; in December, 1578, the name of Edmund Tilney first appears as signing the Revels Accounts;[1] and on July 24, 1579, a patent was issued formally appointing Tilney Master, and providing that his service was to date from the preceding Christmas.  The terms of his patent are precisely like Cawarden's, except for a few slight verbal changes and the additional provision, as in Benger's, that it is to hold in succeeding reigns; no mention is made of the new censoring power conferred on the Master by the patent to Leicester's company five years before.[2]

The new Master, Edmund Tilney, was of good family, a connection of Lord Howard of Effingham, and with some literary achievement to his credit, — *The Flower of Friendship*, a dialogue on matrimony which he had dedicated to Elizabeth in 1568.  Under his energetic hand the reorganization of the Revels Office seems to have proceeded rapidly.  He evidently saw the

[1] Cunningham, *Revels Accounts*, 124.

[2] Tilney's patent is printed at length in Halliwell-Phillipps, *Dramatic Records*, 2–3.

necessity for a commission granting him power to enforce service from workmen, such as the Clerk Comptroller had recommended in 1573; and he must have perceived some of the great possibilities in the extension of his jurisdiction over performances outside the Court. The fruit of his efforts appeared in the very favorable patent granted him on December 24, 1581.[1]

This is entitled "Commissio specialis pro Edo. Tylney, Ar. Magistro Revellorum." It differs from the patents of appointment in various ways. In the first place it is in English instead of Latin; it is a grant of special powers to Tilney personally from the Queen, and is not mentioned as holding in the reigns of her Majesty's successors. Apparently it had to be renewed in the case of succeeding Masters, and we shall find in later years that such declarations of the powers of the Revels Office were made from time to time by the Crown and the Lord Chamberlain. This commission resembles in nature, as we have suggested, the grants issued at intervals to the Masters of the Chapel Children, authorizing them to "take up" singing boys for the Queen's service.

The patent first empowers Tilney to take and retain at competent wages for the royal service, in all parts of England, all such painters, embroiderers, tailors, and other workmen as may be needed in the Revels Office; and to take all necessary materials and carriage at a reasonable price. If any persons refuse to serve, or withdraw from the work, Tilney is authorized to imprison them as long as he may think fit. The workmen of the Revels are to be under the special protection of the Queen during their time of service, and are to be freed from prison by the Master's authority, should they be arrested at the suit of any other persons. They are also to be released from the obligation of completing any other contract or work which they may have undertaken, until they shall have ended their service in the Revels.

Then follows the clause already quoted,[2] giving the Master power, in all places in England, to summon all players, with their playmakers, that they may recite any of their plays before him

---

[1] First printed from the Patent Rolls by T. E. Tomlins, in the *Shakspere Society Papers*, III, 1 ff. It is also in Collier, *English Dramatic Poetry*, I, 247–249, note; and in Halliwell-Phillipps, *Illustrations*, pt. i.     [2] pp. 16–17.

or his Deputy, "whom wee ordeyne, appointe and authorise by these presentes of all suche Showes, Plaies, Plaiers and Playmakers, together with their playinge places, to order and reforme, auctorise and put downe, as shalbe thought meete or unmeete unto himselfe or his said Deputie in that behalfe." The power granted him of imprisoning all recalcitrant actors or playwrights is also notable. "And also likewise we have by these presentes authorised and com'aunded the said Edmunde Tylney, that in case any of them, whatsoever they be, will obstinatelie refuse, upon warninge unto them given by the said Edmunde, or his sufficient Deputie, to accomplishe and obey our comaundement in this behalfe, then it shalbe lawful to the said Edmunde, or his sufficient Deputie, to attache the partie or parties so offendinge and him or them to com'ytt to Warde, to remaine without bayle or mayneprise, untill suche tyme as the same Edmunde Tylney or his sufficient Deputie shall thinke the tyme of his or theire ymprisonment to be punishment sufficient for his or their said offence in that behalfe; and that done to inlarge him or them so beinge imprisoned at their plaine libertie without any losse, penaltie, forfeiture or other damages in this behalfe to be susteyned or borne by the said Edmunde Tylney, or his Deputie; any Acte, Statute, Ordinance or P'vision heretofore had or made to the contrarie hereof in any wise not withstandinge." Finally, all officials are commanded to aid the Master in the execution of his duties.

It is difficult to discover just how far and how rapidly Tilney succeeded in extending and defining the vague and general powers conferred on him by this patent, — in having his authority to license plays, players, and playhouses recognized throughout the kingdom. In the face of the opposition of the powerful Corporation of London, the growth of his authority within that city was necessarily slow. In the spring of 1582, a few months after the issue of his special commission, the Privy Council apparently did not recognize him as having any jurisdiction over plays in London, for, as we have seen, they requested the Lord Mayor to appoint some proper person to overlook and license plays to be performed in the city.[1] In fact, during all the agitation of the

---

[1] See above, p. 17.

years 1582–1584, concerning the admission of actors into London, the Master of the Revels is never mentioned in the voluminous correspondence between the Privy Council and the city authorities.[1]

But Tilney was already claiming authority over plays and players throughout the kingdom almost as extensive as that asserted by his successors. He was certainly licensing players to travel, for, as we found, a company appeared at Leicester in 1583, bearing a commission signed by him and dated February 6 of that year. From the abstract of parts of this document given in the Leicester records, confused though it is, one can see that he was claiming the exclusive right to license players and allow plays.

"In w<sup>ch</sup> Indenture there ys one article that all Justices, Maiors, Sherifs, Bayllyfs, Constables, and all other her Officers, Ministers & subiects whatsoev' to be aydinge & assistinge unto the said Edmund Tilneye, his Deputies & Assignes,[2] attendinge & havinge due regard unto suche parsons as shall disorderly intrude themselves into any the doings & acc'ons before menc'oned, not beinge reformed qualifyed & bound to the orders p'scribed by the said Edmund Tyllneye. These shalbee therefore not only to signifye & geve notice unto all & ev'y her said Justices &c that noñ of there owne p'tensed aucthoritye intrude themselves & presume to showe forth any suche playes, enterludes, tragedies, comedies, or shewes in any place w<sup>th</sup>in this Realm, w<sup>th</sup>oute the ord'lye allowance thereof under the hand of the sayd Edmund.

"Nota. No play is to be played, but such as is allowed by the sayd Edmund, & by his hand at the latter end of the said booke they doe play."[3]

The players who carried this license became involved in a dispute at Leicester with the Earl of Worcester's company, who attacked the validity of their commission. The objection was not, however, against the authority of the Master to issue such licenses, but was based, apparently, on the fact that Haysell, the chief player, to whom the commission had been granted,

[1] On March 10, 1583, Tilney was summoned to Court to select the players for the Queen's new company (Cunningham, *Revels Accounts*, 186); but this was naturally a part of his duty as manager of court entertainments.

[2] Tilney's license evidently quoted the portion of his commission of 1581 calling on all officials to assist him in the exercise of his authority.

[3] Kelly, *Drama in Leicester*, 211–212.

was not present, and the actors bearing it were not really entitled to its protection.[1]   So chaotic, however, are the pronouns of the Leicester scribe, that it is hard to discover just what the ground of the quarrel was.

No other company appeared at Leicester under the Master's authorization until 1623.   Were the records of other towns accessible, it might be possible to ascertain how extensively he exercised such authority during the intervening period.

In London we have no sign of Tilney's activity until 1589. Mr. Chambers thinks that by 1587 the Privy Council had already begun to regard him as primarily responsible to them for the regulation of the theaters, and cites the order for the temporary suspension of performances in and about London issued by the Council on May 7, 1587, copies of which were sent, according to Mr. Dasent's edition of the Council Register, to the Lord Mayor, the Justices of the Peace of Surrey, and the Master of the Rolls.[2]   Mr. Chambers states that " Rolls " must be an error for " Revels," and suggests that this is the Master's first appearance as regulator of the London drama.[3]   But the Master of the Rolls was really the official meant, for it appears from the Council Register that he exercised the authority of a Justice of the Peace in Middlesex.   In 1577 similar orders for the suppression of plays in that county were sent to him and to the Lieutenant of the Tower, who also had jurisdiction in parts of Middlesex, — those adjacent to the Tower.[4]   There are several other examples of the exercise of similar functions by the Master of the Rolls.[5]

Though in the surviving documents the Master of the Revels does not appear in this rôle as early as 1587, it is probable that he was already exercising some supervision over the London drama.

[1] Kelly, *Drama in Leicester*, 212.      [2] *Acts*, XV, 70.      [3] *Tudor Revels*, 76.
[4] *Acts*, IX, 388.
[5] On March 2, 1591, the Privy Council, desiring stricter enforcement of the regulations against killing and eating flesh without license in Lent, sent orders to this effect to the Lord Mayor, to the Justices of the Peace in Surrey who had jurisdiction over parts of Southwark, and to "the Master of the Rolls and Thomas Barnes, esquire, Justices of Peace for the county of Middlesex." (*Acts*, XX, 322–323.)   Similarly, on June 23, 1592, when the Council desired to take precautions against riots in and about London, it sent orders to the Master of the Rolls, among many other Justices of the Peace and various officials. (*Acts*, XXII, 549–551.)

In 1589, when the Martin Marprelate controversy was treated on the stage, Tilney certainly had something to say about the drama in the city, for he appears to have reported to the Privy Council that improper plays were being performed; whereupon the Lords ordered the suppression of all plays in London. "Where by a l're of your Lordships, directed to Mr. Yonge, it appered unto me," wrote the Lord Mayor to Lord Burghley, "that it was your ho: pleasure that I sholde geve order for the staie of all playes within the cittie, in that Mr. Tilney did utterly mislike the same." [1]

This Martin Marprelate trouble and the consequent appointment of the censorship commission, of which Tilney was a member, apparently gave the Master a favorable start on his career as licenser of plays in and about London. Realizing the necessity of some stricter censorship of the drama, and feeling, apparently, that the old system of supervision by the city authorities was inadequate, the Privy Council established, as we have seen,[2] a commission of three persons — the Master of the Revels, an expert in divinity appointed by the Archbishop of Canterbury, and a representative of the city government — to examine, expurgate, and license all plays to be given in and about London. Even if his colleagues on this commission ever served, they apparently soon withdrew from active participation in the work. The Master, supported by the authority of his royal patents and by this new and more explicit grant of power, rapidly extended his jurisdiction, and developed the licensing business into a profitable one.

The earliest surviving manuscript showing Tilney's "reformations" for public performance — that of *Sir Thomas More* — is dated by Dyce about 1590, the year following the appointment of the commission.[3] By 1592 Tilney was evidently exercising wide power, and his authority in London was recognized by the city officials. It is noticeable that he was now licensing playhouses as well as plays. On February 25, 1592, the Aldermen wrote to the Archbishop of Canterbury, informing him of the disorders and corruption caused by the performances of the

---

[1] The letter is printed in Hazlitt, *English Drama*, 34-35.
[2] p. 18.     [3] See below, pp. 93 ff.

players in the City, and beseeching his aid for the remedy of these abuses. "Further, because Her Majesty must be served at certain times by this sort of people, she had granted her Letters Patent to Mr. Tilney, her Master of the Revels, by virtue whereof he had authority to reform, exercise or suppress all manner of players, plays and playhouses, and he had licensed the said houses, which before had been open to the Statutes for the punishment of such disorders. They requested his Grace to call the Master of the Revels before him and treat with him as to the measures to be devised, that Her Majesty might be served with these recreations as she had been accustomed, which might easily be done by the private exercise of Her Majesty's own players in convenient places, and the City freed from these continual disorders." [1]

The Archbishop came promptly to the aid of the City. A few days later the Lord Mayor wrote to him, thanking him for the trouble he had taken for removing the great inconvenience suffered by the municipality through the increase of plays and players. "As touching the consideration to be made to Mr. Tilney for the better effecting the restraint of plays in and about the City, a certain number of Aldermen had been appointed to confer with him thereon." [2]

An endeavor to raise the necessary funds for this "consideration" to Mr. Tilney, appears in the proceedings of the Court of the Merchant Taylors' Company a few days afterward. On March 23 they discussed a "precepte" from the Lord Mayor, which called attention to the evils of plays and suggested "the payment of one Anuytie to one Mr. Tylney, mayster of the Revelles of the Queene's house, in whose hands the redresse of this inconveniency doeth rest, and that those playes might be abandoned out of this citie." The Court sympathized, but "wayinge the damage of the president and enovacion of raysinge of Anuyties upon the companies of London," declined to unloose their purse-strings. [3] Whether the other guilds proved more generous, and the Mayor was enabled to buy off Tilney from

---

[1] *Remembrancia*, 352.       [2] *Ibid.*, 353.
[3] Chambers, *Tudor Revels*, 78, quoting C. M. Clode, *History of the Merchant Taylors*, I, 236.

licensing these obnoxious performances in the City, I have not discovered. It is possible that some such arrangement was actually made for a time, for during the next three years there are no complaints regarding plays within the city limits.

According to the modern code Tilney's methods of administering his office at this juncture may appear distinctly improper; but I doubt if they were considered especially questionable at the time. It was natural that he should desire to make as much money as possible from his licensing business. The practice of buying off men from exercising the rights granted by royal patents apparently existed in other towns than London. A somewhat similar case is found in Leicester in 1579 and 1580, when one Johnson, who held the Queen's commission empowering him to collect the penalty for "unlawful games," was twice paid 20s. by the Leicester officials, " ffor that he shoulde not deale w<sup>th</sup>in this Towne." [1]

During this same year of activity, 1592, Tilney was receiving from Henslowe, manager of the Rose, payments for the licensing of plays presented by Lord Strange's company at that theater, — apparently for seventeen in all, between February 26 and June 14.[2] The Rose was outside the city limits, and probably not included in any arrangement Tilney made with the London officials. He was doubtless licensing plays for other theaters as well, though of these no record has come down to us.

For the next six years we have no light on Tilney's activity except the fragmentary records of Henslowe's payments to him found in the Diary. These indicate that he was still "allowing" plays and that he was also licensing playhouses. On January 2, 1595, Henslowe gave him £10 in payment of a bond and other indebtedness;[3] in February, 1596, he noted that the Master was paid "all I owe him until this time";[4] and between April, 1596, and February, 1598, there are frequent records of payments of 10s. per week, apparently for the license of the Rose, — showing that Tilney was continuing the licensing of playhouses.[5] In January, 1598, there is a payment for the licensing of two plays

[1] Kelly, *Drama in Leicester*, 208–209.
[2] *Henslowe's Diary*, 12. See below, p. 79.    [3] *Henslowe's Diary*, p. 39.
[4] *Ibid.*, p. 28.        [5] *Ibid.*, 40, 46, 54, 72. See below, p. 73.

for the Lord Admiral's company.[1]   It is evident that Tilney's business was progressing favorably.

The Privy Council, however, did not yet recognize him as the person through whom orders regulating the drama should be transmitted, for on January 28, 1593, when, because of the plague, they forbade plays in and about London, they sent their commands only to the Lord Mayor and the Justices of the Peace of Middlesex and Surrey.[2]   Nor did they mention the Master, so far as we know, in granting traveling licenses, in the spring of that year, to the companies of the Earl of Sussex and Lord Strange.[3] He does not appear, moreover, in the troubles and complaints of 1594 and of 1597, resulting finally in the order — never enforced — for the destruction of all theaters.[4]

But in 1598 Tilney appears prominently.   The order of the Privy Council concerning plays issued on February 19 of that year was sent to the Master of the Revels, as well as to the Justices of the Peace of Middlesex and Surrey.   Two companies, those of the Lord Admiral and the Lord Chamberlain, had been especially authorized by the Privy Council to perform, in order that they might prepare themselves properly to appear as usual before the Queen.   A third company, the Council was informed, "have by waie of intrusion used likewise to play, having neither prepared any plaie for her Majestie, nor are bound to you, the Master of the Revelles, for perfourming such orders as have bin prescribed, and are enjoyned to be observed by the other two companies before mentioned."   The Lords therefore order that this third company be suppressed, and none allowed to play but the Lord Admiral's and the Lord Chamberlain's.[5]   The case is significant.   The companies used for court performances were evidently granted special privileges, — amounting to a monopoly of playing.   As in the case of the patent to Leicester's players in 1574, in return for these favors, they were bound to obey the authority of the Master.   The Council thus guarded against any abuse of the privileges granted.   At this time it seems likely that the players had actually given a money bond as surety

<hr/>

[1] *Henslowe's Diary*, 83.    [2] *Acts*, XXIV, 31–32.    [3] *Ibid.*, 209, 212.
[4] See below, pp. 187–188.
[5] *Acts*, XXVIII, 327–328.   Fleay conjectures that the third company was Pembroke's.   (*London Stage*, 158.)

for their obedience, and that this had been for some years the
practice of the favored companies. Such seems the most probable explanation of the entry in Henslowe's Diary on January 2,
1595, in the form of a receipt signed by one of Tilney's servants
on behalf of his master, acknowledging Henslowe's payment of
£10 "in full payment of a bond of one hundred pounds,"
and of whatsoever was due until the following Ash Wednesday.[1]

The other payments to the Master of the Revels noted in
Henslowe's Diary appear to be also in behalf of privileged companies, — those in 1592 for Lord Strange's, which performed
at Court and was granted a special warrant by the Council in
1593; and in 1598 and later years on behalf of the Lord Admiral's
players, one of the two companies granted a monopoly of performances in and about London.[2] We find, moreover, that in
preparing for his new and privileged theater, the Fortune, Henslowe had some dealings or consultation with the Master of the
Revels,[3] and that he afterwards paid him £3 a month for the
license of this playhouse.[4]

All these facts seem to indicate that, though the Master's
authority extended more or less over other players as well, the
companies enjoying privileges granted by the Crown were especially under his jurisdiction. This was very natural. Even
if they were not actually "bound" by the terms of their patent
or warrant, as in 1574 and 1598, they would obviously be inclined to obey the Crown official. Disobedience might result
in the withdrawal of their privileges, and their exclusion from
the court performances, which the Master directed. It was the
necessary preparation for these appearances before the Queen
which was the reason alleged for granting them the right to play
in public. Under the Stuarts also, as we shall see, the companies enjoying royal patents were especially obliged to obey
the Master.[5]

[1] p. 39. I infer from this that part of the £10 was a payment on the bond,
part for some licensing charges for performances until Lent.

[2] *Henslowe's Diary*, 12, 83, 85, 90, 103, 109, 116, 117, 121, 129, 130, 132, 148,
160, 161.　　　[3] *Ibid.*, 158.

[4] *Ibid.*, 132, 160, 161. For further discussion of Henslowe's payments to
the Master of the Revels, see below, pp. 73, 79 ff.

[5] See below, pp. 63-64.

Besides the important council order of 1598, there is another reason for considering that year a significant one. When Herbert was endeavoring to reëstablish the Master's jurisdiction after the Restoration, he based his claims largely on the precedent of his predecessors, and cited the names of certain plays licensed by Tilney in 1598, implying, apparently, that by this date the Master was fully established as censor.[1]

From henceforth he continued to exercise over the stage a general jurisdiction, which grew as the years went on. In 1600 we find that he, in conjunction with the Archbishop of Canterbury and the Bishop of London, had arranged a treaty between the parish of St. Saviour's and some of the Bankside theaters, whereby the players were to contribute money for the parish poor.[2] Before issuing their orders for the restriction of theaters and plays in 1600, the Privy Council had evidently consulted with Tilney, for they state that he has informed them — wrongly, as the case turned out — that the new Fortune was not to increase the number of theaters, but was to take the place of the Curtain, which was to be torn down.[3]

The Master's importance, however, was not yet fully established. In the theatrical regulations which the Council now promulgated, no mention was made of his authority. The Lord Mayor and the Justices of Middlesex were ordered to enforce the rules, and were reproved in December, 1601, for their laxness. In March, 1601, the Mayor was commanded to suppress plays in Lent, and in the following May the Justices of Middlesex were directed to censor plays at the Curtain.[4] Evidently the Master of the Revels was not yet considered, as he was later, the proper agent to carry out the orders of the Council in and about London. Probably, however, the two companies granted a monopoly by the order of 1600 — the Lord Admiral's and the Lord Chamberlain's — were expected to obey him. We know indeed, as I have already mentioned, that he was being regularly paid

---

[1] *1821 Variorum*, III, 263, note. Possibly Herbert cites 1598 merely because the play-books bearing Tilney's license, which were in his possession and which were offered as evidence, happened to bear this date.

[2] Extract from the Parish Register, in Chalmers, *Apology*, 405.

[3] *Acts*, XXX, 395.     [4] See below, pp. 190 ff.

for a license for playing at the Fortune, one of the privileged theaters.[1] The Curtain, where the Justices were ordered to censor, was not occupied by one of the privileged companies, and was therefore not especially under the Master's jurisdiction.

It is clear that by the end of Elizabeth's reign the authority of the Revels Office over performances outside the Court was fairly well established. The system of royal patents for all important companies inaugurated by James, and the concentration of authority in the Crown by the statute of 1604, obviously strengthened the Master's position. As in the past, the players enjoying special privileges from the King naturally obeyed the Crown officer in charge of dramatic performances. In many of the royal patents, indeed, a special proviso was inserted, reserving all the rights and privileges granted to the Master of the Revels.[2] He now advanced rapidly towards the position of sole censor and licenser of plays in and about London.

In the first few years of James' reign, however, his exclusive authority was not yet unquestioned. As we have seen,[3] the royal patent to the Children of the Queen's Revels, in January, 1604, provided that Samuel Daniel should approve all plays to be given by that company. I doubt if Daniel exercised this authority to any extent. *Eastward Hoe*, at least, presented by these players about a year later, was apparently not "allowed" at all. So Chapman implies in a letter to the Lord Chamberlain, written probably during his imprisonment because of the offensive passages in that play.[4] His words suggest also that some sort of direct license by the Lord Chamberlain was sometimes available. "Of all the oversights for which I suffer," writes the poet, "none repents me so much as that our unhappie booke was presented without your Lordshippes allowance, for which we can plead nothinge by way of pardon but your Person so farr removed from our requirde attendance; our play so much importun'de, and our cleere opinions, that nothinge it contain'd could worthely be held offensive."[5] Evidently a license was

<hr>

[1] See above, p. 59.     [2] See below, pp. 63–64.     [3] p. 19.

[4] Possibly this imprisonment, as I shall explain later, was for some other offense, and the play presented without license on this occasion not *Eastward Hoe*. See below, pp. 101 ff.

[5] Letter printed in *Athenæum*, March 30, 1901.

not considered indispensable, and obviously the Master of the Revels, who is not mentioned, was not yet recognized as absolute censor over the London drama.

The extension of the powers of the office was apparently hastened by the granting of it, in reversion, to Tilney's nephew, Sir George Buc, who soon began to act as his uncle's Deputy. The reversion of the Mastership had been promised to Buc by Elizabeth in 1597,[1] and was confirmed by James I in a formal grant dated June 23, 1603. This patent recites the grant of the office to Tilney in 1579, and the terms on which it was bestowed, as in Tilney's patent of that date; it next expressly appoints Buc Master of the Revels, and declares that his term of service is to begin upon Tilney's death, resignation, or forfeiture of his office. It grants all rights, privileges, and pay as in the patents of preceding Masters from Cawarden down.[2] Apparently no further patent of appointment was necessary; but, by virtue of this grant, when Tilney's service ceased Buc's immediately began. A "special commission," like that granted to Tilney in 1581, conferring the same powers, was issued to Buc on the same date as his patent of reversion.[3] This would seem to indicate that he was even then — in 1603 — actively engaged in the management of the Office, as Tilney's Deputy. We know from an entry in the Stationers' Register that he was certainly acting in that capacity on November 21, 1606.[4] From the same source we learn that Tilney was still serving as Master on June 29, 1607;[5] but some time in this year he probably ceased to perform

[1] Chambers, *Tudor Revels*, 57. John Lyly had hoped for the Mastership, and was much disappointed by the promise to Buc. On Lyly's relation to the Revels Office, see Chambers, *op. cit.*, 57 ff.

[2] The patent is printed in Halliwell-Phillipps, *Dramatic Records*, 14–16.

[3] This is mentioned by Lysons in his *Environs* (1800–1811 edition), I, 69, note, among other items from the Patent Rolls, as a "commission to George Buck to take up as many paynters, embroiderers, taylors, &c. as he shall think necessary for the office of the Revels. Pat. 1 Jac. pt. 24. June 23." This is obviously another patent like Tilney's of 1581 and Astley's of 1622. (See below, p. 65.) In the *State Papers, Dom.*, 1603–1610, 16, it is catalogued as a "Commission to the Master of the Revels to take up workmen and stuff," under the date of June 21, 1603. Probably this is the Privy Seal, and the two patents under the Great Seal — this and the reversionary grant — were issued on June 23.

[4] Arber, *Transcript*, III, 333.      [5] *Ibid.*, 354.

his duties, for Buc is referred to as Master of the Revels in the edition of Camden's *Brittania* printed at that date.[1]  By October 4, moreover, Segar was acting as Buc's Deputy,[2] — a fact which would indicate that Buc was now Master.  As late as March 2, 1608, however, the warrants for the payments of expenses in the Revels Office were made out in Tilney's name.[3]  In 1610, at all events, his death left Buc in undisputed possession of the Office.[4]

Buc was a man of literary interests, author of various writings, including a treatise entitled *The Third University of England* and some commendatory verses prefixed to Watson's *Hekatompathia*.  He apparently took his office very seriously, for he wrote, as he himself tells us, a long and "particular commentary" on the "Art of Revels," — unfortunately lost.[5]  His energy and interest are apparent in the extension of the powers of the Revels Office.  Evidently he desired to have more explicit authority over the companies patented by the Crown, and to make sure that their privileges should not weaken his rights.  The earliest patents of James' reign do not mention the Master; but that granted in 1606 to the Prince's company contains the following proviso : —

"Provided alwaies, and our wyll and pleasure ys, that all auctoritie, power, priviledges, and profittes whatsoever, belonging and properlie appertaining to the Maister of our Revells, in respect of his office, and everie clause, article, or graunt contained within the letters patent, or commission, which have heretofore byn graunted or directed by the late Queene Elizabeth, our deere sister, or by ourselves, to our welbeloved servantes, Edmonde Tilney, Maister of the Office of our saide Revells, or to Sir George Bucke, Knight, or to either of them, in possession or reversion, shall be, remayne, and abide entire and in full force, estate, and vertue, and in as ample sorte as yf this our commission had never been made."[6]

A similar proviso is contained in the patents granted in 1609 to the Queen's company,[7] in 1610 to the Duke of York's,[8] and in

[1] *1821 Variorum*, III, 57, note.       [2] Arber, *Transcript*, III, 391.
[3] *State Papers, Dom.*, 1603–1610, 391, 410.       [4] *Ibid.*, 652.
[5] See Chambers, *Tudor Revels*, 59, note.
[6] *Shakspere Society Papers*, IV, 43.       [7] *Ibid.*, 46.       [8] *Ibid.*, 48.

1613 to the Elector's.[1]   According to Sir Henry Herbert's claims,
there was a like clause in those issued in 1620 and in 1630–1631.[2]
It is noteworthy that none of the three patents to the King's
company — in 1603, 1619, and 1625 — contains such a proviso.
Possibly these players, as members of the royal household, were
so obviously under the Master's authority that no specific mention of it was necessary.   Sometimes the Master's approval was
sought before the issuing of a patent, as in 1615, when Buc wrote
to the Lord Chamberlain's secretary, consenting to the proposed
patent for Daniel "as being without prejudice to the rights of
his office." [3]

While thus securing his rights over the patented companies,
Buc was extending his licensing power in various ways.   Without
any specific authority, so far as we know, he began in 1606 to
license plays for printing, and nearly all the dramas entered in the
Stationers' Register during the next thirty years were authorized
by the Revels Office.[4]   Buc also penetrated to other fields besides
the drama, and found profit in authorizing various kinds of
shows.   In 1610, for example, he licensed three men "to shew
a strange lion brought to do strange things, as turning an ox
to be roasted." [5]   Tilney had long before received monthly
payments for licenses for established theaters; but Buc advanced
to the extent of selling a permit for the erection of a new theater
within London — in Whitefriars — a transaction for which he
received £20 in 1613.[6]   These scattered facts which have come
down to us show the development of the Master's jurisdiction.
From the quotations from his Office Book made by Herbert,
and the surviving manuscripts showing his license to act, we
know that he was continuing to censor and license plays for
performance.

On April 3, 1612, Sir John Astley, or Ashley, was granted the
reversion of the Mastership, in a patent like Buc's of 1603, to
take effect on the latter's death or withdrawal from office.[7]
On October 5, 1621, a similar reversionary grant was made

[1] Hazlitt, *English Drama*, 45.
[2] Halliwell-Phillipps, *Dramatic Records*, 93.   See Appendix.
[3] *State Papers, Dom.*, 1611–1618, 294.     [4] See below, pp. 84 ff.
[5] *State Papers, Dom.*, 1603–1610, 631.     [6] *1821 Variorum*, III, 52, note.
[7] Printed in Halliwell-Phillipps, *Dramatic Records*, 11–13.

to Ben Jonson, who was to serve on the death of both Buc and Astley, but who, dying before the latter, never profited by his appointment.[1] In 1622 Buc, old and enfeebled in mind, ceased to act,[2] and Astley took up the office. Buc died on September 22, 1623. On May 22, 1622, a special commission was given to Astley, precisely like that granted to Tilney in 1581,[3] and in November the Lord Chamberlain issued a "Declaration of the Ancient Powers of the Office." We know of this latter document only from Herbert's mention of it after the Restoration.[4] Presumably it resembled the declaration made by the Lord Chamberlain at this later date, notifying all Mayors, Justices, and other officials that no players or other showmen should be allowed to perform without a license from the Revels Office.[5]

Astley acted as Master for only a few months. In July, 1623, Sir Henry Herbert purchased the office from him for £150 per year;[6] and in the next month, as he tells us, was "received" by the King as Master of the Revels.[7] James, that is, apparently recognized and approved the transfer of the office. As Mr. Fleay plausibly suggests,[8] the change in the form of entry in the Revels Office Book indicates that on July 27, 1623, Herbert was in charge. On September 3 Astley for the last time licensed a play for printing.[9] From henceforth until the Civil War Herbert was in undisputed possession of the office, and officially recognized as Master of the Revels. Nevertheless, Astley was technically

---

[1] See Halliwell-Phillipps, *Dramatic Records*, 39 ff. There was also a reversionary grant of the office, apparently, to William Painter, on July 29, 1622, to take effect after Jonson's. *State Papers, Dom.*, 1619–1623, 432.

[2] *State Papers, Dom.*, 1619–1623, 366.

[3] Printed in Hazlitt, *English Drama*, 52–56. It is not a patent of appointment, as Hazlitt states, but a grant of special powers to the man who is already Master, and who is mentioned as such in the opening of this patent. In the State Papers the date is given as May 6. (*State Papers, Dom.*, 1619–1623, 386.) The reversionary grant was the patent of appointment. A Privy Seal was also issued on May 22, 1622, directing the payment of certain Revels funds to Astley, and announcing that Buc was incapable, because of sickness, of performing his duties, and that the Mastership had been conferred on Astley. See Collier, *English Dramatic Poetry*, I, 403–405.

[4] Halliwell-Phillipps, *Dramatic Records*, 91.          [5] *Ibid.*, 59.

[6] Cunningham, *Revels Accounts*, xlix. See also Chalmers, *Apology*, 495, note.

[7] Warner, *Epistolary Curiosities*, I, 3, note.

[8] *London Stage*, 301, 310.          [9] Arber, *Transcript*, IV, 103.

F

Master until his death on January 13, 1641. In 1629 a reversionary grant of the office had been made to Herbert and Simon
Thelwall jointly, and by virtue of this they came formally and
technically into possession on Astley's death.[1]

This rather confused history of grants is of comparatively little
importance from our point of view, but the facts of Herbert's
administration, which lasted from July, 1623, until the outbreak
of the Civil War, and technically for some years after the Restoration, are of the greatest significance. Sir Henry Herbert was
of a noble and famous family, brother to George Herbert and to
Lord Herbert of Cherbury, and kinsman to William Herbert,
Earl of Pembroke, Lord Chamberlain from 1617 to 1630, and
to his brother and successor in that office, Philip Herbert, Earl
of Pembroke and Montgomery. This connection with his
chiefs, the Lord Chamberlains, was doubtless of great advantage
to Sir Henry. The survival of portions of Herbert's Office
Book or Register, and the declarations made by him after the
Restoration, when he was endeavoring to reëstablish his rights,
reveal to us many of the workings of the Office in a vivid and
detailed manner which we can never hope to realize in the years
of Tilney and Buc.[2] During Herbert's administration the Mastership was at the height of its power and importance. This
seems the fitting time, therefore, to expound in detail the or-

---

[1] See the history of these grants given by Herbert in his suit for the reëstablish-
ment of his jurisdiction after the Restoration. (*Dramatic Records*, 39–42.)
It is noteworthy that he bases his claims on these patents of appointment, — all
in terms of the grant to Cawarden, — and that he does not cite the "special
commissions," such as Tilney's of 1581 and Astley's of 1622. See also *ibid.*, 60.

[2] Sir Henry's Office Book, often referred to as *MS. Herbert*, was found in the
same chest with the MS. Memoirs of Lord Herbert of Cherbury. It contained,
Malone tells us, "an account of almost every piece exhibited at any of the
theatres from August, 1623, to the commencement of the Rebellion." (*1821
Variorum*, III, 57, note.) Malone and Chalmers made use of this precious document, but its whereabouts is now unknown. As it was already in a molder-
ing condition when seen by Malone, it has perhaps since perished entirely.
The extracts from it given by Chalmers and Malone are of the greatest value.
Buc's Office Book, we learn from Herbert, was burned. (Chalmers, *Supplemental Apology*, 203, note.)
Many of the documents concerning Herbert's suits after the Restoration are
printed in Halliwell-Phillipps, *Dramatic Records*, and some in *1821 Variorum*,
III.

ganization and operation of the Office, so far as it dealt with the regulation of the drama.

The Revels Office, since early in its history, had included, besides the Master, a Clerk Comptroller, a Clerk, a Yeoman, and various subordinate officers. These were concerned with the making and care of costumes and properties, the purchasing of supplies, and other details of the management of court entertainments. Materials were stored and the work carried on in a building especially devoted to the Revels. The Office moved frequently, being located at various times in Warwick Inn, the Charterhouse, Blackfriars, the Priory of St. John of Jerusalem in Clerkenwell, and St. Peter's Hill, Doctor's Commons. The officers were paid regular fees according to their patents, and besides these were given various wages and allowances and an official residence. The Master's fee, as specified in his patent, was £10 a year, but this represented only a small fraction of his perquisites. Tilney received an extra recompense of £100 a year, and though this was apparently not continued to the later Masters, they were allowed very considerable sums for extra attendance, "diet," lodgings, and various expenses.[1]

With all the intricacies of the Revels Accounts and the internal workings of the Office, we are not here concerned. The subordinate officials just mentioned appear to have confined themselves to their original function, — the preparation of court entertainments. The Master succeeded in keeping in his own hands the more profitable side of his business, — the licensing of public performances. In this he was assisted by his Deputy, who occasionally read, censored, and "allowed" plays in place of his chief; and in an humbler degree by Messengers of the Office and by his personal servants, who collected fees for him and carried his orders to the players. Sometimes he was served also by "Messengers of the Chamber," who summoned for him recalcitrant actors.

As the government official especially in charge of the stage, the Master was recognized as the proper person to transmit to the players the commands of the King and the Privy Council.

---

[1] See Chambers, *Tudor Revels*, 67 ff., and Warner, *Epistolary Curiosities*, I, 180, 182.

For example, when the deaths from the plague rose high, the
Lord Chamberlain sent to Herbert an order for the suppression of plays in London, and he in turn despatched his messenger
to the various companies, bearing his "warrants" for their cessation. Such, at least, was the procedure in 1636, and we may
assume that it was the usual one.[1] Similarly, when the Council
issued its orders for the closing of the theaters in Lent, these were
"signified" to the players by the Master.[2] When the higher
authorities were displeased at the content of plays, they sometimes acted through the Master; as in 1617, when the Council bade him prevent the representation of a play concerning the
Marquess d'Ancre;[3] and in 1640, when the King commanded
Herbert to suppress and punish the performance of an unlicensed play which reflected on his Majesty.[4] But when the
Master had licensed a play of which the Council afterwards disapproved, they sometimes acted over his head, arrested the
players, and called him to account for his indiscretion. A
striking case of this sort is that of the *Game at Chess*, in 1624.[5]

Besides transmitting the orders of his superiors, the Master
exercised extensive authority on his own initiative. His power
to license players remained always somewhat ill defined. There
is no clear case of his ever licensing actors for performances in
and about London. The patented companies who held a practical monopoly of the drama in that city may have made it worth
his while to refrain from any invasion of their exclusive privileges.
Or perhaps direct royal authority was considered necessary for
any such intrusion. The French company which performed
in London in 1635 had special royal permission.[6] Possibly the
same favor was shown to the French players in 1629, who paid
Herbert fees for performances.[7] Concerning the "company of
strangers" who appeared in 1623, we know little.[8]

The litigation regarding Herbert's claims after the Restoration
bears out this view of the limitation of his jurisdiction, — that

[1] *1821 Variorum*, III, 239.
[2] Extract from the Council Register in Collier, *English Dramatic Poetry*, I,
380, note.
[3] See below, p. 113.    [4] See below, p. 132.    [5] See below, pp. 119 ff.
[6] *1821 Variorum*, III, 121–122, note.    [7] *Ibid.*, 120, note.    [8] See below, p. 77.

is, that his license alone was not sufficient for players performing
in London. In a list of the points to be proved he notes, "to
prove the Licensinge of Playhouses and of Playes to Acte,"
and "to prove the suppressinge of Players and their Obedience";[1]
but apparently does not claim the right to license players who have
no previous commission. On several occasions after the Restoration the question of Herbert's jurisdiction came up in court,
and at one of these trials, before a London jury, "the Master of
Revels was allowd' the correction of Plaies and Fees for soe
doeing; but not to give Plaiers any licence or authoritie to play,
it being provd' that no Plaiers were ever authorizd' in London or
Westminster, to play by the Commession of the Master of the
Revels; but by authoritie immediately from the Crowne."[2]

To the London companies patented by the King, however,
the Master of the Revels sold other licenses of various sorts.
He seems to have issued to them special traveling commissions,
which were probably renewed yearly. There was an entry, at
least, in Herbert's Register, of his granting to the King's company on July 1, 1625, a "confirmation of their patent to travel
for a year."[3] When some of the actors of the privileged
companies got together a temporary organization for touring
purposes, it is probable that they generally secured a special
commission from the Master.[4]

Herbert sold to the established companies also licenses of a
different sort, — "warrants of protection," such as the Master
was authorized, by his "special commissions," to issue to men
employed in his Majesty's Revels.[5] A copy of such a warrant
issued on December 27, 1624, gives a list of more than a dozen
names, and certifies that these men are all employed by the
King's Majesty's servants — that is, the King's company — as
musicians and other necessary attendants during the time of the
Revels; "in which tyme they nor any of them are to be arested,

[1] Halliwell-Phillipps, *Dramatic Records*, 26.          [2] *Ibid.*, 48–49.
[3] Chalmers, *Supplemental Apology*, 185, note. Chalmers' reference here to
Rymer's *Fœdera* is to a copy of King Charles' patent to the King's company of
June 24, 1625.
[4] See such a commission from the Master's chief, the Lord Chamberlain,
mentioned above, p. 39.
[5] See above, p. 51.

or deteyned under arest, imprisoned, Press'd for Souldiers or
any other molestacion Whereby they may bee hindered from
doeing his Majesties service, without leave firste had and ob-
teyned of the Lord Chamberlyne of his Maiesties most honorable
household, or of the Maister of his Maiesties Revells. And if
any shall presume to interrupt or deteyne them or any of them
after notice hereof given by this my Certificate hee is to aunswere
itt att his vtmost perill. H. Herbert." [1]

It was doubtless a similar warrant that Herbert meant when
he entered in his Register on April 9, 1627, "For a warrant to the
Musitions of the king's company . . . £1." [2]

Though his authority to license unpatented players in London remained doubtful, the Master's right to license any traveling actors for performances throughout the country seems to
have been well established. We have seen an example of its
exercise under Tilney in 1583.[3] At Leicester in 1623 a company
"that did belong to the M$^r$ of the Revells" was paid for not
playing. In 1626 players appeared there "going about with a
Pattent from the M$^r$ of the Revells"; in 1630 came three companies "with a commission from the Master of the Revells";
and in 1639, "the servants of the Master of the Revells." [4]
Among the entries of strange shows extracted by Chalmers
from Herbert's Register, are some which indicate annual licenses of this sort to traveling players: "a warrant to Francis
Nicolini, an Italian, and his Company, 'to dance on the ropes,
to use Interludes and Masques, and to sell his powders and bal-
sams'; to John Puncteus, a Frenchman, professing Physick,
with ten in his Company, to exercise the quality of playing, for
a year, and to sell his drugs." [5]  Had we still Herbert's complete
Register, we could doubtless find many better examples of annual
licenses to traveling companies.

An interesting case illustrative of the Master's jurisdiction in
such matters appears immediately after the Restoration. On

[1] Halliwell-Phillipps, *Dramatic Records*, 16.
[2] *1821 Variorum*, 112. Malone interprets the entry as "an annual fee for a
license to play in the theatre."
[3] See above, p. 53.
[4] Kelly, *Drama in Leicester*, under the years cited.
[5] Chalmers, *Supplemental Apology*, 209, note.

October 8, 1660, the Mayor and the Recorder of Maidstone wrote to Sir Henry Herbert, notifying him of the arrival in that town of several players bearing his commission. The municipal officials appear to be somewhat ignorant of the laws governing the drama, now that the Puritan prohibition is relaxed. They inform Herbert that they do not question his license to these players "so farre as they shall use the same according to lawe, to which your license doth prudently and carefully tye them. One particular of which theyre lawfull exercise we conceive to be within the verge of his Majesties courte, wherever it shall be, in any parte of England, where they may be under your eye and care, for the reforminge and regulating any abuses of their license, which might be committed by them. But we do not finde that you doe, and presume you did not intend to, grant them a licence to wander abroad all England over, at what distance soever from you." The writers next cite the Statute 39 Elizabeth, permitting noblemen's companies, as the rule which they are following, and refuse to grant further license.[1]

Sir Henry was indignant at such a rebellion against his authority. On the following day he replied sternly to the Mayor of Maidstone. His license, he declares, "is granted upon the conditions of good behaviour to the lawes and ordinances of superiors." But while the players bear themselves properly, the Mayor has no right to suppress them. "You are the first Mayor or other officer, that did ever dispute the authority, or the extent of it; for to confine it to the verge of the Court, is such a sense as was never imposed upon it before, and contrary to the constant practice; for severall grantes have been made by me, since the happy restoration of our gracious sovereign, to persons in the like quality; and seriously, therefore, admitted into all the counties and liberties of England, without any dispute or molestation." Herbert requires the Mayor to permit the men to perform, according to their license, and threatens, if he refuses, to summon him to Court, to answer for his "disobedience to his Majesties authority derived unto me under the great seale of England." To show the peril of questioning the

---

[1] The letter is printed in full in Warner, *Epistolary Curiosities*, I, 59–60.

power of the Revels Office, he even hints that the Mayor has endangered the charter of his corporation.[1]

These claims of Sir Henry's, coupled with what we know of his practice before the Civil War, indicate that the Master clearly had the right to license traveling companies for performances throughout the kingdom, and that such a commission from him was superior to the authority of local officials, who had no right to refuse the bearers of it permission to play. Concerning the extent to which he exercised this power and the price for which he sold such commissions, we have at present no information.

It is apparent from the extracts cited above, showing permission for rope dancing and even the sale of drugs, that the Master did not confine his traffic to the "legitimate" drama alone. All sorts of showmen were authorized by him. From Chalmers' quotations from the Register we learn of licenses for "making show of an Elephant"; for "a live Beaver"; for an "outlandish creature called a Possum"; for two Dromedaries; for a Camel; for a "Showing Glass, called the World's Wonder"; for a "Musical Organ, with divers motions in it"; for "tumbling and vaulting, with other tricks of slight of hand"; for "certain freaks of charging and discharging a gun"; for teaching the art of music and dancing; and for a show of pictures in wax.[2] Some of these are mentioned as licenses for the space of a year; others as being issued *gratis;* and for one the price received is given. The Dutchman who obtained the license "to show two Dromedaries for a year" paid one pound.

The business of licensing such shows must have been a profitable one, for the Master and his Deputy made great efforts to develop it. After the Restoration, Sir Henry Herbert, among suggestions for the confirmation and extension of the powers of the Revels Office, desired that it should have jurisdiction over all dancing schools, "wakes or rural feasts," and lotteries, and should even have the right to license "gaming" contrary to the law.[3] He seems to have claimed authority also over billiards,

---

[1] Warner, *Epistolary Curiosities*, I, 61–63.
[2] Chalmers, *Supplemental Apology*, 208–209, note.
[3] Warner, *Epistolary Curiosities*, I, 185–187.

ninepins, and cock-fighting,[1] — anything, in fact, over which his
jurisdiction could possibly be stretched, and the licensing of
which might be a source of profit.

He tried also to make his licensing power an exclusive one,
necessary to all showmen in the kingdom. In 1661 Herbert
secured from the Lord Chamberlain an order addressed to all
Mayors, Sheriffs, and Justices of the Peace throughout the
realm, declaring that any persons in any city, borough, town corporate, village, hamlet, or parish, acting or presenting any
"play, show, motion, feats of activitie and sights whatsoever,"
without a license now in force under the hand and seal of the
Master of the Revels, must have their grants or licenses taken
from them and sent to the Revels Office; and that all plays or
shows must be suppressed until approved and licensed by Sir
Henry Herbert or his Deputy.[2] We find the Revels Office trying to enforce this wide authority two years later. On July 23,
1663, one of the Messengers of the Office was despatched to
Bristol, where fairs were to be held, there to investigate all
showmen whatsoever, and see that they had commissions from
the Revels, or that such as had not, paid a proper fee or gave a
bond for their future obedience.[3] How extensively the Master
had enforced such rights over the provinces before the Civil
War, it is impossible at present to ascertain.

The facts concerning the Master's licensing of playhouses are
not entirely clear. In Tilney's time, as we have seen from the
entries in Henslowe's Diary, it appears that he received a regular
sum for the licensing of established theaters, which increased
from ten shillings a week in 1596, 1597, and 1598, to three pounds
a month in 1599 and later years.[4] In 1601 the three pounds per
month is specified as a payment for the Fortune theater.[5] Sir
George Buc ventured on a more radical exercise of power, —
the granting, in 1613, of a license to erect a new playhouse in
Whitefriars, then part of the City of London.[6] For this he

---

[1] Halliwell-Phillipps, *Dramatic Records,* 53–56, 59–60.
[2] *Ibid.,* 42–44.    [3] *Ibid.,* 50–51.
[4] *Henslowe's Diary,* 40, 46, 54, 72, 129, 130, 132, 160, 161; *Henslowe Papers,* 58.
[5] *Henslowe's Diary,* 132, 160.    [6] See below, p. 146.

received £20.[1] Sir Henry Herbert copied this entry from Buc's Office Book into his own, apparently to serve as a precedent for similar licenses in future, and after the Restoration he specifically claimed the right to grant permission to erect playhouses.[2] But we have no record of the Master's ever having exercised this right except in the single case of the new White-friars theater in 1613.

Under Herbert the regular monthly fees for licenses for existing playhouses were apparently no longer paid, — possibly because the London theaters were specifically named and performances in them authorized by the royal patents to the favored companies. Instead of these payments, Herbert received from the players other sums, on which we get some light from his claims after the Restoration and the extracts from his Register. In 1628 the King's company, he tells us, "with a general consent and alacrity," arranged to give him two benefit performances a year, one in summer and one in winter, "to be taken out of the second day of a revived play, at his own choice." For five years and a half this arrangement continued, netting Herbert, on an average, £8 19s. 4d. from each performance. In 1633 a change was made, the managers of the company agreeing to pay him the fixed sum of £10 every Christmas and the same at Midsummer, in lieu of his two benefits.[3] When Herbert was asserting his claims in 1662, he declared that his profit from each of the benefit performances amounted to £50, — an astonishing multiplication of his actual receipts which it is hard to understand.[4] Corresponding to this alleged profit from the King's company was the payment from the other actors noted by Herbert as, "For a share from each company of four companyes of players (besides the late Kinges Company), valued at a £100 a yeare, one yeare with another, besides the usuall fees." [5]

There were other payments alleged, in addition to this very considerable sum. For a "Christmas fee," Herbert asserted, he received £3,[6] and the same for a "Lenten fee." [7] Concerning

---

[1] *1821 Variorum*, III, 52, note.   [2] *Ibid.*, 246–248.
[3] *Ibid.*, 176–178.   [4] *Ibid.*, 266.   [5] *Ibid.*
[6] Possibly it was necessary for the companies to pay this for permission to play in the Christmas season.   [7] *1821 Variorum*, III, 266.

this second item, we gain further information from his Office Book. Performances in Lent were prohibited by order of the Privy Council, as we find from numerous entries in the Council Register.[1] In 1615, for example, representatives of the five companies were summoned before the Lords to answer "for playing in this prohibited time in Lent, notwithstanding the Lord Chamberlain's commandment signified to them by the Master of the Revels."[2] But by the purchase of a special license or dispensation from the Master, it was possible for the players to perform as usual, except on the "sermon days," as they were called, — that is, on Wednesday and Friday.[3] Herbert copied into his Register extracts from Buc's Office Book, showing the latter's practice in such cases. In 1617, we find, the Master received 44s. from the King's company "for a lenten dispensation, the other companys promising to doe as muche."[4] Under Herbert the price of these Lenten dispensations appears to have been generally £2. Such is the sum noted for the Cockpit company in 1624, and for the King's company in 1626.[5] Other shows gained the allowance at a cheaper rate, apparently; for the "dancers of the ropes" at the Fortune, in 1625, paid only one pound.[6] Possibly the price rose later, or Herbert's claim after the Restoration of £3 as the regular fee may be another of his exaggerations.

When the French company so much favored by the King and the Queen appeared in London in 1635, the King commanded Herbert that they should be allowed to play "the two sermon days in the week, during their time of playing in Lent," and as a result of this special privilege they took in the sum of £200. At Herbert's intercession for them the King granted also that they might "have freely to themselves the whole week

---

[1] See below, pp. 210–211.

[2] Extract from the Council Register, in Collier, *English Dramatic Poetry*, I, 380, note. Thompson (*Puritans and Stage*, 155) says that about this time the Master of the Revels was forbidden to grant any more Lenten dispensations; but I find no evidence of this. Indeed, it seems probable that his sale of these dispensations may have resulted from this rigorous action by the Council. Apparently it began two years later, in 1617. This date, at least, is that of the first case quoted by Herbert as a precedent.

[3] *1821 Variorum*, III, 65, note.   [4] *Ibid.*

[5] *Ibid.*, 66, note.   [6] *Ibid.*

before the week before Easter," — a favor which so pleased them that they offered the Master a present of £10. "But I refused itt," noted Herbert, "and did them many other curtesys gratis, to render the queene my mistris an acceptable service." [1] The Frenchmen did not escape, however, without some contribution to the Revels Office, for it appears from a later entry that they gave Sir Henry's Deputy "three pounds for his paines." [2] Such relaxation of the law against Lenten performances was naturally distasteful to the Puritans. Prynne, we find, refers to it in his *Histriomastix* in 1632.[3]

The Master of the Revels was also able at times to secure for the players some relaxation of the orders against performances in plague time, or to hasten the opening of the theaters as the infection subsided. In June, 1631, Herbert received from the King's company the profit on a performance of *Pericles* at the Globe, amounting to £3 10s. od., "for a gratuity for their liberty gaind unto them of playinge, upon the cessation of the plague." [4] Other "occasional gratuities," as Herbert called them, helped to swell his income. One profitable contribution of this sort we find in his Office Book: on July 17, 1626, three pounds "from Mr. Hemmings, for a courtesy done him about their Blackfriars house." [5] Besides such gratuities on various occasions, Herbert had also, as he later asserted, "a box gratis" at each of the theaters.[6]

One of the most considerable sources of revenue for the Master was that derived from the exercise of his most important function, the censorship and licensing of plays. He became sole censor of the drama in and about London; his was the responsibility of seeing that nothing was performed in any way seditious or offensive to the authorities. No play, new or old, could be presented — theoretically, at least — without his permission.

During the early years of Herbert's administration, it seems possible that his authority as licenser of plays sometimes extended only over the privileged companies. In 1623 we find a puzzling

[1] *1821 Variorum*, III, 121, note.
[2] *Ibid.*, 122, note.
[3] p. 784. *1821 Variorum*, III, 66, note.
[4] *Ibid.*, 177, note.
[5] *Ibid.*, 229.
[6] *Ibid.*, 266.

entry in his Register, stating, according to Malone, that the play, *Come See a Wonder*, "written by John Daye for a company of strangers," was acted at the Red Bull and licensed without his hand to it, because they — that is, this company of strangers — were none of the four companies.[1] Who else could have licensed the play is not apparent, — the Lord Chamberlain, possibly; and, in the absence of further information, the entry is hard to understand. The French company which appeared in 1629 was apparently subject to the Master's orders; for twice he received from them £2 for the right of playing one day; and on a third occasion he remitted half this fee, "in respect of their ill fortune."[2]

Over the patented companies, at all events, Sir Henry exercised a strict jurisdiction. Their performance of any play without his license was a serious offense, as we learn from the very humble submission tendered to him by the King's company in 1624, when they had offended in this way.

"To Sir Henry Herbert, K^t. master of his Ma.^ties Revells.

"After our humble servise remembered unto your good worship, Whereas not long since we acted a play called The Spanishe Viceroy, not being licensed under your worships hande, nor allowed of: wee doe confess and herby acknowledge that wee have offended, and that it is in your power to punishe this offense, and are very sorry for it; and doe likewise promise herby that wee will not act any play without your hand or substituts hereafter, nor doe any thinge that may prejudice the authority of your office: So hoping that this humble submission of ours may bee accepted, wee have therunto sett our hands."[3]

The Master had the right to suppress a play at any time. Upon any complaint concerning one, he was accustomed to order its withdrawal from the stage until he was satisfied that nothing offensive had been introduced, or it was changed to suit his judgment.

The methods which he followed in exercising his censorship we can trace in some detail. From Tilney's time onward, as we know from his "indenture" of 1583,[4] and from surviving

---

[1] *1821 Variorum*, III, 224.     [2] *Ibid.*, 120, note.
[3] *Ibid.*, 209–210.     [4] See above, p. 53.

manuscripts, it was customary for the book-keeper of the company to submit to him a copy of the play before its performance, that he might read it at his leisure. He demanded that this should be a "fair copy," [1] and complained at times of the illegibility of the manuscripts.[2] The Master went over the play-book with care, striking out or altering single words and whole passages, and noting in the margin that certain objectionable scenes must be radically changed.[3] He then indorsed on the manuscript his license to act.

"This Second Maydens Tragedy (for it has no name inscribed) may with the reformacions bee acted publikely. 31. October. 1611. G. Buc." [4]

"This Play called ye *Seamans honest wife*, all ye Oaths left out in the action as they are crost in ye booke & all other Reformations strictly observed, may bee acted, not otherwise. This 27th June, 1633. Henry Herbert." [5]

In such words the license was given. Sometimes the Master's Deputy made the corrections and wrote the permission, as in the case of the *Lady Mother*, licensed by Blagrave in 1635.[6]

Though the custom was evidently not consistently followed, Herbert desired that copies of the plays should be left with the Master, "that he may be able to shew what he hath allowed or disallowed." [7] He could thus defend himself against blame for improper interpolations made later by the actors, as in the case of Jonson's *Magnetic Lady*, when the players at first "would have excused themselves," says Herbert, "on mee and the poett"; but afterwards confessed that they themselves were to blame for the interpolations.[8] It was naturally difficult for the Master to keep track of what was actually said at the performances. He directed the company's book-keeper to make the alterations in the actors' parts which he had indicated on the play-book; and declared that the players ought not to study their rôles until the text had been allowed.[9]

---

[1] Bullen, *Old Plays*, II, 432.      [2] Chalmers, *Supplemental Apology*, 217.
[3] On the nature of his corrections, see below, pp. 93 ff., 109 ff., 114 ff.
[4] See below, p. 109.      [5] Bullen, *Old Plays*, II, 432.      [6] *Ibid.*, 200.
[7] *1821 Variorum*, III, 208.      [8] *Ibid.*, 233.      [9] *Ibid.*, 208–210.

But there must have been much carelessness in carrying out these rules and many opportunities for interpolations by the actors.

The fee received by the Master for the licensing of a play varied during the period. Under Tilney, as we learn from Henslowe's Diary, it was, in 1592, 5s., then 6s., and later 6s. 8d.[1] In the years 1598-1600, the fee was uniformly 7s. a play.[2]

This seems to be the most fitting place for a discussion of these entries in Henslowe's Diary. There is little doubt that they were actually payments to the Master for licenses to act certain plays. The first group of entries is perhaps the most dubious. It is a series of payments "to Mr. Tilney's man," occurring about once a week from February 26 to June 14, 1592; always for 5s. until May 13, when the sum is 12s., — presumably for two plays; and on the three occasions after that, for 6s. 8d. As Lord Strange's company began to perform at Henslowe's theater, the Rose, on February 19, and continued until June 22 of this year, it seems most probable that these payments were for licensing plays.

The later entries are scattered here and there through the Diary, and are in some such form as, "Paid unto the Master of the Revels' man for the licensing of a book, 7s." These have been generally considered licenses for performance, but Mr. Fleay asserts: "The instances are far too few to allow of this interpretation. It meant licensing for the press independently of the Stationers' Company."[3] This appears very improbable. It is not until 1606 that we have definite evidence of the Master's licensing for printing, and his authorization was then regularly entered on the Stationers' Register.[4] Moreover, it is very unlikely that Henslowe would desire to have the plays licensed for printing, — especially so soon after they were written. In two cases where the name of the play is given, the license was purchased only about a month after the author was paid for his work.[5] The well-known objection of players to the publication of their plays is here illustrated by Henslowe's

[1] *Henslowe's Diary*, 12.
[2] *Ibid.*, 83, 85, 90, 103, 109, 116, 117, 121.
[3] *London Stage*, 107.
[4] See below, pp. 84 ff.
[5] *Henslowe's Diary*, 120, 121.

entry of a gift of 40s. on March 18, 1600, to the printer "to staye the printing of patient grissel." [1]

The smallness of the number of licenses, on which Mr. Fleay bases his assertion, is easily explained. In the first place many of the payments were doubtless entered on the pages of the Diary which are now missing, and others were perhaps not entered at all. Henslowe's accounts were kept in a chaotic manner, and the entries we have appear to have survived casually in groups. The fact that he made payments to the Master which do not appear in the Diary is shown by his noting, on February 27, 1596, "the master of the Revelles payd untell this time al wch J owe hime," [2] whereas there are no entries of any payments to Tilney for a year preceding this; and also by the appearance of one of the Revels receipts among the Henslowe Papers.[3] Moreover, it seems that it was not always Henslowe's duty, as manager of the theater, to pay for such licenses for performance, but that this financial obligation sometimes rested on the company. There are several entries in a form something like this: "*Lent unto the company* to pay unto the Master of the Revels for the licensing of two books." [4] When the company did not borrow the fee from Henslowe, their payment, of course, would not appear in his accounts. Finally, Mr. Fleay himself remarks, in discussing these licenses for printing — as he considers them: "It is curious that in every instance where Henslowe gives a play-name the play is non-extant." [5] That is, the plays were probably never printed.[6]

In view of all this, and also the fact that we know Tilney was licensing plays for performance at this time, and in the absence of support for Mr. Fleay's assertion, it seems most likely that these entries in Henslowe's Diary were payments for licenses to *act* certain plays.

---

[1] *Henslowe's Diary*, 119.        [2] *Ibid.*, 28.        [3] *Henslowe Papers*, 58.

[4] *Henslowe's Diary*, 83, 148. The term "book," it should be said, has no reference to a printed volume, but is the usual word for a play.

[5] *London Stage*, 107.

[6] It might perhaps be suggested that these printing licenses were bought with no intention of publication, but merely to gain a sort of copyright and thereby forestall others who might secure a license and actually print the plays. This does not, however, seem probable.

By the time Herbert took office, the regular fee for licensing a new play had apparently risen to one pound. This was the sum he received from the King's company on April 10, 1624, for Davenport's *History of Henry the First*.[1] In cases where he had exceptional trouble with the corrections, he was sometimes paid double this sum, as on January 2, 1624, for the *History of the Duchess of Suffolk*, "which being full of dangerous matter was much reformed by me," notes Herbert. "I had two pounds for my pains."[2] Apparently this larger sum afterwards became the regular price. In 1632 he received it for Jonson's *Magnetic Lady*,[3] and in 1642 for several plays.[4] After the Restoration he succeeded in establishing his claim to £2 as the regular fee for a new play.[5]

Herbert held that the payment was not for licensing the play, but for his trouble in reading it over. When he refused to license Massinger's *Believe As You List*, in 1631, because of its "dangerous matter," he entered in his Office Book, "I had my fee notwithstanding, which belongs to me for reading itt over, and ought to be brought always with the booke."[6] And in June, 1642, he noted thus briefly a transaction which must have been somewhat irritating to the players: "Received of Mr. Kirke, for a new play which I burnte for the ribaldry and offense that was in it, £2. o. o."[7]

On the revival of old plays, it was generally necessary to get the Master's approval; but there was at first apparently no fee paid, especially if the players still had the copy bearing the former authorization. On August 19, 1623, Herbert notes: "For the King's players. An olde playe called Winter's Tale, formerly allowed of by Sir George Bucke, and likewyse by mee on Mr. Hemmings his word that there was nothing profane added or reformed, thogh the allowed booke was missinge; and therefore I returned it without a fee."[8] A little later Herbert seems to have felt that some present to him was fitting when he allowed an old drama of which the original license was lost. He notes

[1] *1821 Variorum*, III, 229.   [2] Chalmers, *Supplemental Apology*, 217, note.
[3] *1821 Variorum*, III, 231.   [4] *Ibid.*, 240–241.
[5] *Ibid.*, 266; Halliwell-Phillipps, *Dramatic Records*, 36, 37.
[6] *1821 Variorum*, III, 231.   [7] *Ibid.*, 241.   [8] *Ibid.*, 229.

in February, 1625, that "an olde play called The Honest Mans Fortune, the originall being lost, was re-allowed by mee at Mr. Taylor's intreaty, and on consideration to give mee a booke." [1]

In 1633 Herbert became convinced that greater care was necessary in the supervision of old plays. The *Tamer Tamed* was revived by the King's company in October of that year; whereupon complaint was made to the Master that it contained "foul and offensive matters." Herbert ordered the suppression of the play and sent for the book, to find that the accusation was justified and the *Tamer Tamed* indeed much in need of "reformation." In the account of the affair in his Register he declares that "all ould plays ought to bee brought to the Master of the Revels, and have his allowance to them for which he should have his fee, since they may be full of offensive things against church and state; y^e rather that in former time the poetts took greater liberty than is allowed them by mee." [2] This rule he now appears to have put into force, for in the following month he received from the King's company one pound for Fletcher's *Loyal Subject*, licensed by Buc in 1618 and now "perused and with some reformations allowed of " by Herbert. [3] One pound apparently became the Master's regular fee for a revived play. He claimed this after the Restoration and, though its legality was questioned, was for a time successful in establishing it. [4]

Though the Master claimed the exclusive right of censoring and licensing plays throughout the kingdom, [5] it is not probable that he exercised this at all rigorously outside of London. Practically all plays of any importance must have been performed first at the capital. It would scarcely have been possible or profitable for him to enforce his censorship over all the insignificant local productions throughout England.

The Master's possession of the power of forbidding the performance of any play apparently led to his occasional interference

[1] *1821 Variorum*, III, 229. Malone states — on what authority does not appear — that the book given was the *Arcadia*. Were it not for this assertion, one might imagine that Herbert was referring to a copy of the play-book.

[2] *1821 Variorum*, III, 208–210. See below, pp. 124 ff. [3] *1821 Variorum*, III, 234.

[4] *Ibid.*, 266; Halliwell-Phillipps, *Dramatic Records*, 36, 37, 49.

[5] See above, pp. 53, 73.

to prevent a company from stealing a drama belonging to other actors. Though the players or manager who purchased a play from its author seem to have had a property right in it, there was difficulty in enforcing this, except by careful guarding of all copies of the play-book, so that none might be available for performance by others. This was an urgent reason, of course, for avoiding the printing of plays. Probably the prominent London companies had some agreement binding them to respect each other's property; but at times of hostility between the theaters thefts of plays occasionally occurred. About 1600, for example, the Chapel Children appropriated the *Spanish Tragedy*, belonging to the Lord Chamberlain's company; and in 1604 the latter, then the King's men, in retaliation took the boys' *Malcontent*.[1] The simplest way of avoiding such thefts was for a company to get the Master to forbid the performance of its plays by others. In 1627, four years after the publication of the First Folio had made Shakspere's dramas easily available, the King's company paid Herbert the considerable sum of five pounds "to forbid the playing of Shakespeare's plays to the Red Bull company."[2] How frequently the Master's authority was invoked in such cases we do not know.

In 1639 his superior officer, the Lord Chamberlain, interfered on a somewhat similar occasion. William Beeston's company of the "King's and Queen's young players," performing at the Cockpit theater in that year, were anxious to have confirmed their exclusive right to certain plays, many of which they seem to have inherited from the Queen's company, who had previously occupied the Cockpit. Beeston was able to secure from the Lord Chamberlain an edict forbidding the acting of these plays by other companies. This document gives a list of the dramas, "all of which are in his propriety," and requires all masters and governors of playhouses in and about London to forbear to intermeddle with them, "as they tender his Majesty's displeasure."[3] Possibly the authority of the Lord Chamberlain was

---

[1] See Small, *Stage Quarrel*, 115; Fleay, *English Drama*, II, 78; Bullen's Marston, I, 203.

[2] *1821 Variorum*, III, 229.

[3] The edict is printed in Chalmers, *Apology*, 516, and in *1821 Variorum*, III, 159.

used on other similar occasions to protect the King's players.

A new source of revenue for the Master of the Revels was developed in the extension of his licensing power over the printing as well as the performance of plays. Under the Injunctions of 1559, regulating the censorship of the press in London, it was necessary for all "pamphlets, plays and ballads" to be licensed before printing by three Commissioners for Religion.[1] But in practice the license was generally given by the Master and Wardens of the Stationers' Company,[2] — a custom which persisted to a considerable extent in later years. A Star Chamber decree in 1586 constituted the Archbishop of Canterbury and the Bishop of London sole censors and licensers of all printed books; and in 1588 the Archbishop delegated this authority to several licensers.[3] There was evidently some laxness in carrying out the rule, for on June 1, 1599, the Archbishop and the Bishop reminded the Stationers' Company that no plays should be printed "excepte they bee allowed by such as have aucthorytie."[4]

Sir George Buc appears to have been the one who first thought of extending the Master's powers in this direction. Without any especial authority from the Crown or the Lord Chamberlain, so far as we know, but merely as a natural part of his duties as general regulator of the drama, he began to license plays for printing. On November 21, 1606, Buc appears in the Stationers' Register as licenser of the *Fleare*, a comedy.[5] Several plays are then entered under other license; but on April 10, 1607, Buc appears again, and from now on until 1615 every play except two was entered under the license of the Master or his Deputy. He had evidently almost established his authority as sole censor of printed plays. But as Buc's energy waned with his advancing

---

[1] Arber, *Martin Marprelate Controversy*, 49–50.

[2] *Ibid.*, 51–52.    [3] *Ibid.*, 50–51.

[4] Arber, *Transcript*, III, 677. The most convenient account of the censorship of the press at this period is in Arber, *Martin Marprelate Controversy*, as cited above. Additional facts may be found in his *Transcript*, I, xxxviii; III, 15 ff., 690; IV, 26 ff.

[5] Mr. Fleay has tabulated in convenient form (*Life of Shakespeare*, 328 ff.) all the plays entered in the Stationers' Register, indicating the name of the licenser in the case of those allowed by the Master or his Deputy.

years, the administration of the Revels Office apparently grew lax, and a considerable number of plays appeared under other license. As Herbert developed his business, however, he reëstablished this authority, and from 1628 to 1637 he or his Deputy licensed every play entered in the Stationers' Register. After January 29, 1638, the Revels license appears no more, — perhaps as a result of Archbishop Laud's new regulations concerning the censorship of the press.[1]

In some cases the Master extended his authority over the licensing of books of poetry as well as plays. Two interesting entries in Herbert's Office Book show receipts from this new branch of his business. In October, 1632, he received "from Henry Seyle for allowinge a booke of verses of my Lord Brooks, entitled Religion, Humane Learning, Warr, and Honor . . . in mony 1*l. 0s. 0d.*, in books to the value of 1*l. 4s. 0d.*"; and also "more of Seyle, for allowinge of two other small peeces of verses for the press, done by a boy of this town called Cowley, at the same time . . . 0*l. 10s. 0d.*" [2] This new business was not without its drawbacks, however. In the following month, on November 14, 1632, Sir Henry was summoned before the Star Chamber, "by the King's command delivered by the Bishop of London," to "give account why he warranted" Donne's *Paradoxes* to be printed.[3]

During the latter part of our period, as we shall presently see, the Lord Chamberlain frequently acted directly in cases of trouble in the dramatic world, without reference to his subordinate, the Master of the Revels. In 1637 we find him exercising his authority over the press. Difficulties had arisen from the printing of plays belonging to the King's and the Queen's companies, without their consent. The Earl of Pembroke and Montgomery, then Lord Chamberlain, consequently addressed an edict to the Stationers' Company, ordering them not to allow the printing of any dramas belonging to these actors, without first ascertaining whether they consented to the publication.

[1] See Arber, *Transcript*, III, 15, 16.
[2] *1821 Variorum*, III, 231, note. See also Chalmers, *Supplemental Apology*, 209, note.
[3] *State Papers, Dom.*, 1631–1633, 437.

He refers to a similar order by his predecessor, which has been disregarded.[1]

After the Restoration efforts were made by the Revels Office to continue the licensing for the press. Hayward, who had purchased the Deputyship from Sir Henry Herbert, and was finding his bargain an unprofitable one, was especially anxious to increase his income from this source.[2] An interesting document of July 25, 1663, entitled "Arguments to proue that the Master of his Maiesties Office of the Revells, hath not onely the power of Lycencing all playes, Poems, and ballads, but of appointing them to the Press," shows the wide jurisdiction claimed and the attempted justification therefor.

"That the Master of his Maiesties office of the Revells, hath the power of Lycencing all playes whether Tragedies, or Comedies before they can bee acted, is without dispute and the designe is, that all prophaneness, oathes, ribaldry, and matters reflecting upon piety, and the present governement may bee obliterated, before there bee any action in a publique Theatre.

"The like equitie there is, that all Ballads, songs and poems of that nature, should pass the same examinacion, being argued a Majore ad Minus, and requiring the same antidote, because such things presently fly all over the Kingdom, to the Debauching and poisoning the younger sort of people, unles corrected, and regulated.

"The like may bee said as to all Billes for Shewes, and stage playes, Mountebankes, Lotteries &c. because they all receive Commissions from the Master of the Revells who ought to inspect the same, that their pretences may agree with what is granted by their Commissions, otherwise many of them may Divide their Companies and by way of cheat (as hath beene vsuall) make one Commission serve for two Companies, if not for three.

"Now from the premisses, it may bee concluded but rationall, that hee who hath the power of allowing and Lycencing (as the Master hath) should likewise bee authorised to appoint and order the press, least after such examination and allowance, alterations should bee made, and the abuse proue a scandall and reflection vpon the Master, and therefore all sober, considerate persons must from the premisses conclude, that the ordering of the Press doth of right belong to the

[1] The edict of 1637 is printed in Chalmers, *Apology*, 513–514, note ; and in *1821 Variorum*, III, 160–161, note. I have found no other cases of interference by the Master or the Lord Chamberlain to prevent the printing of a company's plays against its will.

[2] Halliwell-Phillipps, *Dramatic Records*, 53–56, 58, 60.

Master of the Revells; and in order to the regulating of this business, and to make it knowne to the world, that not onely the power of it, but the care of well ordering, bounding and correcting all vnsavoury words, and vnbecomming expressions, (not fitt to bee Lycenced in a christian Commonwealth,) belongeth solely and properly to the Master of the Revells, all Poetts and Printers, and other persons concerned, are to take notice, after this manifestation shall come out, or a precept Drawne from thence, bee sent vnto them that they and every of them doe for the future, forbeare their poetry and printing, soe farre as may concerne the premisses, without Lycence first obteined from the Office of the Revells, over against Petty Cannons hall in St. Pauls churchyard, where they may certainely find one or more of the officers every day." [1]

The general supervision of the stage intrusted to the Master of the Revels extended to various cases besides those main lines of his duty which we have been considering. Anything connected with the drama seems to have been within his province. For example, in 1626 a long-standing dispute between the widow of a shareholder and the surviving members of one of the patented companies, was referred to the Master for settlement.[2] A curious case in 1635, showing the extent of the Master's power, is revealed by this entry in Herbert's Register: —

"I committed Cromes, a broker in Longe Lane, the 16 of Febru. 1634, to the Marshalsey, for lending a church-robe with the name of Jesus upon it, to the piayers in Salisbury Court, to present a Flamen, a priest of the heathens. Upon his petition of submission, and acknowledgemer.t of his faulte, I releasd him, the 17 Febr. 1634." [3]

On the whole, the Master's business was an extensive and a profitable one. Herbert apparently paid to Astley during the latter's life, £150 a year for the office,[4] and his receipts beyond this sum were so considerable that, as his brother, Lord Herbert of Cherbury, tells us, "by these means, as also by a good marriage, he attained to great fortunes for himself and his posterity to enjoy." [5] From Sir Henry's rather confused statements after the Restoration, it is difficult to make out exactly how much he

---

[1] Halliwell-Phillipps, *Dramatic Records*, 51–52.
[2] See the documents printed in Fleay, *London Stage*, 271 ff., 294 ff.
[3] *1821 Variorum*, III, 237.    [4] See above, p. 65.    [5] *Autobiography*, 23.

expected the income from his office to be. In his assertion that the failure of the players to pay his fees has cost him £5000 for five quarters, he appears to imply that his receipts had amounted, before the Civil War, to this sum, — that is, to £4000 per year. But this seems impossibly large. In the following accounts he sets down £163 per quarter, or £652 a year, as his expected receipts from some unspecified source.[1] Possibly this is his estimate of the normal profit from the sale of licenses and other gratuities. Together with his salary and allowances the payments from the players must certainly have swelled his yearly income to a handsome sum.

After the Restoration Herbert succeeded, as a result of some legal controversies, in reëstablishing his authority to a considerable extent. At his death in 1673, Thomas Killigrew became Master. The office retained some part of its jurisdiction until, in 1737, the bill for licensing the stage left it no shadow of its old authority.[2]

---

[1] The accounts are printed in Halliwell-Phillipps, *Dramatic Records*, 46–47.

[2] There is no satisfactory account of the office after the Restoration. Some facts will be found in the article on Sir Henry Herbert in the *Dictionary of National Biography;* in Chalmers, *Apology*, 521 ff., and *Supplemental Apology*, 212 ff.; and in Cibber's *Apology*, edited by Lowe, I, 275, 276 ff.

# CHAPTER III

## THE NATURE OF THE CENSORSHIP

OF far greater importance than the development and business organization of the Revels licensing department, which the preceding chapter has attempted to unravel, is the nature of that censorship of which the Master was the official administrator. It is an interesting task to trace the sort of control exercised by the government over the content of plays, and to speculate concerning its effect on the Elizabethan drama. The material throwing light on this subject is by no means so full as we could wish; but it is still possible to ascertain something from the surviving manuscripts showing the Master's expurgations, and from accounts of the instances in which he or his superiors interfered, — of all the cases, that is, in which players or playwrights got into trouble because of the content of their plays.

Judged by the standards of the time, the government supervision was, on the whole, a reasonable and a lenient one. The character of the men chosen for the office of Master of the Revels indicates a sense of fitness on the part of the government, for they were, as we have seen, gentlemen of good family, generally with some literary experience and qualifications, not apt to take any unreasonable or Philistine attitude towards the drama. It is, of course, necessary for us to remember that the idea of censorship at this period was something radically different from that which inspires the uncertain supervision exercised over the stage in England and sporadically in the United States at the present time. The Puritan notions concerning decency and morality scarcely affected the Master of the Revels, who naturally held the views of his class and his time. Scenes which to our modern sense of propriety seem inexpressibly offensive, the Master passed over without a misgiving. His concern was, in general, not a moral, but a practical political one, — the suppression of anything tending to cause disorder or contempt of authority.

As we have seen, the government of Elizabeth disapproved of any presentation upon the stage of "matters of religion or of the governance of the estate of the common weale." [1] In this attitude the authorities persisted, on the whole, throughout the period, frowning upon any controversial treatment of affairs of church and state. The Master and his superiors endeavored to prevent any remarks hostile to the form and theory of government then prevailing in England, — anything likely to stir up dissatisfaction, disorder, or revolt. Similarly, they suppressed anything reflecting on the national religion, or on foreign nations with which the government was anxious to keep on friendly terms. The protection of personages of rank from any disrespectful representation upon the stage was also a frequent concern of the Master. The King himself had to be guarded at times from such irreverence, and foreign sovereigns also — all "modern Christian kings" — the players were forbidden to represent. Neither were they supposed to attack or satirize noblemen, magistrates, or other persons of consequence, — a rule often broken and the cause of frequent interference by the authorities. Another chief concern of the later Masters was the enforcement of the statute of 1606, forbidding the use in plays of the name of the Deity.[2] In obedience to this, the censor tried to excise all oaths, and sometimes, as we shall see, had difficulty in deciding how strong a degree of affirmation was permissible. The nature of all this supervision will become clearer as we follow its history through the period.

We have treated in an earlier chapter the exercise of the censorship during the first part of the Tudor period. Our concern here is with the years during which the Master was in charge. There is nothing to indicate that during the first decade or more of his censorship the policy of the government was a very repressive one, or indeed that there was any considerable need for repression. The dramatists were in sympathy with the people, and the people were loyal supporters of the government

---

[1] See above, p. 15.    [2] See above, p. 19.

of Elizabeth. As Mr. Bond suggests,[1] the Queen herself was apparently not unwilling to see upon the stage a fairly frank representation of current political events, if we may judge from the slightly veiled symbolism which modern critics have discovered in *Endymion* and *Sappho and Phao*.

The first case of rigorous interference by the authorities under this régime was that of the Martin Marprelate controversy, already twice mentioned. The Martinists, the Puritan pamphleteers who assailed the Established Church, could of course expect no sympathy from the players, whom the Puritan party had long bitterly vituperated and endeavored to suppress. Ranging themselves with the government and the Court, the players replied by violent dramatic attacks on the Marprelate party. These controversial plays have not survived, and are known to us only by allusions in contemporary pamphlets. One appears to have been of the morality type, in which Martin was represented as an ape, vilely attacking the lady " Divinitie." In another he appeared with "a cocks combe, an apes face, a wolfes bellie, cats clawes." It seems probable, from an allusion in Lyly's *Pappe with a Hatchett*, that the former play was suppressed — possibly by the city authorities — before the latter part of September, 1589; and that other plays which had been written against Martin had been refused a license.[2] Apparently, however, some of the offensive dramas later got upon the stage, for on November 6 we find that the Privy Council had ordered the suppression of all plays in and about London, "in that Mr. Tilney did utterly mislike the same."[3] The correspondence relative to the establishment of the censorship commission, six days later, informs us that the ground of this disapproval was the players' having "taken upon them to handle in their plays certain matters of Divinity and of State unfit to be suffered."[4] This is rather vague. In the absence of more definite information, we can only conjecture that these controversial plays had caused disorders and complaints; that the authorities disapproved

---

[1] Edition of Lyly, I, 31.

[2] See Bond's Lyly, I, 52 ff., where the extracts from the pamphlets are conveniently given.

[3] See above, pp. 17–18 55 and below, pp. 176–177.     [4] *Acts*, XVIII, 214.

of the public representation of such grave matters in such a scurrilous manner; and that therefore, though the persons attacked were the bitter assailants of the Established Church, the government very properly suppressed all plays until measures could be taken to secure their more effective supervision. There is no indication that any of the players or playwrights were severely punished — the two members of Lord Strange's company imprisoned for disobeying the Lord Mayor were probably soon released — or that performances were interdicted for any considerable length of time.

It has generally been assumed that some similarly offensive representation of the religious controversy was the cause of the suppression of the Paul's Boys in 1590 or 1591. That "the Plaies in Paules were dissolved"[1] about this time, and not renewed until about 1600, is all we positively know concerning the matter.[2] In view of the comparatively lenient attitude generally taken by the government towards such offenses, it seems impossible that such an extremely severe punishment as exclusion from the stage for nearly nine years could have been inflicted because of a controversial play of this kind. What was the real cause of the loss of royal favor and of the decision that the Paul's Boys had best confine themselves for a time to their choral duties, we shall apparently never know.

If we are to believe an anonymous tract issued in 1592, greater freedom was allowed the players at this period for attacks on the Roman Catholic religion than on the Puritans. A pamphlet of 1592, attributed to Parsons the Jesuit, states that certain players have been suffered "to scoffe and jeast at" the King of Spain "upon their common stages," and to deride the Roman Catholic religion by annexing a verse against it to one of the Psalms of David.[3] So soon after the days of the Armada, it was natural to allow a disrespect to Spain and Catholicism which would have been promptly suppressed by the government in later years.[4]

---

[1] Printer's Preface to *Endymion*, licensed October 4, 1591.
[2] See Baker's edition of Lyly's *Endymion*, clv ff.; and Bond's Lyly, I, 62.
[3] Quoted in Collier, *English Dramatic Poetry*, I, 279.
[4] Compare the case of the *Game at Chess*. See below, pp. 118 ff.

Our most vivid glimpse of the sort of censorship exercised by Tilney during his administration is gained from the very interesting manuscript play-book of *Sir Thomas More*, showing the Master's "reformations." This anonymous play has been variously dated,—as early as 1586,[1] and as late as 1596.[2] Probably Dyce's conjecture is the most likely, — that it was written about 1590 or a little earlier.[3] The manuscript — Harleian 7368 — is a very confusing one, consisting of the official copy submitted to the censor and three different sets of alterations and additions, one of which, it has been contended, is actually in the handwriting of Shakspere himself.[4] The play sets forth the rise and fall of Sir Thomas More, — portraying him first as Sheriff of London, suppressing, by his eloquence and sound sense, the insurrection of the citizens against the foreign residents, on the "ill May Day" of 1517; then as Lord Chancellor, entertaining at his house the Lord Mayor and the Aldermen; later, as refusing to subscribe to the "articles" sent him by the King; imprisoned in the Tower; and finally on his way to execution. Throughout he is sympathetically represented as an admirable character, once in error, but greatly loved and respected by the people. Though he protests to the very end his loyalty to the King, he never retracts or repents his refusal to subscribe to the royal articles. "A very learned woorthie gentleman seales errour with his blood," says Surrey, at the end, summing up the portrayal of the Chancellor's character. As for the insurrection against the foreigners, though there are many sound speeches against rioting and sedition, and concerning the obedience due the King, the sympathy of the writer or writers is clearly with the citizens in their protests against the encroachments and outrages of the foreigners.

[1] R. Simpson, in *Notes and Queries*, July 1, 1871.

[2] Fleay, *English Drama*, II, 312.

[3] Dyce's edition, in Shakspere Society Publications, Vol. XXIII, 1844. The play seems to refer to the troubles of September, 1586, rather than to the prentice riots of 1595. But it is unlikely that the players would have ventured to produce the drama immediately after the height of the trouble. We may assume that an interval elapsed, — perhaps about three years or less. See below, p. 94.

[4] See R. Simpson, in *Notes and Queries*, July 1, 1871; and J. Spedding, *ibid.*, September 21, 1872.

The very fact that a playwright dared to treat without disguise such a critical point in the political history of the reign of the Queen's father, shows the freedom allowed to the stage at this time. From Tilney's "reformations" it appears that he was willing to have More's career portrayed, but felt some uneasiness at seeing such a popular and admirable person represented as disobedient to the royal authority. At the point where the Chancellor refuses to accede to the King's demand, the action is set forth without any seditious or disrespectful language whatsoever, and the contents of the "articles" is tactfully left unspecified. Nevertheless Tilney drew his pen through all the concluding portion of the scene, where More's refusal is represented, and wrote in the margin "all altered." [1]

He appears to have been even more afraid of anything tending to arouse, or even suggest, popular discontent or rebellion. Opposite the following speech by Shrewsbury he has written "Mend y$^t$."

> "My lord of Surrey, and Sir Thomas Palmer,
> Might I with patience tempte your graue aduise,
> I tell ye true, that in these daungerous times
> I do not like this frowning vulgare brow:
> My searching eye did neuer entertaine
> A more distracted countenaunce of greefe
> Then I haue late obseru'de
> In the displeased commons of the cittie." [2]

It seems very probable that the play gained much of its point from the similarity of the popular feeling against foreigners which it described, to the sentiment existing at the time the drama was written. This discontent nearly burst into violent acts in September, 1586, when Recorder Fleetwood wrote to Burghley that the apprentices had conspired an insurrection against the French and the Dutch, but especially the French, "all things as like unto yll May day as could be devised, in all manner of circumstances, *mutatis mutandis*." [3] It was natural that Tilney should try to cut out anything tending to inflame this popular

---

[1] Dyce's edition, p. 74.    [2] p. 14.

[3] See R. Simpson, in *Notes and Queries*, July 1, 1871. Mr. Fleay connects the play with the prentice riots of 1595. *English Drama*, II, 312.

feeling that had been so recently dangerous. On the margin, at the commencement of the play, he wrote: "Leave out y$^e$ insurrection wholy, and the cause thereoff, and begin with Sir Tho. Moore at y$^e$ mayors sessions, with a reportt afterwardes off his good service don, being shrive off London, uppon a meeting agaynst y$^e$ Lumbardes, only by a shortt reportt, and nott otherwise, att your own perrilles. E. Tyllney." [1] That is, he desired to have the players omit all the scenes where the citizens are abused by the foreigners and finally rise against their oppressors, and merely have a brief report of More's suppression of the rioting. He was particularly anxious to avoid anything tending to stir up the people against the French, and altered several lines to this end. For example, when Shrewsbury tells of insults offered by foreigners to the citizens, Tilney substitutes "Lombard" for "Frenchman"; [2] and in the account of the Frenchman Bard's impudent assertion that

> ". . . if he had the Maior of Londons wife
> He would keep her in despight of any Englishe,"

Tilney crosses out "Englishe" and writes merely "man." [3]

If this manuscript represents the text actually used for performance, the players apparently disobeyed some of the Master's instructions. The insurrection scene, for example, they seem to have left in, "at their perils"; and it does not appear that they "mended" all the points as he desired. But probably this very confused play-book does not represent the acting version.

Though the trouble in which Kyd and Marlowe were involved in 1593 was not directly caused by their dramas, it should perhaps be alluded to at this point, as showing that the government was keeping an eye on playwrights and guarding against sedition and atheism. The facts of the case are by no means clear. In May of that year Kyd was arrested, imprisoned, and tortured to extract testimony. Suspected at first of some "libell that concerned the State," he was afterwards, because of a Disputation found among his papers, charged with atheism. A week

---

[1] p. 1, note.     [2] p. 16.     [3] p. 15.

after Kyd's arrest, possibly on his testimony, Marlowe was apprehended by a warrant from the Council, but apparently not imprisoned, for the Lords accepted his pledge to appear when wanted. While his case was under investigation, he was stabbed to death, on June 1, 1593. The charge on which Marlowe was arrested is not clearly apparent, but seems to have been atheism. Kyd was soon afterwards released.[1]

The famous name of Falstaff now appears in our history; but concerning the precise circumstances of the trouble in which this character involved Shakspere we know even less than about the Kyd and Marlowe affair. When *Henry IV* was first produced, probably in 1597, the fat knight was entitled Sir John Oldcastle, — a name which Shakspere had innocently taken over from the old play, *The Famous Victories of Henry V*. But the use of the name of the illustrious Lollard martyr, "the good Lord Cobham," for so unedifying a character, aroused protest. According to the tradition handed down by Rowe, the descendants of the famous nobleman protested, and got the dramatist to change the title. "Some of that family being then remaining, the Queen was pleased to command him to alter it." If the production of the play preceded the death of the Lord Chamberlain, Lord Cobham, on March 5, 1597, it was probably he who thus defended the memory of his ancestor. Or if he had already died, others of the family intervened. Shakspere or his company apparently made prompt reparation. The name Oldcastle was altered to Falstaff, and the Epilogue of Part II expressly protested "Oldcastle died a martyr and this is not the man." The play *Sir John Oldcastle*, which the title-page falsely attributed to Shakspere, appeared in 1600 and further defended the character of the Lollard nobleman.

There is no evidence that Shakspere or his company got into any serious difficulties as a result of this indiscretion. Elizabeth's fondness for the character of Falstaff, to which tradition testifies, would certainly have saved them from punishment. But the incident shows that dramatists had to be careful

---

[1] See Boas' Kyd, lvi ff., cviii ff.; and Ingram, *Marlowe and his Associates*, 230 ff. Marlowe had been arrested in 1589, but for what reason and under what circumstances we do not know. See Ingram, *op. cit.*, 148 ff.

not to allude disrespectfully to powerful noblemen or their families.[1]

The last years of Elizabeth's reign show two notable cases in which the drama was used to reflect the growing political unrest of the time. The first of these occurred in the summer of 1597, — the performance of Nash's *Isle of Dogs* at the Rose. Though Nash was apparently held chiefly responsible, he really wrote, he tells us, only the induction and the first act; the other four acts, which bred all the trouble, were supplied by the players, "without my consent, or the least guesse of my drift or scope."[2] Since the *Isle of Dogs* has not survived, we cannot tell how serious the offense was, but the rigorous action taken by the Privy Council indicates that the play contained some seditious attack on the government policy, or upon persons of high rank in the state. Our chief knowledge of the nature of the work and of the imprisonment of Nash and the other players is derived from the following entry in the Council Register, on August 15, in the form of a letter to several Justices of the Peace.

"Upon informacion given us of a lewd plaie that was plaied in one of the plaiehowses on the Bancke Side, contanynge very seditious and sclanderous matter, wee caused some of the players to be apprehended and comytted to pryson, whereof one of them was not only an actor but a maker of parte of the said plaie. For as moche as yt ys thought meete that the rest of the players or actors in that matter shalbe apprehended to receave soche punyshment as theire leude and mutynous behavior doth deserve, these shalbe therefore to require you to examine those of the plaiers that are comytted, whose names are knowne to you, Mr. Topclyfe, what ys become of the rest of theire fellowes that either had theire partes in the devysinge of that sedytious matter or that were actors or plaiers in the same, what copies they have given forth of the said playe and to whome, and soch other pointes as you shall thincke meete to be demaunded of them, wherein you shall require them to deale trulie as they will looke to receave anie favour. Wee praie you also to peruse soch papers as were fownde in Nash his lodgings, which Ferrys, a Messenger of the Chamber, shall delyver unto you, and to certyfie us th' examynacions you take."[3]

[1] Quotations from the sources of our information and further references may be found in any good edition of the play. For Mr. Fleay's conjecture as to its connection with the closing of the theaters in 1597, see below, p. 188.

[2] Nash, *Lenten Stuffe*, Grosart edition, V, 200.     [3] *Acts*, XXVII, 338.

H

At the time of the arrest of the players, the Lords had evidently also ordered the cessation of all performances at the Rose. On August 10 Henslowe entered in his Diary an agreement with a player who is to act with the Lord Admiral's company at that theater, "beginynge Jmediatly after this Restraynt is Recaled by the lordes of the cownsell w$^{ch}$ Restraynt is by the meanes of playinge the Jeylle of dooges." [1] The entries in the Diary concerning Nash's imprisonment in the Fleet, and the news of the restraint's being recalled by the Council, are modern forgeries.[2] Though the offense was apparently considered a serious one, and the search of Nash's lodgings would even indicate a suspicion of some plot, it does not appear that the players' punishment continued long. The theater soon reopened, and six months later this same company, the Lord Admiral's, was one of the two granted special privileges by the Privy Council.[3]

By far the most interesting case of the use of the stage for political purposes is the well-known effort of the Essex conspirators to encourage rebellion by the performance of Shakspere's *Richard II*.[4] Though this drama was certainly not originally written with any treasonable intent, the scene of the King's abdication apparently offended Elizabeth's sensibility in such matters, and was expurgated from the first and second quartos, issued in 1597 and 1598. The conspirators appear to have believed that the public representation of this abdication and of the murder of the King might fire the boldness of the chief traitors and encourage the populace to rebellion against the present Sovereign. They consequently planned to have the play produced at the Globe on February 7, 1601, the day preceding the date set for the uprising. As we learn from the testimony of Augustine Phillips, a prominent member of the company, Sir Charles Percy, Sir Josceline Percy, Lord Monteagle, and several others went to some of the Lord Chamberlain's players and requested them to perform the deposing and killing of King Rich-

---

[1] *Henslowe's Diary*, 203.   [2] *Ibid.*, xl, xli.   [3] See above, p. 58.
[4] There seems to be no doubt that this play of the "deposing and killing of King Richard II" was Shakspere's. It belonged to his company; and, as his drama had been written about seven years before, it might well be referred to as an "old play."

ard II, promising to give them forty shillings "more than their ordinary" to do so. The actors had arranged to play some other play, holding that of King Richard as being so old and so long out of use that they should have a small company at it, but "at this request they were content to play it." [1] On the day of the performance nine of the conspirators met at one Gunter's house, and together went to the Globe, there to derive treasonable inspiration from Shakspere's play.[2]

No other representation of *Richard II* seems to be mentioned in the legal documents concerning the conspiracy. In the following summer Queen Elizabeth, in a conversation with William Lambarde, referring to the Essex Rebellion, said, "I am Richard II, know ye not that?" Lambarde replied, "Such a wicked imagination was determined and attempted by a most unkind Gent. the most adorned creature that ever your Majestie made." "He that will forget God," rejoined Elizabeth, "will also forget his benefactors; this tragedie was played 40tie times in open streets and houses." [3] With all due respect to the Queen, one cannot but feel that the story had grown tremendously between February and August.

Serious as was this conspiracy, resulting in the execution of Essex and several others, the players appear to have suffered no punishment for their part in it. The protection of their patron, the Lord Chamberlain, may have stood them in good stead; or it may have been obvious to the authorities that they had had no treasonable intent. Moreover, Elizabeth probably did not wish to deprive herself of the diversion which their performances afforded her. On February 24, a little more than two weeks after the rebellion, and on the eve of the execution of Essex, the Lord Chamberlain's men played at Court before the Queen.[4] Evidently Shakspere and his fellows stood high in royal favor, and they may well have been thankful for the leniency which spared them any penalty for their grave indiscretion.

---

[1] *State Papers, Dom.*, 1598–1601, 578.
[2] *Ibid.*, 573, 575. See also *State Trials*, I, 1412, 1445.
[3] Nichols, *Progresses of Elizabeth*, III, 552.
[4] Cunningham, *Revels Accounts*, xxxii; Thorndike, *Hamlet and Contemporary Revenge Plays*, in *Modern Language Association Publications*, XVII, 132.

One other case of trouble in Elizabeth's reign, of a much less serious nature, shows the opposition of the authorities to the disrespectful representation upon the stage of persons of rank. On May 10, 1601, as we have already seen,[1] the Privy Council wrote to certain Justices of the Peace in Middlesex, concerning the players at the Curtain, who, it was reported, were representing upon the stage in their interludes "the persons of some gentlemen of good desert and quallity that are yet alive under obscure manner, but yet in such sorte as all the hearers may take notice both of the matter and the persons that are meant thereby." "This beinge a thinge very unfitte and offensive," the Council orders the Justices to stop the play and investigate it. If they find it "so odious and inconvenient as is informed," they are required to "take bond" of the chief players "to aunswere their rashe and indiscreete dealing before us."[2] Apparently the matter was not particularly "odious," for the Council seems to have taken no further notice of it.

During the early years of James' reign there were apparently various attempts to represent current events upon the stage, and even to express there some of the dissatisfaction and contempt felt by many of his subjects for their new Sovereign. Beaumont, the French Ambassador, in a despatch written in June, 1604, forcibly portrays the popular attitude towards James. "Consider, for pity's sake, what must be the state and condition of a prince, whom the preachers publicly from the pulpit assail, whom the comedians bring úpon the stage, whose wife attends these representations to enjoy the laugh against her husband, whom the parliament braves and despises, and who is universally hated by the whole people."[3]

Even the King's own company was indiscreet in representing his Majesty upon the stage. In December, 1604, they produced the tragedy of *Gowry*, which must have portrayed the unsuccessful plot of the Earl of that name against King James, in the year 1600.[4] The play does not survive, and we know of it only from

---

[1] See above, p. 18.     [2] *Acts*, XXXI, 346.
[3] Raumer, *Sixteenth and Seventeenth Centuries*, II, 206–207.
[4] For an interesting account of this conspiracy, indicating the probable nature of the play, see *State Trials*, I, 1359 ff.

Chamberlain's letter to Winwood, of December 18, 1604, wherein he narrates: "The tragedy of *Gowry*, with all the Action and Actors, hath been twice represented by the King's Players, with exceeding Concourse of all sorts of People. But whether the matter or manner be not well handled, or that it be thought unfit that Princes should be played on the Stage in their Life-time, I hear that some great Councellors are much displeased with it, and so 'tis thought shall be forbidden." [1] The phrasing of this letter indicates that it may have been this tragedy which caused the "commandment and restraint," mentioned in 1624, "against the representing of any modern Christian kings in stage-plays." [2] But it is even more likely that this order resulted from the performance of Chapman's *Biron*, which we shall presently consider.[3] The boldness of the actors apparently continued, order or no order, for on March 28, 1605, Calvert wrote to Winwood that the players did not "forbear to present upon their stage the whole course of the present Time, not sparing either King, State, or Religion, in so great Absurdity, and with such Liberty, that any would be afraid to hear them." [4]

Possibly one of the plays which caused this comment was Day's *Isle of Gulls*, produced in 1605. Mr. Fleay thinks that it was almost certainly one of the series of dramas of this time in which royalty was satirized. He points out that it was published surreptitiously; and that the characters who in the extant version are called Duke and Duchess, had in the original version been called King and Queen.[5] There seems to be no proof that this was actually the play alluded to in Calvert's letter of March 28, as Mr. Fleay suggests; but probably it was indiscreet in its first form, and it may have involved its author or producers in difficulty.

It is possible that one of the dramas which caused Calvert's comment was the famous and delightful *Eastward Hoe*, the joint production of Jonson, Chapman, and Marston, acted about this time. The severe procedure against its apparently mild attack on the Scotch would indicate, however, that Calvert must have

---

[1] Winwood, *Memorials*, II, 41.
[2] See below, p. 119.
[3] See below, pp. 105 ff.
[4] Winwood, *Memorials*, II, 54.
[5] Fleay, *English Drama*, I, 108–110.

exaggerated the frankness of the satire which was allowed to go unsuppressed. The play's hit at the King's numerous bestowals of knighthood — granted often, it was hinted, for the sake of the fee — in the line " I ken the man weel, he's one of my thirty pound knights," [1] seems to have passed uncondemned, as did similar allusions in other dramas.[2] But the satirical reference, in Act III, Scene ii, to the Scotch adventurers who had followed the King to London, apparently brought down the royal wrath upon the authors. In the first edition of the play, issued in September, 1605, the leaves containing this passage were cancelled and reprinted, and it occurs only in a few of the original copies. Captain Seagull is describing the wonders of Virginia, — gold, precious stones, and other treasures, — and as an added attraction he remarks : "And then you shall live freely there, without sargeants, or courtiers, or lawyers, or intelligencers, only a few industrious Scots perhaps, who indeed are dispersed over the face of the whole earth. But as for them, there are no greater friends to Englishmen and England, when they are out on't, in the world, than they are. And for my own part, I would a hundred thousand of them were there, for we are all one countrymen now, ye know, and we should find ten times more comfort of them there than we do here." [3] This seems to be the passage meant by Jonson when he says that "he was delated by Sir James Murray to the King, for writing something against the Scots, in a play called Eastward Hoe." [4] But perhaps at the performance of the comedy these lines were made even more offensive.

The trouble about this comedy caused Jonson's imprisonment for a time. The question of his various incarcerations because of his plays, which this incident brings up, is a puzzling one, not yet satisfactorily solved. Before the year 1605 he had apparently already been twice in difficulties. In just what trouble the *Poetaster*, acted in 1601, had involved him, we do not know;

---

[1] Act IV, Scene i.

[2] See the *Phœnix*, in Bullen's Middleton, I, 135, note.

[3] Act III, Scene ii; Chatto and Windus edition of Chapman, 467. The portion expunged began at the words "only a few," and continued through the passage as it is here quoted.

[4] Jonson's *Conversations with Drummond*, Gifford's edition of Jonson, IX, 390.

but the play seems to have been suppressed at some time, or there was an attempt to suppress it. Jonson's Dedication to Mr. Richard Martin, in the 1616 Folio, states that this gentleman had formerly "preserved" the play, "which so much ignorance and malice then conspired to have supprest." In the Apologetical Dialogue at the end, itself condemned by the authorities after one recital, we find that the author had been accused of "taxing the law, and lawyers; captains, and the players, by their particular names." Jonson protests that he has attacked no persons by name, only general vices. He denies any allusion to "the laws or their just ministers," both of which he deeply reverences. He did not attack the military profession in any way, he contends, and only *some* players. The details of this episode in the war of the theaters must apparently remain obscure.

At a later date, probably soon after the accession of James, Jonson was in trouble because of his *Sejanus*. Henry Howard, Earl of Northampton, who was, Jonson tells us, the poet's mortal enemy, had him summoned before the Council because of this play, and accused "both of poperie and treason." [1] As *Sejanus* was altered before publication, it is impossible to say what justification, if any, there was for this charge.[2] Nor do we know the result of Jonson's appearance before the Council.

His next difficulty of this sort, and apparently by far the most serious, was that caused by *Eastward Hoe*. There is some difference of opinion concerning the details of this affair, which we need not attempt to settle conclusively here. Jonson's own account, as reported by Drummond, is plain enough. "He was delated by Sir James Murray to the King, for writing something against the Scots in a play called Eastward Hoe, and voluntarily imprisoned himself with Chapman and Marston, who had written it amongst them. The report was, that they should then have had their ears cut and their noses." But this fate they escaped. "After their delivery he banqueted all his friends." [3]

This story may be literally true, as it has come down to us.

---

[1] Jonson's *Conversations with Drummond*, Gifford's edition of Jonson, IX, 393.

[2] *Ibid.*, note.      [3] *Ibid.*, 390–391.

But a group of letters, most of them discovered only recently, indicate that it may be inaccurate. These epistles were written by Jonson and Chapman in the year 1605, to the King, the Lord Chamberlain, and various influential patrons. They show that the two distinguished poets were at this time in prison, and seriously concerned about their fate, — "committed hether," as Jonson complained, " unexamyned, nay unheard (a rite not commonlie denyed to the greatest offenders)." Their alleged crime was a play, not named, which had apparently given offense to the King. It had been utterly misconstrued and misapplied, the poets asserted, and the offensive matter was only in "two clawses, and both of them not our owne." [1]

Was this imprisonment that which resulted from *Eastward Hoe*? Or were Jonson and Chapman twice in custody together during the year 1605? Recent opinion has tended to the view that the letters refer to the *Eastward Hoe* affair. This seems indeed probable, though in that case Jonson's account of the matter, as reported by Drummond, is inaccurate. He did not imprison himself voluntarily with his fellow-authors; and Marston was not in prison with them. Mr. Dobell, the discoverer of most of the letters in question, adopts this view,[2] as does Mr. Schelling, in his recent edition of *Eastward Hoe*.[3] Mr. Fleay, who knew only one of the letters, thought that this imprisonment of the two poets resulted from *Sejanus*, in which they had collaborated.[4] The latest writer on Jonson, M. Castelain, in an elaborate discussion of the affair, holds that this trouble for Chapman and Jonson was the result neither of *Sejanus* nor of *Eastward Hoe*, but probably of *Sir Giles Goosecap*, an anonymous comedy which seems to have caused some difficulty with the censor on the occasion of its publication.[5]

---

[1] Jonson's letter to the Earl of Salisbury is printed in Gifford's edition of his works, I, cxvii–cxviii. The other letters were first published in the *Athenæum*, March 30, 1901. All are conveniently reprinted in Schelling's edition of the play in the Belles Lettres Series.

[2] *Athenæum*, March 30, 1901.      [3] Belles Lettres Series.

[4] *English Drama*, I, 347.

[5] Castelain, *Ben Jonson*, 901 ff. On *Sir Giles Goosecap* see also Fleay, *English Drama*, II, 322–323; and T. M. Parrott, *The Authorship of Sir Gyles Goosecappe*, in *Modern Philology*, IV, no. 1 (July, 1906).

The cases made out for *Sejanus* and *Sir Giles Goosecap* seem by no means convincing. In the present state of our knowledge we may say that the letters in question apparently refer most probably to *Eastward Hoe*, though this solution also presents difficulties. From our point of view the problem is not of great importance. We know, at all events, that two of the most distinguished poets of their time were imprisoned because of political or personal allusions, in one or more plays, distasteful to the King and others; that for a time they feared serious consequences, but that their appeals to powerful patrons soon brought about their release.

According to Mr. Fleay, the trouble about *Eastward Hoe* caused the inhibition of the Children of the Queen's Revels, who lost the Queen's patronage and for some time thereafter acted as "their own masters," under the name of the Children of the Revels.[1] How the company could have retained the right to perform, if it had lost its royal patent, is not apparent; nor does it seem likely that so severe a penalty would have been imposed for this offense. But until the very confused history of the children's companies during this decade is at least partially cleared up, it is impossible to say how dearly the Revels company paid for its indiscretion.

The same players were again in trouble a few years later — in 1608 — because of their production of *Biron's Conspiracy* and *Biron's Tragedy* by Chapman, whose fondness for treating contemporary foreign history, and disrespectful portrayal of foreign royalty, now involved him in difficulties. M. de Beaumont, the French Ambassador, had tried to prevent the performance of the plays, but without avail. "I caused certain players to be forbid from acting the history of the Duke of Biron," he writes on April 5, 1608. "When however they saw that the whole court had left town, they persisted in acting it; nay, they brought upon the stage the Queen of France and Mademoiselle de Verneuil. The former, having first accosted the latter with very hard words, gave her a box on the ear.

---

[1] *London Stage*, 209. See also Thorndike, *Influence of Beaumont and Fletcher on Shakspere*, 20.

At my suit three of them were arrested; but the principal person, the author, escaped." [1]  From a letter of Chapman's, thanking the Duke of Lennox for a safe retreat, it appears probable that that nobleman sheltered the poet during this difficulty.[2]

There is extant another letter by Chapman which seems to refer to the two parts of *Biron* and which was apparently written a little later, when he was endeavoring to have them licensed for the press.[3]  He is evidently addressing the censor —presumably Sir George Buc, though no name is given—and is highly indignant at this gentleman's refusal to allow the printing of the plays.  It appears from the poet's words that at some time—whether after or before the Ambassador's complaint is not apparent — the Privy Council had thrice given special permission for the performance of the two dramas. " If the thrice allowance of the Counsaile for the Presentment gave not weight enoughe to draw yours after for the presse, my Breath is a hopeles adition."  On Chapman's application for license to print, the censor had evidently complained that offensive lines were spoken at the performance, and refused his allowance for the press.  The poet retorts indignantly that he did his " uttermost " to suppress the offensive passages and could do no more.  " I see not myne owne Plaies; nor carrie the Actors Tongues in my mouthe."  The objection to these plays he considers highly unreasonable and unjust.  " Whosoever it were that first plaied the bitter Informer before the frenche Ambassador for a matter so far from offence; And of so much honor for his maister as those two partes containe, perform'd it with the Gall of a Wulff, and not of a man." Driven by his wrath to cast prudence aside, Chapman boldly reproaches Buc for his refusal and withdraws the request for a license.  " But how safely soever Illiterate Aucthoritie setts up his Bristles against Poverty, methinkes yours (being accompanied with learning) should rebate the pointes of them, and soften the fiercenes of those rude manners; you know S$^r$, They are sparkes of the lowest fier in Nature that fly out uppon

---

[1] Raumer, *Sixteenth and Seventeenth Centuries*, II, 219.
[2] Letter printed in *Athenæum*, April 6, 1901.
[3] *Ibid.*

weaknes with every puffe of Power; I desier not you should drenche your hand in the least daunger for mee: And therefore (with entreatie of my Papers returne) I cease ever to trouble you." This spirited letter is signed "By the poore subject of your office for the present."

Possibly some of Chapman's powerful patrons again came to his aid. At all events, negotiations with the censor were evidently resumed almost at once and a compromise effected, for on June 5 of the same year, 1608, the two parts of *Biron* are entered in the Stationers' Register under Buc's license.[1] To secure this allowance Chapman had to sacrifice a considerable portion of the plays, to which he refers in the Dedication as "these poor dismembered poems." Act II of the *Tragedy* is entirely omitted, — presumably the part containing the scene which offended the French Ambassador. From the *Conspiracy* it appears that Chapman had also been indiscreet in representing English royalty. Act IV is obviously a recasting in narrative form of a scene at the English Court in which Queen Elizabeth had appeared and discoursed at length upon political affairs, and which probably contained imprudent allusions to the Essex Rebellion.[2] The sadly mutilated condition of the two plays shows that the censor had been aroused to severe measures, and it seems very likely, as has been already suggested, that it was the scandal attendant upon these dramas which caused the edict against " the representing of any modern Christian kings."[3]

In the same despatch in which Beaumont tells of *Biron* he informs us that some of the players were still recklessly satirizing the King upon the stage. "One or two days before, they had brought forward their own King, and all his favourites, in a very strange fashion. They made him curse and swear because he had been robbed of a bird, and beat a gentleman because he had

---

[1] Arber, *Transcript*, III, 380.
[2] See Fleay, *English Drama*, II, 62–64; *London Stage*, 185; Koeppel, *Quellen-Studien zu den Dramen George Chapman's*, 24 ff. Koeppel's conclusions as to the sources of the plays are corrected by F. S. Boas in the *Athenæum*, January 10, 1903.
[3] See below, p. 119.

called off the hounds from the scent. They represent him as drunk at least once a day, &c. He has upon this made order that no play shall be henceforth acted in London; for the repeal of which order, they have already offered 100,000 livres. Perhaps the permission will be again granted, but upon condition that they represent no recent history, nor speak of the present time." [1]  Possibly the Ambassador was exaggerating the rigor of the order which resulted from these plays. But apparently one or more companies got into rather serious trouble because of their impertinence.

That severe measures were sometimes taken against sacrilegious and libellous performances, appears from a report of a Star Chamber trial in May, 1610.  The case was that of Henry, Earl of Lincoln, against Sir Edward Dymock and others, "for contriving and acting a stage play on a Sabbath day, on a Maypole green near Sir Edward Dymock's house, containing scurrilous and slanderous matter against the said Earl by name." After the play ended, one of the actors, it appears, "attired like a minister, went up into the pulpit attached to the Maypole with a book in his hands, and did most profanely, in derision of the holy exercise of preaching, pronounce vain and scurrilous matter, and afterwards affixed to the Maypole an infamous libel against the said Earl." The punishments ordered for these offenses were extremely heavy.  The three principal actors were sentenced to be pilloried and whipped at Westminster Hall; and then to be taken into Lincolnshire and suffer the same punishments again.  Here they were also to "acknowledge their offenses and to ask God and the Earl forgiveness," and to pay a fine of £300 apiece.  Sir Edward Dymock, as privy and consenting to the performance, was to be committed to the Fleet during the King's pleasure, and to be fined £1000. [2]  The offense was evidently a serious one; and the severity of the punishments ordered shows what fate might befall players who were, as these seem to have been, without patent or powerful patron.

At about this time Tilney died, and Buc came into complete

---

[1] Raumer, *op. cit.*, II, 219–220.
[2] *Historical MSS. Commission Reports*, III, 57.

possession of the Revels Office. An interesting manuscript play-book, dating from 1611, the year after Tilney's death, illustrates the sort of "reformations" which Buc made in the plays submitted to him for license. This is Lansdowne MS. 807, of the play which Buc named the *Second Maiden's Tragedy*, apparently from its slight resemblance to the *Maid's Tragedy*, by Beaumont and Fletcher. "This Second Mayden's Tragedy (for it has no name inscribed) may with the reformacions bee acted publikely. 31. October. 1611. G. Buc." It was generally customary to name the play in the license to act, and as this lacked a title, Buc thus supplied one.[1]

The manuscript contains some markings and erasures by the author or the manager, to shorten it for acting purposes, and it is not always possible to distinguish these from the censor's expurgations. Sometimes Buc made a cross in the margin to call attention to his reformations, but not always.

The plot represents the love of a Lady (unnamed) for the deposed King, Govianus, and the efforts of the usurping Tyrant to force her to become his mistress, — a fate which she finally escapes by her suicide. Evidently the censor was sensitive on the subject of kings' mistresses and vice in high places, and he struck out many lines portraying or denouncing the royal lust, — apparently on the ground that such suggestions were disrespectful to the Sovereign. For example, in Act II, Scene i, in Helvetius' speech urging his daughter to become the King's mistress, nine and a half lines, beginning "That glister in the sun of prince's favours," are marked for omission.[2] In the same scene, where Govianus bitterly reproaches Helvetius for urging his daughter to this dishonor, thirty-one lines, commencing "Hadst thou been anything beside her father," are marked in the margin, apparently for expurgation. They consist of violent denunciation of

---

[1] In view of Buc's explicit statement that it had no name, it is surprising to find Mr. Fleay conjecturing, "I think the Master of the Revels objected to the true title, *The Usurping Tyrant*, and substituted this." (*English Drama*, II, 331.)

The play is printed in the *Old English Drama*, I; in Hazlitt's Dodsley, X; and, with the best text, in the Chatto and Windus edition of Chapman's Works (1875) among "Doubtful Plays and Fragments."

[2] Chatto and Windus edition, 356; Lansdowne MS. 807, folio 36.

Helvetius and of "the lustful king, thy master." One line is crossed through as especially obnoxious and reflecting upon morals in high places, — the second of the following: —

> "To end the last act of thy life in pandarism,
> (As you perhaps will say your betters do)."

In Helvetius' reply, when he repents, and thanks Govianus for his conversion, "Smart on, soul!" and the five following lines — a passage where the now repentant father speaks of the loathsomeness of his offense — are marked for omission.[1] Similarly, in Act II, Scene iii, when Helvetius violently reproaches the King for his unlawful passion, the six lines beginning "You'll prefer all your old courtiers to good services," and the last three of the same speech, are marked.[2] So also in Act V, Scene ii, are twelve lines of Govianus' denunciation of the Tyrant, beginning "O thou sacrilegious villain!"[3]

In view of the many lustful tyrants freely portrayed in the drama of the period, and notably in the recent *Maid's Tragedy*, to which Buc's note refers, one may wonder why the censor, if the marks are his, or the manager, chose these passages for omission. That no mere feeling of decency caused the expurgations is evident from many of the points left unmarked. There is no doubt, however, about the final passage condemned as disrespectful to royalty. In Act V, Scene ii, when the expiring Tyrant exclaims "Your king's poison'd!" Buc drew a line through these words, substituted "I am poison'd!" and made a cross in the margin to call especial attention to this reformation, — the propriety of which is evident from the disrespectful exclamation with which Memphonius greets the news, "The king of heaven be praised for it!"[4]

Besides these passages reflecting on royalty, the censor has expurgated lines for various other causes. His care for religion is apparently shown in the omission of the speech of the humorous First Soldier, in Act V, Scene ii, beginning "By this hand, mere idolatry," and in its reference to Latin prayers seeming to allude disrespectfully to the Roman Catholic religion.[5] An

---

[1] Chatto and Windus edition, 357; Lansdowne MS., 807, folio 37.
[2] p. 361; f. 40.    [3] p. 378; f. 54.    [4] p. 379; f. 55.    [5] p. 377; f. 53.

amusing instance of consideration for the feelings of the gentry is to be seen in Act IV, Scene i, where the Wife of Votarius, in speaking of the loose behavior of maidservants, remarks "There's many a good knight's daughter is in service," and "knight" has been carefully altered to "man."[1] In Act I, Scene i, Govianus' speech beginning "Weighty and serious," a fiercely satirical portrait of the Third Nobleman, is marked for omission.[2] As it has nothing to do with the plot, it may have been a hit at some actual nobleman, and expurgated for this reason.

One rather surprising set of "reformations" is to be found in several passages reflecting on the character of women. Such consideration for the feelings of the weaker sex is hardly to be expected in the drama of the period; yet the purpose of these alterations seems evident, and some of them are unmistakably by the censor. In Act I, Scene i, in a speech by the Tyrant, the four lines beginning "A woman to set light by sovereignty!" are struck out.[3] They are rather mild, referring to women's desire to rule, and expressing surprise that the Lady should cleave to the deposed king, and not turn her affections to the usurper. A clearer case is found in Act III, Scene i, when, after the Lady has killed herself to escape the Tyrant's passion, Govianus ironically remarks that few women would have acted thus, and declares "They'll rather kill themselves with lust than for it." Lines are drawn through this and the preceding two lines, and Buc's cross in the margin makes clear his disapproval.[4] He was even more particular in Act IV, Scene iii, where the Tyrant laments over the dead body of the Lady, and asserts that most women would have advised her against the death in which she sought refuge from his lawless passion.

> "Hadst thou but asked th' opinion of most ladies,
> Thoud'st never come to this!"

Buc marks a large cross in the margin and alters "most" to "many," producing a dire effect on the meter, and not vastly greater courtesy to the feminine sex.[5]

The Master's care in expunging oaths, in conformity with the

[1] p. 368; f. 44.  [2] p. 348; f. 29.  [3] p. 349; f. 30.
[4] p. 366; f. 43.  [5] p. 372; f. 49.

statute of 1606,[1] is frequently apparent, and generally disastrous to the meter. "'Sheart" or "Heart," and "'Slife" or "Life," he often crosses out; nor will he permit "By th' mass."[2] But he frequently nods, and passes over "Life." "Faith," he seems never to object to, as Herbert did later.[3]

Early in 1613 occurs a case of interference by the authorities which is not altogether easy to understand, and indeed not of any particular importance. Some London apprentices, apparently ambitious in amateur theatricals, gave an invitation performance of Taylor's *The Hog hath Lost his Pearl*, in the Whitefriars theater. The Sheriffs broke up the assemblage and imprisoned some of the actors. We learn of all this from the following letter of Sir Henry Wotton to Sir Edmund Bacon: —

"On Sunday last at night, and no longer, some sixteen Apprentices (of what sort you shall guess by the rest of the Story) having secretly learnt a new Play without Book, intituled, *The Hog hath lost his Pearl;* took up the *White Fryers* for their Theatre: and having invited thither (as it should seem) rather their Mistresses than their Masters; who were all to enter *per buletini* for a note of distinction from ordinary Comedians. Towards the end of the Play, the Sheriffs (who by chance had heard of it) came in (as they say) and carried some six or seven of them to perform the last Act at Bridewel; the rest are fled. Now it is strange to hear how sharp-witted the City is, for they will needs have Sir *John Swinerton* the Lord *Maior* be meant by the *Hog*, and the late Lord Treasurer by the *Pearl*."[4]

Just what is the meaning of "a new Play without Book" no one seems to hav conjectured. Possibly it refers to the absence of a licensed play-book, — that is, of authorization by the Master of the Revels. The Prologue, in the edition of 1614, bears out this idea, for it states that the play was "tossed from one house to another," until it had "a knight's license" and might "range at pleasure," — that is, until it received Sir George Buc's authorization. That he did at some time license this play, we know from a note by Herbert in later years.[5] Whether the Sheriffs broke up the first performance because the apprentices had no

---

[1] See above, pp. 19–20.
[2] For examples of these corrections, see folios 34, 35, 38, 43, 49, etc.
[3] See below, p. 128.  [4] *Reliquiæ Wottonianæ* (1672 edition), 402–403.
[5] *1821 Variorum*, III, 263, note.

license for their acting or for the play; or because, as Mr. Fleay states, the production was on Sunday;[1] or because of the supposed representation of the Lord Mayor and the late Lord Treasurer, we cannot now say. The Prologue indicates that there had been considerable question of these alleged allusions, for it expressly disclaims any "grunting at state-affairs" and "invecting at city vices."[2]

The next few years of Buc's administration show several cases of interference by the government. The first of these is apparently an interesting survival of a sort of Roman Catholic controversial morality. In 1614, at Sir John York's house in Yorkshire, there was a private performance of a "scandalous play acted in favor of Popery," in which the Devil declared that all Protestants were eternally lost, and carried King James off on his back to the fiery lower regions. For this seditious performance, Sir John York, his wife, and his brother were fined and imprisoned.[3] A less flagrant case occurred in 1617, when the Privy Council interfered to prevent the production of a play representing Marshal d'Ancre. On June 22 they wrote as follows to the Master of the Revels. "We are informed that there are certain Players, or Comedians, we know not of what Company, that go about to play some enterlude concerning the late Marquesse d'Ancre, which for many respects we think not fit to be suffered. We do therefore require you, upon your peril, to take order that the same be not represented or played in any place about this City, or elsewhere where you have authority."[4] As the responsibility for the Marshal's death was assumed by the young King Louis XIII, this proceeding was directed by obvious political caution.[5]

[1] *London Stage*, 251.

[2] The title-page — not the Wotton letter, as Mr. Fleay says — states that the play was "divers times publicly acted by certain London Prentices." See Fleay, *English Drama*, II, 256.

The play is printed in Hazlitt's Dodsley, XI.

[3] *State Papers, Dom.*, 1611–1618, 242; 1628–1629, 333; *Historical MSS. Commission Reports*, III, 63.

[4] Collier, *English Dramatic Poetry*, I, 391–392; Chalmers, *Apology*, 492.

[5] See Ward, *English Dramatic Literature*, III, 234, note; and an interesting document in *State Papers, Dom.*, 1611–1618, 461.

I

By far the most interesting example of the censorship in Buc's administration is that of the admirable historical tragedy, *Sir John Van Olden Barnevelt*, probably by Fletcher and Massinger.[1] The patriot Barnevelt, devoted and successful servant of his country, but opponent of the warlike policies of the ambitious Maurice of Orange, was arrested for treason and executed by order of that Prince on May 13, 1619. In view of the great interest felt by the English in the affairs of the Low Countries, and the dramatic features of the story, it is not surprising that the subject should have been chosen for a play. Within three months after Barnevelt's death, his career was ready for presentation on the London stage. On August 14 Thomas Locke wrote to Carleton, the English Ambassador at The Hague, "The Players heere were bringing of Barnevelt vpon the stage, and had bestowed a great deale of money to prepare all things for the purpose, but at th' instant were prohibited by my Lo: of London."[2] "My Lord of London" apparently means John King, Bishop of London,[3] who may have objected to the play on account of its connection with the Arminian controversy, which had aroused some excitement in England. Barnevelt, in the drama, professes himself an Arminian.[4] Whatever the Bishop's objection, it was apparently not insuperable, for on August 27 another letter from Locke to Carleton says, "Our players have fownd the meanes to goe through w<sup>th</sup> the play of Barnevelt, and it hath had many spectators and receaued applause."[5] The surviving manuscript[6] shows the corrections made by the Master of the Revels, but no license to act. Possibly this was written on some sheet now lost; or it may have been refused, and the play performed without his authorization. We have, however, no further indication that

[1] Printed in Bullen, *Old Plays*, II, 201 ff. On the authorship, see note by Boyle, *ibid.*, 434 ff.

[2] *State Papers, Dom.*, 1619–1623, 71. Printed in full in Bullen, *Old Plays*, IV, 381.

[3] See Sidney Lee, in Bullen, *op. cit.*, IV, 381. The title is so interpreted also in the *State Papers*. Mr. Fleay understands it otherwise. See above, p. 19, note.

[4] Act I, Scene ii.

[5] *State Papers, Dom.*, 1619–1623, 73. Printed in full in Bullen, *Old Plays*, IV, 381.

[6] British Museum Add. MS. 18,653.

the tragedy was offensive to the government, except the fact that it was never printed, either in the Fletcher Folios or elsewhere.

This striking political tragedy preserves in tone a balance between sympathy for Barnevelt and support of the Prince of Orange. In the earlier scenes, the great Advocate is not presented as an admirable character, — rather as a political intriguer, ambitious, proud, and egotistical. In the latter part, however, he is nobly and sympathetically portrayed, — as one who has done great services for his country, as the beloved leader of the people, as the spokesman of political liberty. The Prince of Orange is throughout treated with almost unvarying respect. He is sympathetically represented as a brave and noble leader, generously unwilling to punish Barnevelt and the other conspirators, but finally submitting to the insistence of the Council.[1] The unimportant character of the Englishwoman seems to be introduced chiefly to speak in favor of the Prince and in contempt of his opponents. As the play goes on, however, and Barnevelt appears more admirable, the figure of Maurice becomes less attractive.

Though the attitude of the authors towards the English Sovereign is unfailingly respectful, the references to James, to the Gowry conspiracy, and to the Gunpowder Plot being in phrases of impeccable loyalty, the dangerous political analogy of the play is obvious. As Mr. Boyle has very well put it, "There is no doubt that the audience wandered away in their thoughts from Sir John Van Olden Barnevelt, the saviour of his country from the Spanish yoke, as he professed himself in his defense on his trial, and Spain's determined enemy, to Sir Walter Raleigh, whose head had just fallen on the block, the victim of a perfidious foe and of a mean, shuffling king." [2] Nor could the passion for civil liberty, which breaks in one scene into fiery eloquence, have gone unrebuked under the Stuart despotism.

If Buc's corrections of the *Second Maiden's Tragedy* show the sort of "reformation" he administered to romantic tragedies and tragi-comedies, this manuscript reveals his attitude towards

---

[1] See especially Act III, Scene ii.
[2] Note by Boyle, in Bullen, *Old Plays*, II, 434.

political and historical dramas. He was evidently somewhat disturbed at the representation upon the stage of the Prince of Orange. To make the indiscretion less obvious, he twice strikes out " Prince of Orange," and substitutes "the valiant Prince," or "this Prince that contemns us," adding his warning cross in the margin.[1] In Act I, Scene iii, the Prince has been speaking of the ingratitude and disrespect shown him, and the Guard now refuses him admittance to the Council Chamber. At this point Buc notes in the margin, "I like not this: neither do I think that the pr. was thus disgracefully used, besides he is too much presented," and signs his initials, "G. B."[2]

Some of Buc's expurgations were made so effectively that it is impossible to decipher the text beneath. In Act I, Scene i, for example, on the first folio of the manuscript, he has twice marked out words and placed a cross on the margin; but the condemned phrases are illegible. And at the end of the same scene, a speech thirteen lines long is entirely obliterated.[3] Similarly, in Act II, Scene i, when Barnevelt is speaking against the Prince of Orange and against tyranny, six lines are scored through and two crosses made.[4] In the trial scene, also, after the Prince's speech rehearsing Barnevelt's faults, twenty lines are expurgated by the censor's pen.[5] Mr. Bullen thinks that these last, as well as twenty-six lines shortly before and about twenty immediately following, were cut out by the author, to shorten the scene. But it seems possible in this play to distinguish the two sorts of correction. Buc draws a horizontal line through the text, and puts crosses in the margin, — three of them, in the course of these twenty lines. The author makes a sort of curly line through the text, without marginal mark. It was he, apparently, who cut out the other forty or more erased lines in this scene, probably to make it harmonize with the censor's reformations.[6]

On the whole, the Master's corrections evidently involved a

[1] Bullen, *Old Plays*, II, 218, 231; Add. MS. 18,653, folios 4, 7. At two other points, however, the full title of Prince of Orange is left undisturbed (pp. 233, 245, folios 9, 11).

[2] p. 222; f. 5. And see Bullen, *op. cit.*, II, 204.

[3] p. 216; f. 3.  [4] p. 233; f. 9.  [5] p. 289; f. 23.

[6] A similar erasure by the author is to be seen on folio 9, at the opening of Act II, Scene ii.

considerable portion of the play. But it does not appear that Buc was unreasonably severe. He left in some passages which might have been judged at the time irreverent to royalty. For example, the eloquent speeches of Barnevelt in Act III, Scene i, in which he proudly refuses to submit to the Prince and seek his mercy, are unexpurgated, — notably the lines —

> "What is this man, this Prince, this God ye make now,
> But what our hands have molded?" [1]

In the strikingly fine speech of Barnevelt at the end of his trial, however, the voice of protest against despotism and eulogy of political liberty rang out too unmistakably; and Buc saw the danger. The alterations here are undoubtedly by the censor's pen, showing his horizontal lines through the text and his warning crosses in the margin. The significant passage of the speech is the following close: —

> "You rise, and I grow tedious; let me take
> M/ farwell of you yet, and at the place
> Where I have oft byn heard; and, as my life
> Was ever fertile of good councells for you,
> It shall not be in the last moment barren.
> *Octavius*, when he did affect the Empire
> And strove to tread upon the neck of *Rome*
> And all hir ancient freedoms, tooke that course
> That now is practisd on you; for the *Catos*
> And all free sperritts slaine or els proscribd
> That durst have stir'd against him, he then sceasd
> The absolute rule of all. You can apply this:
> And here I prophecie I, that have lyvd
> And dye a free man, shall when I am ashes
> Be sensible of your groanes and wishes for me;
> And when too late you see this Goverment
> Changd to a Monarchie youll howle in vaine
> And wish you had a *Barnevelt* againe.
> Now lead me where you will: a speedy Sentence:
> I am ready for it and 'tis all I ask you."

The shocking application which might be made of all this was apparent to Buc. He evidently first corrected the most

---

[1] p. 248; f. 12.

offensive phrases. He struck out "tooke that course That now is practisd on you," and wrote in the margin "cutt of his opposites." He crossed out the too significant "You can apply this"; and he altered "to a Monarchie" to read "to another forme." Then, apparently deciding that the whole passage was too dangerous, and should be entirely omitted or radically altered, he drew a line through all the text from "Octavius" through "howle in vaine."[1] The example is an interesting one, and shows in an unmistakable manner the fate that awaited any expression in the drama of revolt against the Stuart tyranny and craving for the ancient liberties of Englishmen.

No other notable case of censorship occurs until the administration of Herbert, whose Office Book gives us many vivid glimpses of the sort of supervision he exercised over the drama. Stage historians have been accustomed to regard Sir Henry as a rather pedantic, interfering censor, with sensibilities almost puritanical. But we get this impression of him chiefly because we know so much about him. His Office Book, often more like a diary, reveals him intimately as a somewhat pompous person, rather particular in his duties at times. If we had Tilney's and Buc's Registers, however, the earlier Masters might appear to have been equally exacting. Indeed, Herbert's "reformations" were apparently no more detailed and fussy than those of Buc in the *Second Maiden's Tragedy;* and I see no reason for accusing him of Puritan sympathies except the expurgation of oaths, to which he was bound by the statute and which Buc had practised before him.[2] He said he was more strict with the poets than his predecessors had been;[3] but the scenes which he passed without comment indicate that his concern was by no means a puritanically moral one.

The first important case of his administration shows him as rather lenient than otherwise. For years public feeling had been running high against James' feeble policy of friendship with Spain, culminating in the project of the marriage of Charles, Prince of Wales, with the Infanta Maria. In Gondomar, Spanish Ambassador at London, the people saw the very incar-

[1] p. 292; f. 24.  [2] See above, pp. 111–112.  [3] See above, p. 82.

nation of the Spanish and Jesuitical intrigue which they so hated. But the proposed match fell through. In October, 1623, to the joy of the English, Charles and Buckingham returned from Madrid without the Spanish bride; James' policy was finally overturned; and Buckingham now headed the movement against Spain. In March, 1624, war was declared between the two countries, and in August the playwright Middleton seized this opportunity of catching the popular fancy by embodying in a symbolical play the hatred of Spanish intrigue and the joy at its defeat. His famous *Game at Chess*, under the thin disguise of the pieces on a chess-board, sets forth a story of perfidious Jesuit plotting and, more notably, a portrayal of the visit of Charles and Buckingham to the Spanish Court. The White and Black Kings and Queens respectively represent the English and Spanish sovereigns. The White Knight seems to be Charles, the White Duke, Buckingham, and — to omit the other characters — the Black Knight is a scurrilously bitter portrait of Gondomar.[1]

In spite of the almost unparalleled boldness of this treatment of current events, the play obtained Herbert's official license, and was acted by the King's company at the Globe nine times, amid great enthusiasm. Then, upon the complaint of the Spanish Ambassador to the King, the *Game at Chess* was suppressed. The official correspondence, which has survived, throws an interesting light on the affair.[2] On August 12 Mr. Secretary Conway sent the following letter to the Privy Council: —

"His Majesty hath received information from the Spanish Ambassador of a very scandalous comedy acted publickly by the King's players, wherein they take the boldness and presumption, in a rude and dishonourable fashion, to represent on the stage the persons of his Majesty, the King of Spain, the Conde de Gondomar, the Bishop of Spalato, &c. His Majesty remembers well there was a command-ment and restraint given against the representing of any modern Christian kings in those stage-plays; and wonders much both at the

[1] For a full and excellent account of the play and the circumstances of its production, see Ward, *English Dramatic Literature*, II, 524 ff. On the identification of the characters, see also Fleay, *English Drama*, II, 106.

[2] Printed in part in Chalmers, *Apology*, 496 ff.; in Dyce's edition of Middleton; and, in full, in Bullen's edition of Middleton, I, lxxviii ff.

boldness now taken by that company, and also that it hath been permitted to be so acted, and that the first notice thereof should be
brought to him by a foreign ambassador, while so many ministers of
his own are thereabouts, and cannot but have heard of it.  His Majesty's pleasure is, that your Lordships presently call before you as
well the poet that made the comedy as the comedians that acted it:
And upon examination of them to commit them, or such of them as
you shall find most faulty, unto prison, if you find cause, or otherwise
take security for their forthcoming;  and then certify his Majesty
what you find that comedy to be, in what points it is most offensive,
by whom it was made, by whom licensed, and what course you think
fittest to be held for the exemplary and severe punishment of the present offenders, and to restrain such insolent and licentious presumption for the future." [1]

On August 21 the Privy Council replied.  They have called
some of the principal actors before them, they report, and
"demanded of them by what license and authority they have
presumed to act" the scandalous comedy.  "In answer whereto
they produced a book being an original and perfect copy thereof
(as they affirmed) seen and allowed by Sir Henry Herbert, Knt.,
Master of the Revels, under his own hand, and subscribed in
the last page of the said book:  We demanding further, whether
there were not other parts or passages represented on the stage
than those expressly contained in the book, they confidently
protested they added or varied from the same nothing at all."
The poet, one Middleton, the Lords report, has "shifted out
of the way";  but they have sent a messenger to apprehend him.
They have sharply reproved the players, forbidden them to act
this comedy any more, or any play whatsoever until his Majesty's pleasure be further known, and made them give bond
for their attendance upon the Council when wanted.  Instead
of telling the King the offensive passages, they send the book,
subscribed by the Master of the Revels, so that Conway, or some
one appointed by the King, may peruse the play, and "call Sir
Henry Herbert before you to know a reason of his licensing
thereof, who (as we are given to understand) is now attending
at court." [2]

The responsibility of the affair was now shifted to the shoul-

---

[1] Bullen's Middleton, I, lxxviii-lxxix.    [2] *Ibid.*, lxxix-lxxx.

ders of the Master of the Revels, who seems to have interceded at once with his kinsman and superior officer, the Earl of Pembroke, Lord Chamberlain. On August 27 Conway wrote again to the Council, expressing the King's satisfaction with their procedure, and bidding them "examine by whose direction and application the personating of Gondomar and others was done; and that being found out, the party or parties to be severely punished, his Majesty being unwilling for one's sake and only fault to punish the innocent or utterly to ruin the company."[1] Pembroke had evidently been soothing the King's feelings and had settled the affair. On the same day he wrote to the Lord President of the Council, reviewing the history of the case, and stating that the players had petitioned the King that they might be allowed to perform again. "His Majesty now conceives the punishment," writes the Lord Chamberlain, "if not satisfactory for that their insolency, yet such as since it stopps the current of their poore livelyhood and maintenance, without much prejudice they cannot longer undergoe. In consideration therefore of those his poore servants, his Majesty would have their Lordships connive at any common play lycensed by authority, that they shall act as before." But the players are to be "bound" not to repeat the *Game at Chess*, and the Lords are to continue their efforts to find out who was originally responsible for the production of the play.[2]

As Middleton had "shifted out of the way," his son Edward was brought before the Council, but released with the injunction to attend again whenever required.[3] There seems to be no reliable evidence for the story that Middleton himself was imprisoned because of the play, and freed on sending to the King a petition in humorous doggerel.[4] It appears, then, that for this grave indiscretion the only punishment inflicted was the suppression of the company for about two weeks. This leniency is not hard to understand. The players and the poet were absolved from real responsibility by the license of the Master of the Revels, who was, in his turn, protected from serious consequences by his influence with the Lord Chamberlain. Moreover,

---

[1] Bullen's Middleton, I, lxxx–lxxxi.    [2] *Ibid.*, lxxxi–lxxxii.    [3] *Ibid.*, lxxxii.
[4] *Ibid.*, lxxxiii; and see Ward, *English Dramatic Literature*, II, 497.

the King's Spanish policy was now reversed, Charles and Buckingham were in command, and the all-powerful "White Duke" must have looked kindly on the play which celebrated the course he was now guiding.

The eagerness with which the public welcomed dramatic representation of such vital current politics is strikingly evident in the great enthusiasm which greeted the *Game at Chess*. This is made vivid by a letter from Chamberlain to Carleton, dated August 21, 1624, in which he speaks of the "famous play of Gondomar, which hath been followed with extraordinary curiosity, and frequented by all sorts of people, old and young, rich and poor, masters and servants, papists, wise men, &c., churchmen and Scotsmen." [1] The exceptional applause which the play won was remembered as a stage tradition for many years.[2] But the authorities continued to frown upon it, and the early printed editions apparently had to be issued surreptitiously, without license, for they are not entered in the Stationers' Register.[3]

Perhaps the trouble over the *Game at Chess* made Herbert more careful. In the following December he evidently threatened the same company of players with serious consequences for having performed without his license a play called the *Spanish Viceroy*. Their humble submission on this occasion has already been quoted.[4] There is no evidence to show that the play contained dangerous political allusions. It has not been positively identified, but has been supposed to be by Massinger.[5]

In 1625 the Privy Council interfered again to guard the feelings of a foreign government. "The East India Company," writes Locke to Carleton, "have ordered Greenbury, a painter, to paint a detailed picture of all the tortures inflicted on the English at Amboyna, and would have had it all acted in a play, but the Council was appealed to by the Dutch ministers, and stopped it, for fear of a disturbance this Shrovetide." [6]

A case of trouble for the poet Massinger appears in Herbert's

---

[1] Bullen's Middleton, I, lxxxiv.
[2] See *ibid.*, lxxxvi.
[3] See Fleay, *London Stage*, 256.
[4] See above, p. 77.
[5] See Ward, *English Dramatic Literature*, III, 8–9.
[6] *State Papers, Dom., Add.*, 1623–1625, 48.

Office Book on January 11, 1631, when the Master noted that he had refused to license a play by that dramatist because "it did contain dangerous matter, as the deposing of Sebastian, king of Portugal, by Philip, there being a peace sworn 'twixt the Kings of England and Spain."[1] Massinger thereupon thoroughly revised the play, duly removing the most "dangerous matter" and altering names and scenes. He then submitted it again to Herbert. This time the Master licensed it without question, and it appeared under the title *Believe As You List*, with an apology in its prologue for coming "too near a late and sad example." This second draft which Massinger submitted to the Revels Office still survives in his autograph manuscript, showing Herbert's license.[2] In several places the author at first inadvertently wrote the original names, and then corrected them. "Sebastian" appears twice, "Carthage" is written over "Venice," and there are other similar slips. To what extent the original play was altered in other respects it is impossible to say, as, except in a few instances like these, the process of revision was completed before the author made his fair copy for the licenser.[3]

Gardiner's paper on the *Political Elements in Massinger*[4] points out in *Believe As You List* a striking analogy to Charles' attitude at this date towards his brother-in-law Frederick, Elector Palatine and titular King of Bohemia. In this play, as well as in several others, Gardiner thinks that Massinger was representing, under a thin disguise, current political events; and portraying them from the standpoint of the faction to which belonged his patrons the Herberts, Earls of Pembroke and Montgomery. In the *Bondman*, for example, in the character of Gisco he satirized the Duke of Buckingham, then opposed by Pembroke; but in the *Great Duke of Florence*, some four years later, he exhibited towards the favorite the new and

---

[1] *1821 Variorum*, III, 229–231.

[2] The license is reproduced in facsimile in the edition of the play in the Percy Society Publications, XXVII, 105.

[3] See *An Autograph Play of Philip Massinger*, in the *Athenæum*, January 19, 1901. The MS. is now in the British Museum.

[4] *New Shakspere Society Transactions*, 1876; reprinted from *Contemporary Review*, August, 1876.

friendly attitude now felt by the brothers Herbert. *The Maid of Honor*, again, according to Gardiner, shows a striking similarity to the policy followed by Charles and James towards the Elector Frederick.

The analogies which Gardiner points out are interesting and often plausible. It is possible that Massinger was indeed putting into the plays this political significance; and if he was doing it in support of the faction favored by Pembroke, that nobleman, as Lord Chamberlain, perhaps protected him from trouble with the censor. At all events, the allusions seem to have been sufficiently veiled to avoid stirring up much public notice or the wrath of the King.

In 1632, the year following *Believe As You List*, Herbert noted in his Register his displeasure at Shirley and Chapman's *The Ball*. The offense in this case was the manner in which "divers lords and others of the Court" were represented. On receiving promises of omissions, however, and of not "suffering it to be done by the poet any more," Herbert allowed the play.[1] In the next year, 1633, there appears to have been a veritable epidemic of offensive language among the playwrights. In May, 1633, Inigo Jones complained of his being represented in the character of Vitruvius Hoop, in Jonson's *Tale of a Tub*, "as a personal injury unto him"; and the Lord Chamberlain commanded Herbert to allow the play only on condition that Vitruvius Hoop's part and "the motion of the Tub" be "wholly struck out."[2] In June, in allowing the *Seaman's Honest Wife*, Sir Henry was so offended by its numerous oaths that he appended to his license the following note: "I command your Bookeeper to present mee with a faire Copy hereaft. and to leave out all oathes, prophaness & publick Ribaldry as he will answer it at his perill. H. Herbert."[3] The trouble with Fletcher's *Woman's Prize*, or *The Tamer Tamed*, followed in October, and resulted, as we have seen, in Herbert's closer supervision of revived plays.[4] On complaint

---

[1] *1821 Variorum*, III, 231–232. On the altered passages, see Fleay, *English Drama*, II, 239.

[2] *1821 Variorum*, III, 232.  [3] Bullen, *Old Plays*, II, 432.

[4] See above, p. 82.

of the "foul and offensive matters" which it contained, the Master suppressed the play and sent for the book, which he returned to the company three days later, "purgd of oaths, prophaness, and ribaldrye," and with the following note "subscribed and directed to Knight, their book-keeper," who had evidently already tried his hand at expurgating it.

"Mr. Knight,
"In many things you have saved mee labour; yet wher your judgment or penn fayld you, I have made boulde to use mine. Purge ther parts, as I have the booke. And I hope every hearer and player will thinke that I have done God good servise, and the quality no wronge; who hath no greater enemies than oaths, prophaness, and publique ribaldry, wh^{ch} for the future I doe absolutely forbid to bee presented unto mee in any playbooke, as you will answer it at your perill. 21 Octob. 1633."

The incident was closed three days later, when, as Herbert tells us, the players apologized. "Lowins and Swanston were sorry for tl.eir ill manners, and craved my pardon, which I gave them in presence of Mr. Taylor and Mr. Benfeilde." [1]
Though the publisher of the Fletcher Folio asserts that the text is restored to its original form, we may not have the *Tamer Tamed* in its full and "offensive" state, and can therefore not determine just what passages were complained of. Herbert's comments would indicate that the offense was chiefly profanity. There seems to be no foundation for the statement that the fault consisted in the attacks on the Puritans. Weber, in his edition of Beaumont and Fletcher,[2] asserts that the persons who complained were probably Puritans, and "the passages reprobated . . . were probably those levelled at the sect, which seems to have stood high in the favor of Sir Henry." This is highly unlikely. Certainly Herbert, chief fosterer of the stage and dependent upon it for his income, and in sentiment "more royalist than the King," would have been the last person to sympathize with the Puritans. And the year during which the Puritan Prynne, for his attack on the drama, was lying in prison, pre-

---

[1] See Herbert's full account of the affair in *1821 Variorum*, III, 208–210.
[2] V, 254.

paratory to his further punishment on the pillory, was an unlikely time for the exhibition of much consideration towards that sect. The passages in the *Tamer Tamed* to which Weber alludes [1] are rather mild and commonplace hits at the Puritan opposition to May-poles, morris-dances, and players. As for the scene in which, according to Weber, "Fletcher seems to have thrown the glove of defiance before these pious foes, by introducing the most disgusting obscenity," [2] I fear that the poet did not need the added inducement of this opposition to egg him on. Certainly the play is indecent enough, and some of its offenses in this respect may perhaps have shocked even Sir Henry Herbert. Apparently the *Tamer Tamed* did not suffer from this temporary cloud. About a month later it was acted at Court, and, Herbert tells us, "very well likt." [3]

In the same busy month — October, 1633 — two other troubles confronted the Master. The High Commission Court had apparently interfered in the case of Jonson's *Magnetic Lady*, on account of some offensive interpolations, mostly oaths, made by the actors. The players, in their first petition to the Court, laid the blame on the Master and on the author; but in their second petition "they did mee right," notes Herbert, "in my care to purge their plays of all offense." Whereupon "my lords Grace of Canterbury bestowed many words upon mee, and discharged me of any blame, and layd the whole fault of their play called The Magnetick Lady, upon the players." [4] Offensive personalities, as well as oaths, the actors seem to have been making use of; for in this same October, the Master tells us, "Exception was taken by Mr. Sewster to the second part of The Citty Shuffler, which gave me occasion to stay the play, till the company had given him satisfaction; which was done the next day, and under his hand he did certifye mee that he was satisfyed." [5] It would seem that Mr. Sewster had been offensively satirized in this production.

One bright spot cheered Herbert in this year of struggling

[1] Act II, Scene v; Act III, Scene ii. Weber's edition, 312, 330.
[2] *Ibid.*, 330, note.   [3] *1821 Variorum*, III, 234.
[4] *Ibid.*, 233. And see Fleay, *English Drama*, I, 385–386.
[5] *1821 Variorum*, III, 172, note.

against "oaths and ribaldry." In July, 1633, Shirley's *Young
Admiral* aroused his warm approval, and caused him to enter
in his Register this patronizing eulogy: —

"The comedy called The Yonge Admirall, being free from oaths,
prophaneness, or obsceanes, hath given mee much delight and satisfaction in the readinge, and may serve for a patterne to other poetts,
not only for the bettring of maners and language, but for the improvement of the quality, which hath received some brushings of late.
When Mr. Sherley hath read this approbation, I know it will encourage him to pursue this beneficial and cleanly way of poetry, and when
other poetts heare and see his good success, I am confident they will
imitate the original for their own credit, and make such copies in
this harmless way, as shall speak them masters in their art, at the first
sight, to all judicious spectators. It may be acted this 3 July, 1633.
I have entered this allowance for direction to my successor, and for
example to all poetts, that shall write after the date hereof." [1]

Any one who would see Herbert's ideal of dramatic writing
has therefore but to read the *Young Admiral*. It is indeed far
more "cleanly" than many dramas of the period, but various
passages in it give us added proof that Herbert's concern was
more with the abhorred oaths than with modern notions of
decency.

Herbert's reputation as a puritanical person, "pious" and
"delicate," rests chiefly on the affair of D'Avenant's *Wits*.
Though the inference usually drawn from his account of this
seems to me hardly justified, the story does certainly reveal him
in an amusingly pedantic light. The Master, it appears, had
"reformed" this play so rigorously that the ire of the author was
aroused. The exasperated D'Avenant secured the aid of Endymion Porter, to whom he afterwards dedicated the comedy.
At the intercession of this gentleman, the King himself consented
to intervene, and actually went over the play-book with Herbert,
to moderate his censorial zeal, and restore some of the expurgated words. The Master's record of the affair shows a comical

---

[1] *1821 Variorum*, III, 232. At this period Shirley seems to have been in close
and friendly relations with the Master and even with the King. In this same year
Charles suggested to the dramatist, through Herbert, the plot for his *Gamester*, —
which his Majesty afterwards naturally thought "the best play he had seen for
seven years." See *ibid.*, 236.

mixture of his respect for the royal judgment and his obstinate persistence in his own views. "The king is pleased to take faith, death, 'slight for asseverations and no oaths, to which I do humbly submit as my master's judgment; but under favour conceive them to be oaths, and enter them here to declare my opinion and submission." King Charles' tactful consideration for the feelings of his Master of the Revels is apparent from the latter's statement that "the kinge would not take the booke at Mr. Porters hands; but commanded him to bring it to mee, which he did, and likewise commanded Davenant to come to me for it, as I believe; otherwise he would not have byn so civill."[1] The tone of the *Wits* is, to the modern taste, consistently indecent throughout, and one situation is, as Mr. Ward puts it, "of a breadth which would have suited the most frolic pages of Boccaccio"; but these things naturally did not concern Herbert, intent on his search for profanity.

The Master's condemnation of oaths extended over printed plays as well as stage presentations. It is worth while to glance at his activity in this line during these years. Since the passage of the statute of 1606 such expurgation had been attended to with more or less rigor. Later editions of plays originally printed before the statute, frequently show reformations of this sort. The Jonson Folio of 1616, for example, exhibits such substitutions as "Believe me" for "By Jesu." Later reissues of plays often show still more rigorous emendations. Herbert's energy in eliminating oaths seems, during part of his administration at least, to have been applied vigorously to the press. Interesting examples of his very fussy alterations in this line may be seen in the fourth quarto of *Philaster*,[2] published in 1634, the same year in which the Master tried to be so severe with the profanity in D'Avenant's *Wits*. In *Philaster*, too, "Faith" is cut out, or changed to such words as "Marry" or "Indeed." "By Heaven" is altered to "By these hilts." Even the heathen gods were not to be invoked without caution. "By the gods" is frequently displaced by "And I vow," "By my sword," "By

---

[1] *1821 Variorum*, III, 235.

[2] The first edition of *Philaster*, in 1620, was not licensed by the Revels Office. (Arber, *Transcript*, III, 662.)

my life," "By all that's good." Instead of "By the just gods," the poet is allowed to asseverate "By Nemesis." [1] If the Revels Office attended thus minutely to the new editions of many plays, the Master and his Deputy must indeed have been kept busy.

To return to cases of dramatic performance, — the Queen's company seems to have been in trouble in 1637. The Prologue of Brome's *English Moor*, produced by them in that year, informs us that the actors had been "restrained" for a time, but does not tell us the cause of their punishment. The players promise, in the Prologue, that they will submit to the "high powers," and will "utter nothing may be understood offensive to the state, manners or time." [2] We know nothing further about the case. Presumably the company had presented some play containing indiscreet allusions to affairs of state.

A case of a different sort arose in June, 1638. There had been some difficulty about the licensing of Massinger's *King and Subject*, which had been finally laid before the King himself for his opinion. After expurgating some apparently seditious lines, Charles bade the Master allow the play. Herbert's account of the matter is amusingly characteristic.

"At Greenwich the 4 of June, Mr. W. Murray gave mee power from the king to allowe of the play, and tould me that he would warrant it.

> "'Monys? Wee'le rayse supplies what ways we please,
> And force you to subscribe to blanks, in which
> We'le mulct you as wee shall thinke fitt. The Cæsars
> In Rome were wise, acknowledginge no lawes
> But what their swords did ratifye, the wives
> And daughters of the senators bowinge to
> Their wills, as deities,' &c.

This is a peece taken out of Philip Messinger's play called The King and the Subject, and entered here for ever to bee remembered by my son and those that cast their eyes on it, in honour of Kinge Charles,

---

[1] All such alterations are registered in the foot-notes in the Variorum Edition of Beaumont and Fletcher, I. A multitude of such examples could doubtless be collected from the books of the time.

[2] Brome, *Works*, II, 1.

K

my master, who, readinge over the play at Newmarket, set his marke upon the place with his owne hande, and in thes words:

"'This is too insolent, and to bee changed.'

"Note, that the poett makes it the speech of a king, Don Pedro king of Spayne, and spoken to his subjects." [1]

Certainly the passage on the raising of supplies was indiscreet, in view of the bitter trouble between King and Parliament. It is striking to find that it is by the same hand which probably penned the one notable protest against despotic government which we have encountered, — the closing speech of Barnevelt at his trial. [2]

The care still taken to suppress any disrespect shown to religion is illustrated in the following year, 1639, when, according to a letter, the players of the Fortune were fined a thousand pounds — one may doubt the sum — for setting up on the stage an altar, a basin, and two candlesticks, and bowing down to them. The actors alleged that it was an old play revived, and the altar merely one to the heathen gods; but the authorities decided that the performance was in contempt of the ceremonies of the church. [3]

In the same year the Aldermen of London and the profession of proctors were also in need of protection against the stage. A complaint was made in September, we learn, to the King in Council, "that the stage-players of the Red Bull have lately, for many days together, acted a scandalous and libellous play, wherein they have audaciously reproached, and in a libellous manner traduced and personated, not only some of the Aldermen of the City of London and other persons of quality, but also scandalized and defamed the whole profession of Proctors belonging to the Court of Probate, and reflected upon the present Government." The Council ordered that the Attorney-General should call before him "not only the poet who made the said play, and the actors that played the same, but also the

---

[1] *1821 Variorum*, III, 240. Herbert tells us that the name of the play was changed. It does not seem to have survived.

[2] See above, p. 117.          [3] *State Papers, Dom.*, 1639, 140–141.

person who licensed it"; and that, having ascertained the truth of the complaint, he should proceed "roundly" and expeditiously against the offenders, in order that their "exemplary punishment may prevent such insolence betimes." [1] The name of this production was the *Whore New Vamped*. Another document informs us of its objectionable passages: the dubbing of all proctors "arrant knaves," and the even more shocking assertion, "The alderman is a base, drunken sottish knave, I care not for the alderman; I say the alderman is a base, drunken, sottish knave!" [2]

As the storm of the Civil War draws near, it is most fitting that the last important case we have to chronicle should be one of disrespect to the King and defiance of the authority of his servant, the Master of the Revels. The offenders were William Beeston's company at the Cockpit theater, sometimes known as the "King's and Queen's young company." We learn of the affair from Herbert's Register and from the following order issued by the Lord Chamberlain on May 3, 1640.

"Whereas Wm. Bieston and the company of players of the Cockpit in Drury Lane have lately acted a new play without any license from the Master of his Majesty's Revells, and being commanded to forbear playing or acting of the same play by the said Master of the Revells, and commanded likewise to forbear all manner of playing, have notwithstanding in contempt of the authority of the said Master of the Revells and the power granted unto him under the great seal of England, acted the said play and others to the prejudice of his Majesty's service and in contempt of the office of the Revells, whereby he, they, and all other companies ever have been and ought to be governed and regulated: These are therefore in his Majesty's name and signification of his royal pleasure to command the said Wm. Bieston and the rest of that company of the Cockpit players, from henceforth and upon sight hereof to forbear to act any plays whatsoever until they shall be restored by the said Master of the Revells unto their former liberty." [3]

Herbert informs us that on the following day Beeston was committed to the Marshalsea, and that for three days the com-

---

[1] *State Papers, Dom.*, 1639, 529.
[2] *Ibid.*, 530–531; Chalmers, *Apology*, 504–505, note.
[3] Chalmers, *Apology*, 517, note.

pany "laye still." But on the fourth, "at my Lord Chamberlen's entreaty," and "upon their petition of submission subscribed by the players," Herbert restored to them their liberty
of playing. "The play I cald for," he notes, "and, forbiddinge
the playinge of it, keepe the booke, because it had relation to the
passages of the K.'s journey into the Northe, and was complaynd
of by his M.<sup>tye</sup> to mee, with commande to punishe the offenders."[1]
As a result of this trouble, Beeston was removed from the management of the "King's and Queen's young company," and D'Avenant appointed by the Lord Chamberlain to take charge of it.[2]
The reckless insubordination of a royal company on this occasion is hard to understand. Their reflections upon the "King's
journey into the North," cannot, however, have been danger-
ously disrespectful, or they would have been more severely
punished.

The catastrophe now approached to which the loyal Master
of the Revels in after years referred as "the Late Horrid Rebellion, when sir Henry Herbert owned not their uniust and
Tyranicall Authority."[3] His task was over, and in the Office
Book which had chronicled so many famous dramas he made his
last entry, — "Here ended my allowance of plaies, for the war
began in August, 1642."[4]

That industrious and practical playwright, Thomas Heywood, evidently understood very well the nature of the censorship
which we have been following. In his *Apology for Actors*,
written in 1612, he thus sums up the errors against which the
dramatists must be especially on their guard. "Now, to speake
of some abuse lately crept into the quality, as an inveighing
against the state, the court, the law, the citty, and their governe-
ments, with the particularizing of private men's humors (yet
alive), noble-men and others: I know it distastes many; neither
do I in any way approve it, nor dare I by any meanes excuse it."[5]
Other dramatists, also, show evidences of guarding against

---

[1] *1821 Variorum*, III, 241.
[2] See the warrant appointing D'Avenant, printed in Chalmers, *Apology*, 519, note.
[3] Halliwell-Phillipps, *Dramatic Records*, 33.     [4] *1821 Variorum*, III, 242.
[5] Printed in the Shakspere Society Publications, III, 61.

such accusations as these.   The prologues and epilogues of the
period contain many protestations that the author is not inveighing against the state or any other institution, and is not
attacking or satirizing any individual persons.   The poets even
protest at times that they have avoided indecency and immorality.   Fear of the presence of spies who might misinterpret
their lines and involve playwright and players in trouble with
the authorities also seems to disturb them occasionally.   The
most striking and amusing expression of these ideas is in the
Induction of Jonson's *Bartholomew Fair*, which ridicules such
interpretations of a play as the City had made in the case of
the *Hog hath Lost his Pearl* in the preceding year,[1] and satirizes
the official condemnation of profanity.   "It is agreed by the
aforesaid hearers and spectators, That they neither in themselves conceal, nor suffer by them to be concealed, any state-
decypherer, or politic picklock of the scene, so solemnly ridicu-
lous as to search out who was meant by the gingerbread-woman,
who by the hobby-horse man, who by the costardmonger, nay,
who by their wares.   Or that will pretend to affirm on his own
inspired ignorance, what Mirror of Magistrates is meant by the
justice, what great lady by the pig-worn n, what concealed
statesman by the seller of mousetraps, and so of the rest.   But
that such person, or persons, so found, be left discovered to the
mercy of the author, as a forfeiture to the stage, and your
laughter aforesaid.   As also such as shall so desperately, or
ambitiously play the fool by his place aforesaid, to challenge the
author of scurrility, because the language somewhere savours
of Smithfield, the booth, and the pigbroth, or of profaneness,
because a madman cries, *God quit you*, or *bless you*."   Other
writers appear at times to take the matter more seriously, and
to be really in fear of condemnation for sedition or slander.[2]

These were indeed the faults which brought down the wrath
of the censor.   On the whole there was, throughout the period,
a fairly rigorous suppression of anything touching on current

---

[1] See above, p. 112.
[2] See, for example, the Preface to Marston's *Malcontent*, the Prologues to
Beaumont's *Woman-Hater* and *Knight of the Burning Pestle*, and the Prologue
to Taylor's *Hog hath Lost his Pearl*.

political and religious questions, and a frequent effort to suppress offensive personalities. The nature of the whole Elizabethan drama is sufficient evidence that the censor was not concerned with decency and morality in our modern sense. It would, of course, be absurd to expect him to have been. In summing up such a survey of the censorship, one should also be careful to bear in mind that it was probably enforced no more regularly and consistently than the laws which we have investigated in an earlier chapter. Doubtless many plays, especially before Herbert's day, went quite uncensored and unlicensed. And we ought never to be surprised if we find passages permitted which seem far more flagrant than some that brought down rebuke upon players and poets. In Buc's expurgations of the *Second Maiden's Tragedy*, for example, we saw rather rigorous suppression of disrespectful allusions to the wicked Tyrant. But the drama of the period abounds in apparently unrepressed portrayals of weak and vicious kings who meet avenging death, and of intriguing and pernicious favorites. The *Maid's Tragedy*, supposed to have seemed offensive to Charles II in later years, apparently aroused no protest in the early Stuart period. Such examples as these show the real freedom allowed in many cases to the dramatists of this time.

The punishment of erring actors was on the whole extremely lenient. We have encountered scarcely a case of real severity. When we consider the customs of the time, and compare the dire penalties meted out to some offending Puritans — John Stubbes' loss of his right hand, Prynne's mutilation and suffering in the pillory — it is evident how effectively the protection of their patrons and the favor of the Court sheltered the players and the playwrights.

It is always dangerous to speculate on how things would have turned out if conditions had been quite different from what they were. But the problem of the effect of the censorship on the drama of the period is too interesting to avoid. What would the Elizabethan drama have been, had it been free from this supervision? Not materially different, I imagine, from what it was. The dramatists would no doubt have been spared much annoyance, for it must have been peculiarly exasperating to them to have their verses spoiled by such "reformations" as we have seen; but the general content and spirit of their plays would probably have been much the same. They would undoubtedly have indulged in much more personal satire and scurrilous abuse of living individuals, — a loss to which we can easily reconcile ourselves, as we can to the expurgated oaths. They would doubtless have written more plays treating current politics, and especially foreign relations and affairs. The great popular approval which greeted the *Game at Chess,* shows how eager the public was for representations of really vital events such as these; and the case of Massinger also indicates the willingness of some playwrights to deal with these themes. But even when the drama did touch politics, it was rather, especially under the Stuarts, the mere expression of the views of one faction of the Court party, as in Massinger's case, than any discussion of the great political and religious questions which were stirring so profoundly the heart of the nation. This was not due to the censorship. Nearly all those seriously concerned for civil liberty and religious reform were comprised in the party loosely called Puritan, and to them the stage was anathema. Under no circumstances could it have served as a voice for their views and aspirations. The dramatists were the spokesmen of the party then dominant, — Court, Royalist, Cavalier, — almost completely out of touch and sympathy with the great movements which were so soon to triumph.

The Elizabethan drama was, indeed, essentially non-controversial. It was chiefly romantic, concerned not with how things ought to be, but with how they might appear most splendid, most thrilling, most effective. Or when it assumed a realistic attitude, it dealt rather with the analysis of human character, of the foibles of human nature, than with political and social problems. It is difficult to imagine Beaumont and Fletcher, for instance, using the stage as a weapon in religious or political controversy; or, to take the most illustrious case of all, to think of Shakspere as having been restrained by the censorship from entering the controversial arena. Obviously in sympathy with the government and the customs prevailing in his time, the great poet seems to have looked with some contempt upon the populace and their desire for civic rights. But on the whole such political questions interested him little, — and religion apparently scarcely at all. The persons with whom he associated, the audiences for whom he wrote, the patrons who assisted him, had no real concern with these ideas which were about to revolutionize the nation. Nor can we imagine him, dispassionate though sympathetic observer and portrayer of human nature as he was, — so dispassionate that we can scarcely guess his views on any of the great questions of society, — we cannot imagine such a man ever becoming under any circumstances the mere mouthpiece of a political or religious party, ever desiring to use his art for a controversial purpose. These things were not his concern. When the manuscripts of his plays were submitted to the Revels Office, the pen of Tilney or of Buc, we may feel sure, marred with no considerable "reformations" his unblotted lines; nor would his dramas have been materially different from what they are, had there been no necessity of guarding against the condemnation of the censor.

# CHAPTER IV

## LOCAL REGULATIONS IN LONDON, 1543-1592

IT is now necessary for us to retrace our steps chronologically, and to follow the history of conditions in London, of the orders and ordinances applying particularly to the stage in and about that city. Before one can clearly understand the course of these local regulations, and especially the disputes between the City and the royal government concerning plays, it is essential to consider briefly the constitution of the municipal government and the topographical limits of its jurisdiction. This is an interesting and complex subject, full of contradictions, anomalies, and uncertainties. Strange relics of medieval customs, precincts which were at the same time both within and not within the City, conflicts of jurisdiction, privileged persons, edicts which were never enforced, — all these make the situation hard to grasp. As late as 1675 there were disputes on the old and unsettled question as to whether the Lord Mayor and the Court of Aldermen had power to veto decisions and orders of the Common Council; [1] and a capital example of the uncertainty of the municipal jurisdiction is afforded by the fact that it seems never to have been decided whether the Temple is in the City or no.[2] Of course, no attempt at a complete elucidation of all such matters is necessary here; we need only a brief statement of the general situation in the municipality under Elizabeth and the early Stuarts, so far as this affects our immediate subject and so far as it can be definitely ascertained.

The city government, the powers and privileges of which had been granted and confirmed to the citizens by the charters of many kings, was carried on by a Lord Mayor, a Court of

---

[1] Sharpe, *London and the Kingdom*, II, 454.
[2] Loftie, *History of London*, I, 228.

Aldermen, and a Common Council, together with Sheriffs and
various minor officials. By a strange survival of medieval
institutions, the election of these officers, and thus the practical
control of the city government, was in the hands of the so-called
"Livery Companies." These were the twelve great trading
companies or medieval guilds, called "Livery" from the uniform
in which their members of higher grade were privileged to array
themselves. Their control of the corporation was exerted as
follows: The Mayor and the Sheriffs were elected by the Common Council, which included the masters and wardens of the
guilds.[1] The Mayor was chosen annually from among the
Aldermen, to serve for one year, beginning on October 28.[2]
There were from each ward one Alderman, elected for life, and
four Common Councilmen, chosen annually.[3] These Aldermen
and Councilmen were voted for by the *freemen* in the various
wards who were also householders and who paid the taxes known
as "scot and lot."[4] This rank of freeman, or possession of
the "freedom of the city," originally connected with the right to
trade, could be obtained only through membership in one of the
great trading companies. Thus the control of the municipal
franchise was in the hands of the guilds, — a strange state of
affairs which prevailed until 1835, and is not yet entirely abolished.[5]

In view of the strong opposition to plays shown by the city
authorities, it is interesting to investigate the organization of
these powerful guilds and the classes of society represented in
their membership, in order to discover what portions of the
community probably withheld from the drama their approval
and patronage. In earlier times the guilds had to a considerable
extent regulated each its own industry — by putting down
adulteration, for instance — and had besides this exercised various religious and charitable functions. By the end of the sixteenth century, however, they had practically ceased to be of

[1] Merewether and Stephens, *Boroughs and Municipal Corporations*, III,
1938 ff.; Stubbs, *Constitutional History*, III, 576.
[2] Stow, *Survey*, 196.      [3] Stubbs, *op. cit.*, III, 576.
[4] *Ibid.;* Merewether and Stephens, *op. cit.*, III, 1486, 1986, 2046; Hazlitt,
*Livery Companies*, 80; Besant, *Stuart London*, 119.
[5] Hazlitt, *Livery Companies*, 80.

any use for industrial purposes; and with the Reformation their religious function had also passed away. They continued to exercise hospitality and charity and, as we have seen, to control indirectly the municipal government.[1] Their organization consisted of three parts: the ordinary members, or freemen; the "Livery," or members of higher grade, privileged to wear the uniform of the company; and the "Court," or governing body. Membership might be gained in four ways: (1) by apprenticeship; (2) by inheritance, whereby all sons and daughters of a freeman obtained the freedom; (3) by redemption or purchase, a means by which many non-residents became freemen; and (4) by gift, a method whereby honorary membership was conferred on many kings, princes, noblemen, and prelates.[2]

The twelve Livery Companies, which had absorbed many smaller guilds, and dominated by recognized right over the thirty-six less important companies, were the Mercers, the Grocers, the Drapers, the Fishmongers, the Goldsmiths, the Skinners, the Merchant Taylors or Linen Armorers, the Haberdashers, the Salters, the Ironmongers, the Vintners, and the Cloth-workers. As indications of the classes of people represented, these names are somewhat misleading. Some of the companies, such as the Mercers and the Grocers, appear to have consisted, to a great extent, of merchants and wholesale dealers; others, such as the Fishmongers, of shopkeepers and their apprentices; some, like the Goldsmiths and the Cloth-workers, deriving their names from "arts and misteries," of master manufacturers and their artisans. But because of membership by inheritance and by purchase, and a system of apprenticeship which did not require any actual practice of a trade, the companies had consisted, from the earliest times, largely of non-craftsmen. Their organization was, moreover, usually aristocratic. Their governing bodies consisted generally of the principal capitalists and employers of labor, and of distinguished citizens not connected with commerce or manufacture.

---

[1] Hazlitt, *Livery Companies*, 65.
[2] Stubbs, *Constitutional History*, III, 576; Hazlitt, *Livery Companies*, 75; Besant, *Stuart London*, 9.

There was practically always a property qualification for membership in the "Livery."[1]

On the whole, then, the municipal government was controlled, as one might expect, by the upper middle class, the well-to-do merchants and city capitalists; and it is evident that this respectable, prosperous, and conservative portion of society was, on the whole, hostile to the drama, and, to a considerable extent, withheld its patronage from the theaters throughout most of our period.

The municipal government so constituted and controlled exercised jurisdiction over an irregular and somewhat uncertain territory. The question of the topographical limits of its authority is an important one for stage history, since it determined the location of the playhouses. In their efforts to escape from the hostility of the Lord Mayor, while keeping within reach of their city patrons, the players erected their theaters just outside his jurisdiction. This placed them in close proximity to the disreputable houses and other disorderly resorts which clustered just beyond the controlling hand of the city authorities, on the borders of Southwark, in Shoreditch, and elsewhere, — an unfortunate association which must have affected the quality of the audience throughout most of the period.

London in the reign of Elizabeth was a city of considerable size, wealth, and power. It included, according to the usual estimate, about a hundred thousand inhabitants within the city proper, north of the Thames; and there were about as many more scattered through the Borough of Southwark, across the river, the neighboring city of Westminster, and the adjoining suburbs.[2] On the north or Middlesex side of the Thames, the old city walls inclosed a space which bore in shape a rough resemblance to a strung bow, of which the string represents the southern line along the Thames, from the Tower on the east to Blackfriars on the west.[3] The wall on the land side, the bent

[1] Hazlitt, *Livery Companies*, 64–65, 75.

[2] Campbell, *The Puritan*, I, 330; Stephenson, *Shakespeare's London*, 69.

[3] For the topography of London at this period the best maps are Agas', c. 1561–1576, published with notes by W. H. Overall; Norden's, 1593, published with notes by H. B. Wheatley in Furnivall's edition of Harrison's *Description*

shaft of the bow, curved irregularly northward between these
two points, passing Aldgate, not far north of the Tower, curving
westward past Bishopsgate, Moregate, and Cripplegate, and
southward past Aldersgate, Newgate, and Ludgate to the precinct of the Blackfriars by the Thames. We may gain some
notion of the size of the city from Stow's statement that the
circuit of this wall, on the land side, was "two English miles
and more by 608 feet." [1] The territory within this space was,
of course, under the jurisdiction of the Lord Mayor — with
some exceptions to be noted later. The city jurisdiction had
been extended also beyond the walls in various directions, to
points where "bars" marked the limits of the municipality.
Up to the bars on the east, outside Aldgate, lay "Portsoken
Ward without the walls"; [2] north of Bishopsgate extended part
of Bishopsgate Ward; [3] and north of Cripplegate, part of
Cripplegate Ward. [4] West of the wall lay the ward of "Farring-
don Without," and here the limits of the City were marked by
Gray's Inn Bars and Temple Bar. [5]

Over London Bridge, on the south or Surrey side of the
Thames, lay the Borough of Southwark. This had been possessed in part by the City of London under grants of Edward III
and Edward IV. [6] By a charter of April 23, 1550, [7] Edward VI
ceded to the City all royal liberties and franchises in that Borough, and declared the inhabitants thereof subject to the city
laws and jurisdiction. In this same year, 1550, the Lord Mayor
marched through the Borough in solemn procession, taking formal
possession. It was intended, no doubt, that Southwark should
be incorporated for all municipal purposes with the City, as the
ward of "Bridge Without." But this was never done. The
inhabitants have never elected an Alderman nor sent representatives to the Common Council; they have refused to "take up

of England; and Ryther's, 1604, reproduced in Loftie, History of London,
I, 282. These, with Stow's Survey, first written in 1598, give a fairly good idea
of the city. A convenient collection of maps may be found in Baker, Development of Shakespeare.

[1] Stow, Survey, 5.  [2] Ibid., 46–47.  [3] Ibid., 150.
[4] Ibid., 109.  [5] Ibid., 138–139.
[6] Sharpe, London and the Kingdom, I, 443 ff.; Rendle, Old Southwark, 7 ff.
[7] Printed in Birch, Historical Charters of London, 110 ff.

their freedom" and bear the burdens of citizenship. For some time an Alderman for this ward was appointed by the other Aldermen; but this practice was given up, and the status of Southwark remained uncertain until, in 1836, a Committee reported to the Common Council that the Borough had never formed part of the City of London, the charter of Edward VI notwithstanding.[1]

However, we may imagine that the Lord Mayor, with the charter of Edward VI to support him, would certainly have used his authority over Southwark had the theaters on the Surrey side been placed within that Borough. They were not; they were situated outside the limits of the Borough, in the "Liberties." This word is the cause of some confusion to any one investigating the documents of the time. It is sometimes used to indicate the rights and privileges of a city or other division, and hence the geographical and governmental limits of that city. Thus a company of players is authorized to perform "within the liberties and freedoms of any of our Cities . . . and without the same." Or a "Liberty" may mean a locality or administrative division outside the Lord Mayor's jurisdiction, possessing, as an inheritance from feudal or ecclesiastical customs, certain privileges or exemptions. Thus we read of "the Manor or Liberty of the Clink," "the Liberty of Holywell," etc. The "Liberties of London" may thus mean either those portions *within* the Mayor's jurisdiction, or those divisions lying *outside* his jurisdiction. "A Liberty," however, seems to refer always to one of the latter. With these facts in mind, one can generally tell from the context the meaning of the term.

On the Surrey side of the Thames, as we have seen, just south of London Bridge, lay the Borough of Southwark. To the west of this, outside the Mayor's jurisdiction, though just across the narrow river from the heart of London, were two Liberties bordering on the "Bankside" along the Thames.[2] First lay the Manor

---

[1] Sharpe, *op. cit.*, I, 443. An interesting and more detailed account of this anomalous situation is given in Benham and Welch, *Mediæval London*, 41–42.

[2] The best authority for this locality is Rendle, who gives Norden's map of 1593, with comments, and a smaller map, in his *Old Southwark*, xxii–xxiii and 200. See also Ordish, *Early London Theatres;* and Wheatley and Cunningham, *London Past and Present*, III, 29–30.

or Liberty of the Clink (so called from the Clink prison), a manor of the Bishop of Winchester, under whose seigniorial protection disorderly houses flourished. Within this Liberty were three theaters, — the Globe, the Rose, and the Hope or Bear Garden. Adjoining this on the west was the Manor or Liberty of Paris Garden, where the Swan was situated.[1] West of Paris Garden lay Lambert Marsh. The parish of St. Saviour's, of which we often hear in connection with theatrical affairs, included much of the Borough of Southwark and the Liberties of the Clink and Paris Garden.[2]

Southwest of Southwark, beyond the open space of St. George's Fields, lay Newington. The boundaries of Southwark extended almost to the parish church of this town,[3] and just outside the borough limits was the Newington theater,[4] — also, of course, beyond the Lord Mayor's jurisdiction.

On the Middlesex side of the Thames, north of the wall, beyond the bars which marked the limits of Bishopsgate Ward, were several Liberties, especially the Liberty of Holywell, the precinct of the former priory of St. John the Baptist. Here, near Finsbury Field and Shoreditch, were the Theater and the Curtain.[5] Farther to the west, north of Cripplegate, near Golding Lane, and just outside the bars bounding the portion of Cripplegate Ward without the walls, was the Fortune theater, in the Liberty of Finsbury.[6]

These theaters "in the fields," on the Surrey and the Middlesex sides of the Thames, were under the jurisdiction of the Justices of the Peace for these counties, to whom the Privy Council sent its orders concerning the players and upon whom it relied for their enforcement.

Most puzzling of all to the modern American mind are various Liberties which were scattered through the City proper, sur-

---

[1] Some confusion is caused by the fact that the term "Paris Garden" was sometimes used loosely to mean all this locality of the Bankside.

[2] Rendle, *Old Southwark*, 110, 121–122.  [3] Stow, *Survey*, 150.

[4] Concerning this theater see Ordish, *Early London Theatres*, 142 ff.

[5] Stow, *Survey*, 158; Halliwell-Phillipps, *Outlines of the Life of Shakespeare*, 335 ff.

[6] Stow, *Survey*, 109; contract for erection of the Fortune, Halliwell-Phillipps, *Outlines*, 462; *Henslowe Papers*, 50.

rounded by the Lord Mayor's jurisdiction but exempt therefrom, holding special privileges from the Crown by reason of their being the precincts of dissolved monasteries, which in their day had, of course, been exempt from civic authority.[1] The most important of these districts, from the theatrical point of view, were Whitefriars, on the north bank of the Thames, just east of the Temple, the site of the Whitefriars and other later theaters; and especially Blackfriars, also bordering on the river, a little farther east, where Burbage had his famous private theater. The exemption of these districts within the City was naturally a thorn in the side of the municipal authorities. Shortly after the dissolution of Blackfriars monastery and its surrender to the Crown in 1538, the Lord Mayor endeavored to obtain from the King the abolition of the district's privileges; but Henry replied that he was as well able to maintain the liberties of the precinct as ever the friars were.[2] Other attempts to invade the Liberty were made by the municipal authorities. In 1574, for example, we find that the City of London had "pretended interest" in Blackfriars, and that the Privy Council commanded the Mayor "not to intermeddle to the impeachment of such liberties and franchises until further orders."[3] In 1596, therefore, when Burbage established his Blackfriars playhouse, that precinct was outside the Lord Mayor's jurisdiction, and the inhabitants of the Liberty, when they wished the theater prohibited, appealed for protection to the Privy Council.

Since the Liberties of Blackfriars and Whitefriars were apparently not under the jurisdiction of the Middlesex Justices of the Peace, who were expected to enforce order at the Holywell and Finsbury theaters, one is puzzled at first to decide under whose jurisdiction they actually were. Of course the authority of the Crown and of the Privy Council was supreme over them, after the precincts passed from the possession of the Church. But what officials were actually in charge, with a jurisdiction

[1] Some idea of the ecclesiastical foundations in London which later became Liberties may be obtained from a map of the City in the 13th century, in Loftie, History of London, I, 120.

[2] Wheatley and Cunningham, London Past and Present, I, 193-194; Stow, Survey, 127.

[3] Acts, VIII, 240, 257.

corresponding to that of the Lord Mayor and the Justices of the Peace in the neighboring districts? An order issued by the Privy Council in 1597 seems to answer this question definitely enough. No officials whatsoever were in charge. Some dispute had arisen concerning payments for repairs in Blackfriars, and this was referred by the Privy Council, on January 26, 1597, to a commission consisting of the Lord Chief Justice, Lord Hunsdon and others, who were to report to the Lords their opinion on this question, and also, according to the Council order, "concerninge an other point in the peticion for the government of the said libertie of the Black and White Fryers, which being grown more populus than heretofore and without any certaine and knowen officer to keepe good orders there, needeth to be reformed in that behalfe, and herein we shall be glad to have your Lordships advise and opinion." [1]

There was, of course, a parish organization which served for some purposes of local government; but in the time of dangerous disorders or other emergencies the situation of Blackfriars and Whitefriars was an awkward one. The Lords seem to have been in the habit of meeting the difficulty on such occasions by appointing, in each of the precincts, some prominent man of rank to take temporary charge. In June, 1592, when serious riots were feared on Midsummer Night, and the Privy Council desired to take stringent measures against disorder, they commanded that an armed watch of householders should be organized in and about London. [2] A list of the persons to whom these orders were sent may be found in the Council Register. It is an illuminating example of the divided jurisdiction exercised over the metropolitan district, and the complicated difficulty of getting such a general command enforced. Orders were sent to the Lord Mayor of London; to the Master of the Rolls [3] and four other Justices of the Peace of the County of Middlesex, for Holborn, St. Giles in the Fields, Clerkenwell, and neighboring places; to three Justices of the Peace of the County of Surrey, for the precincts of Newington, Kentish Street, Barmondsey Street, the Clink, Paris Garden, and the Bankside; to the Lieu-

---

[1] *Acts*, XXVI, 448–449.    [2] See below, pp. 179 ff.    [3] See above, p. 54.

L

tenant of the Tower and the Master of St. Catherine's for the precincts of St. Catherine's and East Smithfield; to Lord Wentworth for Ratcliffe, Shoreditch, and Whitechapel; to Lord Cobham for the Blackfriars; to Sir Thomas Shirley for the Whitefriars; and to the Bailiff of Westminster for Westminster, St. Martin's, and the Strand.[1] It will be noticed that Lord Cobham was called on to organize the watch and preserve order in Blackfriars. His residence was in that precinct,[2] and he was a nobleman of distinction, — Lord Warden of the Cinq Ports, Lord Lieutenant of Kent, a member of the Privy Council, and later Lord Chamberlain. He seems therefore to have been chosen for this duty as the most prominent and powerful resident of the Liberty. The duty in Whitefriars was similarly assigned to Sir Thomas Shirley, then Treasurer at War for the Low Countries.

In spite of the investigation intrusted to the commission in January, 1597, no action seems to have been taken. Blackfriars and Whitefriars apparently remained in the same uncertain jurisdiction until after James' accession; though we find that in March, 1599, in the case of certain taxes the Lord Mayor was intrusted with the assessment of Blackfriars.[3]

But in 1608 a decisive step was finally taken to remedy this anomalous state of affairs; and the two famous Liberties came at last under the jurisdiction of the Lord Mayor. On September 20 of that year James granted a new charter to the City of London, confirming all former charters and customs and extending the city liberties through various districts, including "the several circuits, bounds, limits, franchises and jurisdictions of . . . the late dissolved house or priory of Preaching Friars within and at Ludgate, London, commonly called Blackfriars; and also the late dissolved house or priory of Friars of the Order of the Blessed Virgin Mary of Mount Carmel, called Whitefriars." These places shall be for all time to come "within the circuits, precincts, liberties, franchises and jurisdictions of the same our City of London. . . . And all and singular the

[1] *Acts*, XXII, 549, 551.
[2] See the deed quoted in Fleay, *London Stage*, 153.
[3] *Acts*, XXX, 149–150.

inhabitants and dwellers within the same, or any of them, shall be, and every of them is and for all time to come shall be and remain under the rule, government, jurisdiction, oversight, search, correction, punishment, precepts and arrests of the said Mayor and commonalty and citizens . . . and the Sheriffs of London . . . any liberties, franchises, privileges, exemption or authority whatsoever to the contrary thereof notwithstanding." It is provided, however, that the inhabitants of Blackfriars and Whitefriars (though not those of the other districts concerned) shall be exempt from certain taxes and from holding certain offices.[1]

Some privileges of sanctuary also remained to portions of these districts. Before the breaking up of the monasteries, the priories of the Black and the White Friars had possessed these rights of sanctuary. Such privileges were, however, restricted by laws of Henry VIII to minor offenders, and not available for murderers, thieves, and like criminals.[2] After the dissolution of the monasteries the privileges clung irregularly to portions of the two precincts. Blackfriars became a respectable and in part aristocratic quarter, inhabited largely by Puritans, many of them feather-makers, and by noblemen. It therefore seems to have taken little if any advantage of the sanctuary privileges. But Whitefriars was a notoriously disreputable district, and the criminal classes who flocked there claimed all the privileges allowed by law and far more. Though the exemptions seem to have extended legally only to cases of debt, other refugees from justice fled thither, and Whitefriars, or "Alsatia," as it was called, became the resort of the outcasts of society, — a community so lawless that even the warrant of the Chief Justice of England could not be executed there without the help of a company of musketeers.[3] By the Statute 21 James I, cap. 28 (1623-1624), all rights of sanctuary in England were abolished absolutely. But Whitefriars continued to claim them in

---

[1] Charter of James I, September 20, 1608. Printed in Birch, *Historical Charters of London*, 139 ff.

[2] Stephen, *Criminal Law of England*, I, 491.

[3] See Wheatley and Cunningham, *London Past and Present*, I, 41-42; III, 503. "Alsatia" is best known from Scott's *Fortunes of Nigel*, but was treated earlier by Shadwell in *The Squire of Alsatia*.

defiance of the law, and, as the Sheriffs were afraid to enforce writs in the precinct, was long successful in maintaining some of its exemptions. The Statute 8 and 9 William III, cap. 27 (1697), shows the strange state of affairs which was still surviving, by making it penal in Sheriffs not to execute process in certain "pretended privileged places" such as Whitefriars and the Savoy.[1]

Theoretically and legally it would seem that these fragmentary and anomalous privileges of sanctuary could have had no effect on the Lord Mayor's jurisdiction over the theaters in the precincts of Blackfriars and Whitefriars. After 1608 his authority certainly extended over these districts.[2] In the peaceable precinct of Blackfriars, it does not seem to have been questioned; but the lawless community of Whitefriars no doubt made difficult the enforcement of any sort of municipal order.

I have treated the status of these two Liberties thus elaborately because disregard of the change made by the charter of 1608 has slightly confused some histories of the stage. As we shall see, the Lord Mayor endeavored later to exercise his authority over Blackfriars against Burbage's theater; but not until a date when royal authority was paramount, and the players had little to fear from the hostility of the municipality.

In spite of the charters granted to the City, the right of the royal government to interfere in this district over which the Lord Mayor ruled was apparently limited only by motives of expediency. It has generally been underrated by historians of the stage. We must remember that the authority of the Crown, under the Tudor and Stuart despotism, was considered paramount. Royal patents, as we have seen, were given a power superior even to the statutes, and were expressly granted "any act, statute, proclamation or commandment to the contrary notwithstanding." During the period, moreover, as we have observed in the case of the laws regulating the status of players and the censorship, there was a steady centralization of power,

[1] Stephen, *Criminal Law of England*, I, 491–492. The Savoy was another Liberty to the west of the City.

[2] See the recognition of this in the case of Blackfriars by the Lord Chief Justice in 1615, mentioned below, pp. 199–200.

a removal of administration from the hands of local officials to the royal government. This course of policy is evident in the dealings of the Crown with the Corporation of London in connection with theatrical affairs. Its interference became bolder and more arbitrary, passing from requests to commands.

But there were some limits to such coercion of the municipality. The powerful and wealthy Corporation of London was too important to be utterly antagonized. Before Elizabeth's day the capital had been the determining factor in the making and unmaking of kings; and even when the great Queen feared no such extremity, she was in frequent need of the money and men which the loyal metropolis could supply. Hence, during most of her reign, the tone of royal despotism was softened at times; and the City, conscious of its power and its rights, occasionally assumed a bold attitude in asserting its privileges. But as the years passed and the Stuarts reigned, its manner grew more subservient. However much the Puritan spirit was increasing within, outwardly and officially the municipality as a rule submitted respectfully to the royal will. Such, at all events, is the course seen in dramatic affairs.

The long conflict concerning the admission of plays into London, which is the most interesting feature in the history of local stage regulation, arose from the essentially differing attitudes held by the Crown and the Privy Council, on the one hand, and the city government, on the other, towards the performance of plays in London. The Privy Council, representing, of course, the views of the Queen, held the traditional English attitude toward the stage, — that plays are not in themselves evil, but, on the contrary, entirely justifiable, — "for honest recreation sake," as the Lords once put it. The Queen, as is well known, went even further than this in her extreme fondness for dramatic performances, and many of the Councillors were also warm friends of the drama and patrons of companies. The position of the royal government was therefore on the whole one of generous and sympathetic patronage of the stage. The chief reason advanced by the Privy Council for the admission of the players into London — a reason reiterated on all occasions and respectfully received by the City — was that the actors must have practice in order to perfect themselves for their performances before the Queen. This was the root of all the difficulty, and the ground of the granting to the favored players of those special and exclusive privileges which developed into the monopolistic system of patented companies.

Under certain circumstances, of course, the Privy Council believed that no plays should be allowed in and about London; and they frequently ordered their suppression: — in times of plague or danger of plague; because of the representation of unfit matters, seditious or personal, upon the stage; because of disorders at the theaters, or, when riots were expected, fear that such assemblages might foment disorder. They sometimes restricted the number of performances, because frequent representations led people to wasteful and riotous living. They forbade them on Sunday, in Lent, and sometimes on Thursday, because on that day they interfered with the Queen's bear baiters. But under proper restrictions they saw nothing wrong in them.

The city authorities agreed with the Lords in desiring plays stopped for these reasons. They too, and even more acutely, feared the danger of infection. They dreaded, much more deeply, the disorder growing from such assemblages of the baser elements of the population. Far more important, — they feared the effect of the drama upon the morals of the people. Not only did plays lead the citizens to wasteful expenditure, and interfere with their industry, but, to the minds of the London authorities, they corrupted the morals of the city and led astray its youth. Finally, apart from all matters of expediency, in the opinion of many of the municipal officials and citizens, all plays were essentially sinful and irreligious, — an abomination in the sight of God. This was the new, the Puritan attitude. Though no doubt many of the London officials opposed the stage on the other grounds, independent of any Puritan principles, it was this deep religious conviction on the part of most of the city which made the opposition of the municipal government to plays especially bitter. The Lord Mayor felt himself the guardian of the moral and spiritual welfare of the citizens. Roger Ascham, in his *Scholemaster*, written shortly before his death in 1568, recognizes in an interesting passage this moral zeal in the chief officer of the municipality. "Yea, the Lord Maior of London, being but a Ciuill officer, is commonlie, for his tyme, more diligent in punishing sinne, the bent enemie against God and good order, than all the bloodie Inquisitors in Italie be in seauen yeare." [1]

These were the attitudes held, in general, by the Crown and the City during the controversy of the last quarter or more of the sixteenth century. But we must not expect to find them preserved with entire consistency. A new Lord Mayor was elected each year; the Lords upon the Privy Council frequently changed; and as different individuals and different influences came into play, the policy of the authorities varied. Sometimes the Privy Council seems strongly opposed to plays; sometimes the City seems lax in suppressing them.

Though the real controversy does not begin until about 1573, some facts have come down to us which show that thirty years before this the Lord Mayor was already appealing to the Privy Council against actors. On March 31, 1543, he complained to the Lords of the "licentious manner of players." [2] A few days later, on April 10, two companies, we learn from the Council Register, had to be suppressed. One, a nobleman's company, — four players "belonging to my Lord Warden," — "for playing contrary to an order taken by the Mayor on that behalf, were committed to the Countours." [3] On the same day a craftsman company was in trouble. "Certain joyners to the number of xx having made a disguising upon the Sonday morning without respect either of the day or the order which was known openly the Kings Highness intended to take for the repressing of plays, were therefore committed to warde." [4] Most of the joiners, "after a good lesson," were restored to liberty four days later; [5] but three of them, who had been committed to the Tower, were not released until more than two weeks had passed. [6] Just why the Council punished these players is not entirely clear. Probably the Mayor's complaint of March 31 had resulted in some royal order against plays, and it was for breach of this that the actors were imprisoned. But the reference to their lack of re-

[1] Arber's edition, 84.  [2] *Acts*, I, 103–104.  [3] *Ibid.*, 109.
[4] *Ibid.*  [5] *Ibid.*, 110.  [6] *Ibid.*, 122.

spect for Sunday seems to show that there was already some feeling against performances of certain sorts on that day.

In an earlier chapter we have considered the most significant points in the regulation of the London drama during the reigns of Edward VI and Mary: the suppression of occasional seditious plays, and the delegation of censoring power to the Bishop of London.[1] Elizabeth's proclamation of May 16, 1559, as we have seen,[2] gave to the municipal authorities the power to censor and license plays in cities; and under such a system London lived for some years. The great importance and power of the London Corporation enabled it to take towards traveling companies a firmer attitude than was possible for the smaller towns of England. But the prescriptive right to play possessed by a properly authorized company seems to have had some effect even at the capital. The municipal authorities were sometimes chary of refusing a nobleman's request that his company be allowed to perform within the City. The royal authorization they rarely dared to oppose.

The first definite expression in London of the Puritan attitude towards the drama occurs in 1563, in the voice of Grindal, later Archbishop of Canterbury, but at this time Bishop of London, known for his Puritan leanings. In 1563 a great plague was raging in the city, and Grindal appealed to the Privy Council to stop all plays. The assemblages which they caused, he urged, were the most dangerous means of spreading the infection. Moreover, the players, he said, were "an idle sort of people, which had been infamous in all good commonwealths"; and "God's word was profaned by their impure mouths, and turned into scoffs." He therefore advised that a proclamation be issued inhibiting all plays within the City or three miles thereof for the space of a year — "and if it were for ever, it were not amiss."[3] What action the government took as a result of this appeal does not appear. In 1572, however, we have record that "plays were banished for a time out of London, lest the resort unto them should engender a plague, or rather disperse it, being already begonne."[4]

[1] See above, pp. 8 ff.    [2] p. 14.    [3] Strype, *Life of Grindal*, 121–122.
[4] Extracts from MSS. of Harrison's *Chronologie*, in Harrison's *Description of England*, edited by Furnivall in the New Shakspere Society Publications, Pt. I, liv.

The opposition to plays in the City had apparently by this time risen high, and the success of this temporary prohibition of them perhaps encouraged the municipal authorities, who now began their long and bitter war against the London stage. The first campaign may be said to have lasted from 1573 to 1576, and to have resulted in the building of the regular theaters in the Liberties.

The first gun seems to have been fired in July, 1573, when the Privy Council apparently began its practice of securing special privileges within the City for favored performers. On July 14, we learn from the Council Register, the Lords requested the Mayor "to permit liberty to certain Italian players to make show of an instrument of strange motions within the City." [1] But the municipal authorities were apparently already showing the comparative boldness and independence which characterized their attitude during all this first campaign. Five days later the Council had to write to the Lord Mayor again, reiterating their demand and "marveling that he did it not at their first request." [2] The sequel does not appear, but one fears that the Mayor had to acquiesce.

The demand for license to play in the inn-yards within the City was now so considerable, and the difficulty of securing such permission from the municipality so great, that it apparently occurred to some one to devise a sort of "licensing patent," something like those which we have already considered,[3] granting to the patentee the right to license playing places within the City. The privilege would probably have been a profitable one, as the Master of the Revels proved in later years. The scheme had evidently been suggested several times. We have our first definite knowledge of it, however, in March, 1574, when the Lord Chamberlain proposed to grant such a privilege to one Holmes. But before carrying out the plan, the Chamberlain, with due regard, in this instance, for the rights and feelings of the city authorities, requested their assent. Our knowledge of the affair is derived wholly from the letter in which the Mayor and the Corporation replied to this request. It is particularly interesting

---

[1] *Acts*, VIII, 131.    [2] *Ibid.*, 132.    [3] See above, p. 45.

as showing the bold and jealous guardianship of their liberties and privileges which the municipality dared at this time to assert against the encroachment of the royal officials. One should note, however, that the request had apparently not been made in the Queen's name, but solely by the authority of the Lord Chamberlain.

"Our dutie to your good L. humbly done. Whereas your Lord. hath made request in favour of one Holmes for our assent that he might have the appointment of places for playes and enterludes within this citie, it may please your L. to reteine undoubted assurance of our redinesse to gratifie, in any thing that we reasonably may, any persone whom your L. shall favor and recommend. Howbeit this case is such, and so nere touching the governance of this citie in one of the greatest matters thereof, namely the assemblies of multitudes of the Queenes people, and regard to be had to sundry inconveniences, whereof the peril is continually, upon everie occasion, to be foreseen by the rulers of this citie, that we cannot, with our duties, byside the precident farre extending to the hart of our liberties, well assent that the sayd apointement of places be committed to any private persone. For which, and other reasonable considerations, it hath long since pleased your good L. among the rest of her Majesties most honourable counsell, to rest satisfied with our not granting to such persone as, by their most honourable letters, was heretofore in like case commended to us. Byside that, if it might with reasonable convenience be granted, great offres have been, and be made for the same to the relefe of the poore in the hospitalles, which we hold as assured, that your L. will well allow that we prefer before the benefit of any private persen. And so we commit your L. to the tuition of Almighty God. At London, this second of March, 1573." [1]

The opposition to plays on the part of the city officials was now very decided, and the players evidently appealed against it to their patrons and to the Privy Council. On March 22, a few days after the letter just quoted, the Council wrote to the Lord Mayor, asking him "to advertise their Lordships what causes he hath to restrain plays, to thintent their Lordships may the better answer such as desire to have liberty for the same." [2] The Mayor's presentation of the causes of restraint was appar-

[1] Printed in Hazlitt, *English Drama*, 23-24. Hazlitt, however, does not understand its significance, and gives it an inaccurate and misleading title.
[2] *Acts*, VIII, 215.

ently not entirely convincing to the royal government; or at all events one company, so fortunate as to have for its patron the Queen's favorite, and also to be able to give her Majesty "solace and pleasure" by its court performances, had powerful enough influence to override the opposition of the City. The Earl of Leicester's players obtained from the Crown, in May, 1574, less than two months after the Council's request for the Mayor's reasons, the patent under the Great Seal of England which I have already quoted:[1] This, according to the text of the Privy Seal directing the issue of the Great Seal, explicitly authorized performances "within our City of London," except in "time of common prayer, or in the time of great and common plague in our said City of London,"—any act, statute, proclamation, or commandment to the contrary notwithstanding. The copy of the instrument preserved among Rymer's unpublished papers,[2] however, does not contain the important clause respecting performances in London; and it has been suggested that this was omitted from the Great Seal.[3] This theory seems improbable. Rymer's copy contains at the end the telltale "plague in our *said* City of London," showing that the previous clause had once been in. Why it was dropped out from this copy we cannot tell. But surely it is not likely that it was omitted from the patent actually issued, since the authorization to play within the City must have been the chief thing desired by the players and the chief point of the granting of the patent. That the authority of a patent under the Great Seal should be used to override the municipal government is not at all surprising, in view of what we have seen of such grants, some of which were issued expressly to supersede even Statutes of the Realm.[4]

It does not appear, however, that the Lord Mayor acquiesced promptly and completely in the newly authorized performances. He seems to have needed a further reminder. On July 22 following the Privy Council wrote, requiring him to "admit the

---

[1] pp. 33-34.　　[2] Printed in *1821 Variorum*, III, 47, note.

[3] See Collier, Introduction to Northbrooke's *Treatise*, Shakspere Society Publications, XIV, xiii. No justification is apparent for Collier's statement that the right granted by this clause was certainly never exercised.

[4] See above, p. 45.

comedy players to play within the City of London, and to be
otherwise favorably used," [1] — a request which probably refers
to the recently patented company. But performances could not
have continued long during this summer, for the plague increased and grew so virulent that on October 24 the Lords of
the Council refused to go to the proposed feast of the new
Lord Mayor, because of the danger of infection. They even
suggested that the feast ought not to be given, but that the
money intended therefor should be devoted to the poor.[2] One
wonders whether they took any ironical pleasure in administering this pious reproof to the puritanical city government.

In anticipation of the renewal of plays after the plague should
cease, the City Council, on December 6, 1574, passed a long and
interesting ordinance carefully and rigorously regulating dramatic performances in London.[3] If they were to be forced to
have plays in the City, they evidently determined that the productions should be thoroughly supervised. Though the general
tone of the phrasing of the act is decidedly Puritan, as is also
its concern for decency and morality, it does not show the absolute condemnation of all plays as sinful which the extreme Puritans, and later the city officials themselves, vehemently urged.
It even admits that there may be a "lawful, honest and comely
use of plays." Its preamble gives us an interesting picture of
some of the conditions surrounding the inn-yard performances
of the period, and a summary of the chief arguments of the city
fathers against plays.

"Whereas heartofore sondrye greate disorders and inconvenyences
have beene found to ensewe to this Cittie by the inordynate hauntynge
of greate multitudes of people, speciallye youthe, to playes, enterludes
and shewes; namelye occasyon of frayes and quarrelles, eavell practizes of incontinencye in greate Innes, havinge chambers and secrete
places adjoyninge to their open stagies and gallyries, inveyglynge and
alleurynge of maides, speciallye orphanes, and good cityzens children
under age, to previe and unmete contractes, the publishinge of unchaste, uncomelye, and unshamefaste speeches and doynges, with-

---

[1] *Acts*, VIII, 273.    [2] *Ibid.*, 303.
[3] Printed at length in Hazlitt, *English Drama*, 27–31; and in Collier, *English
Dramatic Poetry*, I, 208–211, note.

drawinge of the Quenes Majesties subjectes from dyvyne service on Soundaies & hollydayes, at which tymes such playes weare chefelye used, unthriftye waste of the moneye of the poore & fond persons, sondrye robberies by pyckinge and cuttinge of purses, utteringe of popular, busye and sedycious matters, and manie other corruptions of youthe, and other enormyties; besydes that allso soundrye slaughters and mayhemminges of the Quenes Subjectes have happened by ruines of Skaffoldes, Frames and Stagies, and by engynes, weapons and powder used in plaies. A· d whear in tyme of Goddes visitacion by the plaigue suche asseinoles of the people in thronge and presse have benne verye daungerous for spreadinge of Infection."

The act also cites the restraint of plays by the Privy Council in times of plague, and further states that the city officials fear lest "vppon Goddes mercyfull w^{th}drawinge his hand of syckenes from vs (w^{ch} God graunte) the people, speciallye the meaner and moste vnrewlye sorte, should w^{th} sodayne forgettinge of his visytacion, w^{th}owte feare of goddes wrathe, and w^{th}owte deowe respecte of the good and politique meanes, that he hathe ordeyned for the preservacion of commen weales and peoples in healthe and good order, retourne to the vndewe vse of suche enormyties, to the greate offence of God, the Queenes ma^{ties} commaundements and good governance."

In order that all these perils may be avoided, and "the lawfull, honest, and comelye vse of plaies, pastymes, and recreacions in good sorte onelye permitted, and good provision hadd for the saiftie and well orderynge of the people thear assemblydd," the Lord Mayor and "his bretheren th' aldermen, together w^{th} the grave and discrete Citizens in the Comen Councell assemblyd," enact that "from henceforthe no playe, comodye, tragidie, enterlude, nor publycke shewe shalbe openlye played or shewed w^{th}in the liberties of the Cittie, whearin shalbe vttered anie wourdes, examples, or doynges of anie vnchastitie, sedicion, nor suche lyke vnfytt, and vncomelye matter, vppon paine of imprisonment by the space of xiiij^{ten} daies of all persons offendinge in anie suche open playinge, or shewinges, and v^{li}. for evrie suche offence."

The following explicit provisions for licensing are then laid down. No innkeeper or any other person shall allow any play to be given in his house yard or other place unless (1) the play has been perused and allowed by the persons appointed for that purpose by the Lord Mayor and the Aldermen; (2) the players have been authorized by the Mayor and Aldermen; (3) the place has been approved by them; and (4) the house owner has given security for the keeping of good order. Moreover, no performances whatsoever shall be given at any times — such as those of sickness — forbidden by the city authorities; or during the hours of Divine Service upon Sundays and Holy Days; upon pain of a fine of £5 for every offense. All duly licensed housekeepers shall contribute to the poor and the sick of the City; and all fines and forfeitures shall be devoted to the same purpose. Performances in private houses, at weddings or other festivities, where no money is collected from the audience, are exempted from the provisions of this act, except those "touchinge the publishinge of unchaste, sedycious and vnmete matters," — an offense which is under no circumstances to be tolerated.

Though perhaps somewhat stringent, the regulations laid down by this act seem on the whole very sensible, showing a due regard for the safety and well-being of the citizens. But the law, as enforced, was apparently very irksome to the players. The expense of the required contributions to the poor, the fines, and the bonds, must have been considerable; and the growing Puritan feeling among the citizens probably made the enforcement of the licensing regulations unduly restrictive and oppressive, and the suppression of performances too frequent to suit the taste of the actors. It was apparently these hardships which drove Burbage and others to seek refuge in the Liberties, beyond the reach of the city officials, and caused the erection, in 1576, of the first permanent playhouse, the Theater, where Leicester's company performed, and almost immediately afterward of its neighbor, the Curtain.

It has been customary for stage historians to attribute the building of these theaters in the Liberties to an undated order of the municipal government wholly prohibiting all plays in the City, which has generally been placed in the year 1575.[1] But, as Mr. Chambers has shown,[2] this date was carelessly and in-

[1] It is so dated by Collier, Fleay, and Ordish.
[2] *Academy*, August 24, 1895.

accurately indorsed on the documents in Lansdowne MS. 20 which relate to this edict and were apparently written soon after its issue. They refer to it as having been separated by a considerable interval of time from the city ordinance of December, 1574. Moreover, they themselves, as will be shown later, cannot have been written earlier than 1584, and they seem to have followed rather soon after this order of expulsion. In view of these facts it seems probable that the latter edict was not promulgated until some years after 1575. I have tentatively placed it in 1582, and shall consider it at that point in this narrative.[1]

Indeed, one would not expect, in the very next year, such a sudden change of policy and reversal of the careful ordinance of December, 1574; nor is the absolute prohibition of plays in the City necessary to explain the actors' resort to the Liberties. It is certain that, contrary to the impression given by some historians, plays in the inn yards within London continued for many years after 1575. This will appear as we follow the subsequent history of the controversy over the city stage. The theaters were not yet sufficient to accommodate all the companies performing; nor were they desirable in the winter months, when the players still wished to act in the more accessible and convenient inn yards.

During the years immediately following this first stage of the contest, the Puritan disapproval of the drama was finding expression in violently denunciatory sermons and pamphlets, such as Northbrooke's *Treatise*, in 1577, and Gosson's *Schoole of Abuse*, in 1579. But the City seems to have made, for the present, no further definite move against the players, except, presumably, the more or less rigid enforcement of the regulation of 1574. The Privy Council, however, several times took action affecting the London stage. On August 1, 1577, they ordered the suppression of all plays in and about the City until Michaelmas — September 29 — because of the danger of infection in hot weather.[2] In the following January they again sought special privileges in London for certain players, requesting the Lord Mayor to permit Drousiano, the Italian comedian, and his company, to play within the City.[3] In the next December (1578),

[1] See below, pp. 163 ff.　　[2] *Acts*, IX, 388.　　[3] *Ibid.*, X, 144.

apparently after another outbreak of the plague, they ordered the resumption of performances in and about London, with proper precautions against infection; and wrote to the Lord Mayor, requiring him to "suffer the Children of her Majesty's Chapel, the servants of the Lord Chamberlain, of the Earl of Warwick, of the Earl of Leicester, of the Earl of Essex, and the Children of Paul's, and no company else, to exercise playing within the City." [1] These companies are to be allowed, the Lords state, because "they are appointed to play this Christmas before her Majesty." The granting of these exclusive privileges is an early example of the monopoly allowed favored players. But the large number of companies here named is in contrast to the practice of the later years of Elizabeth's reign.

On March 13, 1579, we find the first explicit statement of a law against performances in Lent. The Privy Council on that day bade the Lord Mayor and the Justices of Middlesex — *i.e.* those with authority over the Theater and the Curtain — suppress all plays during Lent and until after Easter week; and commanded also that this order should be observed thereafter yearly in the Lenten season.[2]

Urged on by the Puritan denunciations of the drama in general, and of the Theater and the Curtain in particular, as sinks of abomination and iniquity, the city authorities now resumed, more energetically, their war against plays. The second and the most bitter stage of this contest lasted from 1580 to 1584, — years filled with appeals, arguments, and orders from Common Council and Privy Council, resulting in temporary victory for the City, but ultimate defeat.

Early in 1580 the campaign opened with an attack on the Theater. The Lord Mayor seems to have appealed to the Middlesex Justices and brought about the indictment of John Braynes and James Burbage for causing unlawful assemblages of people at that playhouse, and thus provoking great affrays, assaults, tumults, and other breaches of the Queen's peace.[3] Probably this indictment followed a particularly great disorder which

---

[1] *Acts*, IX, 435, 436.    [2] *Ibid.*, XI, 73–74; and see below, pp. 210–211.
[3] See the indictment, quoted from the Middlesex County Records, in the *Athenæum*, February 12, 1887.

occurred at the Theater on a Sunday in April of that year, and concerning which the Lord Mayor wrote to the Privy Council on April 12.[1] Though the playhouse was outside his jurisdiction, the Mayor, moved by the fact that "those players do make assemblies of citizens and their families of whom I have charge," had started, he reported, to investigate the matter. He had consulted with the Under-Sheriff of Middlesex and had summoned some of the actors before him. Upon learning that the Privy Council had taken up the affair, however, he ceased to act. But he begged the Lords to consider "that the players of plays which are used at the Theater and other such places, and tumblers and such like, are a very superfluous sort of men and of such faculty as the laws have disallowed, and their exercise of those plays is not only a great hindrance to the service of God, who hath with His mighty hand so lately admonished us of our earnest repentance,[2] but also a great corruption of youth, with unchaste and wicked matters, the occasion of much incontinence, practices of many frays, quarrels and other disorders within the City." He therefore begged that order might be taken to prevent such plays, not only within the City, but also in the Liberties.[3]

It does not appear that the Theater was much troubled as a result of this agitation. Within a month after the Mayor's appeal, however, the opponents of plays had obtained an ally in the shape of the plague, which caused the Privy Council in May to forbid performances.[4] This order was apparently not rigorously enforced in the Liberties, for in June the Lord Mayor again appealed to the Lords, reporting the steps taken in the City to stop the spread of the disease, and requesting the aid of the Council "for the redress of such things as were found dangerous in spreading the infection and otherwise drawing God's wrath and plague upon the City, such as the erecting and frequenting of infamous houses out of the liberties and jurisdictions of the

[1] The indictment is for causing an unlawful assemblage on February 21 and other days before and after that date. It might have been drawn as late as April.

[2] This apparently refers to the recent earthquake of April 6.

[3] *Remembrancia*, 350; Halliwell-Phillipps, *Outlines*, 348–349.

[4] *Acts*, XII, 15.

M

City, the drawing of the people from the service of God and honest exercises, to unchaste plays." [1]

Whether the Lords attempted to remedy these bitter grievances by more rigorous suppression of the theaters, we do not know. In the following summer the plague again caused the prohibition of performances. On July 10, 1581, the Privy Council commanded the Mayor and the Justices of the Peace, in order to prevent the spread of the disease, to permit no more plays until the end of September. [2] The general measures for the avoidance of infection, apart from the closing of the playing places, the city authorities did not carry out to the satisfaction of the Privy Council. In September and again in October the Lords administered to the Mayor and the Aldermen a severe scolding for their negligence, and reproached them because the disease had spread so that the Queen had had to remove to a greater distance from London. [3] With these reproofs fresh in their minds it must have been exasperating to the city officials to receive in November a request for the allowance of what they considered the most dangerous cause of infection, — the assemblages at plays. The demand of the Privy Council on November 18, 1581, was couched in the usual terms. "As the sickness was almost ceased, and not likely to increase at this time of year, in order to relieve the poor players, and to encourage their being in readiness with convenient matters for her highness's solace this next Christmas," the Lords required the Mayor forthwith to "suffer the players to practise such plays, in such sort, and in the usual places, as they had been accustomed, having careful regard for the continuance of such quiet order as had been before observed." [4] The Mayor apparently did not accede promptly to this request, and because of his opposition the players petitioned the Privy Council for further aid. The Lords therefore wrote again on December 3, ordering the Mayor to permit the petitioning companies — who are not named — to perform in and about the City, as they had been accustomed to do, in order that they might support their families and because they were to perform before the Queen at Christmas. But, perhaps as a concession to the municipal

---

[1] *Remembrancia*, 330.  
[2] *Ibid.*, 331.  
[3] *Ibid.*; *Acts*, XIII, 234.  
[4] *Remembrancia*, 350.

authorities, the players are to be allowed to act only on week days, and never on the Sabbath, either in the forenoon or in the afternoon.[1]

In this same December, 1581, the patent was issued which gave to the Master of the Revels such wide authority over the stage. Possibly some inkling of the trouble which his licensing power was to cause reach ed the city officials, and combined with their indignation at the abuses of the theaters to urge them to the extreme measure they seem to have taken about this time. This was the passage of the act totally prohibiting all plays within the City, which has generally been dated 1575, but which, as Mr. Chambers has pointed out and as I have stated above,[2] almost certainly belongs in these years of agitation between 1580 and 1583, and perhaps early in 1582. The order of expulsion is referred to in a letter from the municipal officials in 1584[3] as being contained in Article 62 of an Act of the Common Council for the Relief of the Poor. This is clearly identical with Article 62 of an undated pamphlet printed by Hugh Singleton and entitled "Orders appointed to be executed in the Cittie of London for setting roges and idle persons to worke, and for the releefe of the poore." [4] The municipal letter of 1584 states that this edict preceded the Paris Garden disaster, and it must therefore be of a date somewhat earlier than January 13, 1583. It was apparently as late as 1580, and probably a year or two after that; for the city officials speak of it as having been separated from the act of December, 1574, by a considerable period of time, during which the abuses of the stage grew flagrant, and there was much agitation and many denunciatory sermons.[5] Moreover, Rawlidge's *Monster Lately Found Out*, published in 1628, in an account of this controversy states that it was soon after 1580 that the citizens expelled the players and "quite pulled down and suppressed" the playhouses in the City.[6] During the years 1580–1582 the agitation against the stage was bitter and continuous,

[1] *Acts*, XIII, 269. Possibly this is the same letter as that just mentioned, dated November 18 in the city archives.

[2] pp. 158–159.        [3] See below, p. 172.

[4] Collier, *English Dramatic Poetry*, I, 212; Chambers, in *Academy*, August 24, 1895. The order is sometimes referred to as the "Singleton order."

[5] See below, pp. 172–173.        [6] Chambers, in *Academy*, August 24, 1895.

and the edict would fit appropriately into almost any part of that period. The early spring of 1582 is perhaps the most probable date, for at that time the City was suffering from the plague, as the order implies, the Mayor was begging the Lords to continue the restraint of plays, as the last clause of the edict suggests, and all the other requirements seem to be met by this date. The order is characteristically Puritan in its phrasing and sentiment, more extreme than the ordinance of December, 1574.

"For as much as the playing of enterludes, and the resort to the same, are very daungerous for the infection of the plague, wherby infinite burdens and losses to the Citty may increase, and are very hurtfull in corruption of youth with incontinence and lewdness, and also great wasting both of the time and thrift of many poore people, and great provoking of the wrath of God, the ground of all plagues, great withdrawing of the people from publique prayer, and from the service of God, and daily cried out against by the preachers of the word of God; therefore it is ordered, that all such enterludes in publique places, and the resort to the same, shall wholy be prohibited as ungodly, and humble sute made to the Lords, that lyke prohibition be in places neere unto the Cittie." [1]

Whether or no this edict was actually promulgated in the spring of 1582, there was evidently some opposition to plays on the part of the City at this time; for the Privy Council again came to the aid of the actors. They wrote to the Mayor, requesting him to allow performances in London, since the city was free from infection. As usual, they advanced as a reason the Queen's delight in plays and the necessity of the actors' having practice in order that they might the better gratify her Majesty. Perhaps somewhat impressed by the municipal arguments, they forbade plays not only on the Sabbath, but also on the ordinary Holy Days until after evening prayer; and they suggested that the City should appoint a censor, in order that those dramas which contained "matter that might breed corruption of manners and conversation among the people" might be forbidden. [2] Such a direct request from the Privy Council the Mayor

[1] From the text given by Collier, *English Dramatic Poetry*, I, 211–212, quoting the Singleton pamphlet.

[2] *Remembrancia*, 351; *Acts*, XIII, 404. The first gives the date as April 11, the second as May 20.

of course dared not refuse; but in his reply he again rehearsed the inconveniences and perils of theatrical performances, and begged that the Lords would continue their restraint of them. The suggestion as to a censor he gladly adopted. The plan of restraining plays on Holy Days until after evening prayer, however, he respectfully condemned, since this would delay the action of the performances to a very inconvenient time of night, especially for servants and children.[1]

Not only did the Mayor and the Aldermen have to submit to the interference of the Privy Council, but they had also to deal with the demands of individual noblemen that their servants might have the privilege of performing within the inn yards of the City. An example of this occurred in the following July, when the Earl of Warwick requested of the Mayor a license for his servant, John David, to play "his provost prize in his science and profession of defence" at the Bull in Bishopsgate Street.[2] Apparently the Mayor was obdurate, for three weeks later the Earl again addressed him, expressing surprise at the prohibition of playing prizes by his servant, and desiring that more favor might be shown him.[3] To this the Mayor replied at some length, standing by his first prohibition, but endeavoring to pacify the offended nobleman by some concession. If the Earl's servant will arrange to perform at the Theater or some other open place outside London, the Mayor will permit him, "with his company, drums, and show, to pass openly through the City, being not upon the Sunday, which is as much as I may justify in this season."[4]

In the following winter an accident occurred which vindicated some of the assertions of the city authorities concerning the danger of assemblages at shows, and, by arousing feeling against theaters, temporarily gave the municipality great help in its warfare upon them. On Sunday, January 13, 1583, a scaffold fell during a performance at Paris Garden, killing some of the spectators and injuring many. The Mayor reported the affair to Lord Treasurer Burghley on January 18, attributing the disaster to the hand of God, on account of the abuse of the Sab-

---

[1] *Remembrancia*, 351.  [2] *Ibid.*; *Athenæum*, January 23, 1869.
[3] *Ibid.*  [4] Halliwell-Phillipps, *Outlines*, 376.

bath Day, and requesting Burghley to give order for the redress of such contempt of God's service.[1] The Lord Treasurer appears to have been moved by the Mayor's report. He replied that he would bring the matter before the Council, and get some general order passed prohibiting such exhibitions. In the meantime he recommended the Lord Mayor, with the advice of the Aldermen, to issue a command to every ward for the prevention of such profane assemblies on the Sabbath Day.[2] Supported by this pronouncement of the Lord Treasurer, and justified further by another outbreak of the plague, the city authorities now seem to have proceeded to rigorous measures. It appears probable that in this spring of 1583 they actually suppressed, for a time, all the city inn yards used for performances.[3] They certainly took vigorous steps against them, as we shall presently see.

Had it not been for the royal favor, the state of the players would now have been lamentable. But just at this time a step was taken which added considerably to their prestige and influence. This was the formation of a company directly in the Queen's service, to be known as Her Majesty's Players. On March 10, 1583, Sir Francis Walsingham summoned Tilney to Court, to select these actors.[4] As a result, twelve of the best were chosen from the noblemen's companies, and, according to Howes' account, written about 1615, "were sworn the Queen's servants and were allowed wages and liveries as grooms of the chamber."[5] Save that they were apparently more distinguished actors, their status seems to have resembled that of the household players kept by the Queen's predecessors and by Elizabeth herself during the first decade or so of her reign.[6] The new company, as we shall shortly see, appears to have had no formal patent or warrant. Its position in London did not differ very essentially from that of the noblemen's companies which served the Queen at times, when they were backed, as they often were,

---

[1] *Remembrancia*, 336.　　　　[2] *Ibid.*

[3] See Fleay, *London Stage*, 54; and the passage from Rawlidge's *Monster Lately Found Out* (1628), quoted in the *1821 Variorum*, III, 46.

[4] Cunningham, *Revels Accounts*, 186.

[5] See the passage from Howes' additions to Stow's *Chronicle*, edition of 1615, quoted in the *1821 Variorum*, III, 49, note.

[6] See above, pp. 23, 26–27.

by letters of the royal Council requiring that they be allowed to perform. But on its travels the very name of her Majesty's servants must have brought it consideration and profit, since the treatment accorded to players was so generally dependent upon the rank and influence of their patron. Even in London the Queen's name must often have overawed the city officials and protected the actors from trouble. Moreover, the Privy Council was even more energetic and urgent in securing for Her Majesty's Players the privilege of performing than it had been on behalf of the favored noblemen's companies. It does not, however, seem to me certain that, as most historians assume, the new company was formed for the express purpose of overcoming the opposition of the city officials. Such a course was not necessary. The Privy Council had at any time the power to get any players admitted to the City, and they had, as we have seen, frequently exercised it. The formation of the company may have been due to some desire to limit the number of performers necessary at Court; to a willingness to favor certain players; and, most likely, to some plan for the better organization of court performances. Besides such motives as these, the royal officials may have felt that they could better supervise and control the Queen's own servants, when the Lords secured for them, for their necessary practice, playing privileges in London. The favored noblemen's companies were less directly responsible to the authorities, and perhaps less easy to keep in order.

It seems probable that, supported by the power of the Queen's name, her players performed in London in the spring of 1583, in spite of the growing plague and the opposition of the City.[1] But they could not have played long, for the infection soon became serious, and all performances in the City must have been stopped.[2] Writing to Sir Francis Walsingham on May 3, in reference to the plague, the Mayor points out that the restraints in London are useless, unless like orders are carried out in the

---

[1] This may perhaps be inferred from the Council's request to the Mayor, in the following autumn, that this company be allowed to play *as heretofore*. *Remembrancia*, 352.

[2] See the Mayor's letter to a Middlesex Justice on April 27, 1583. *Athenæum*, January 23, 1869.

adjoining Liberties, and he requests the Privy Council to take steps to redress this danger.[1] He again forcibly urges the evils and demoralization caused by such performances, and the disreputable classes who frequent them. "Among other we finde one very great and dangerous inconvenience, the assemblie of people to playes, bearebayting, fencers and prophane spectacles at the Theatre and Curtaine and other like places, to which doe resorte great multitudes of the basist sort of people . . . and which be otherwise perilous for contagion, biside the withdrawing from Gods service, the peril of ruines of so weake byldinges and the avancement of incontinencie and most ungodly confederacies."[2]

The severity of the plague seems to have prevented performances in the summer of 1583; but as the winter drew on the Privy Council wrote, on November 26, to the Lord Mayor on behalf of the new company. As the infection within the city had ceased, they desired that "Her Majesty's players might be suffered to play as heretofore, more especially as they were shortly to present some of their doings before her."[3] However much the municipality might resent this action, the officials dared not refuse such a direct command from the Crown. They relaxed their prohibition and allowed the players within the City; but with certain restrictions which caused dissatisfaction. A few days later — on December 1 — Sir Francis Walsingham wrote to the Mayor in the name of the Privy Council, reiterating the request of November 26. "With regard to the letter of the Council on behalf of her Majesty's players, which the Lord Mayor had interpreted to extend only to holidays, and not to other week-days, the Council, considering that without frequent exercise of such plays as were to be presented before her Majesty her servants could not conveniently satisfy her recreation and their own duty, desired that they should be licensed to perform upon week-days and workdays, at convenient times, between this and Shrovetide, Sundays only excepted."[4] Reluctant though the City was, it apparently had to submit. In spite of the municipal prohibition

[1] *Remembrancia*, 337.
[2] Halliwell-Phillipps, *Outlines*, 352.
[3] *Remembrancia*, 352.
[4] *Ibid.*

of plays the Queen's company performed within the Mayor's jurisdiction in the winter of 1583, and, fortified with this practice, appeared at Court during the Christmas festivities of that year.[1]

In the following summer, however, the tables were turned, and the City gained a temporary victory. Fleetwood, the Recorder of London, was in the habit of writing to Lord Burghley concerning events in the city, and our knowledge of this affair comes from one of these letters, written in June, 1584. According to his account, the Lord Mayor sent to the Court two Aldermen, with a request for the suppressing and pulling down of the Theater and the Curtain. Presumably the municipal officials had already stopped all performances within London. The royal government was at this time apparently anxious to conciliate the City, for all the Lords acceded to the request, except the Lord Chamberlain and the Vice-Chamberlain, — the natural friends and protectors of the players. "But," says Fleetwood, "we obtained a letter to suppress them all." On the same night the Recorder summoned before him the Queen's company and Lord Arundel's, who were then performing; and they all obeyed the Lords' letters. But when he sought to "bind" the "owner of the Theater" to obedience, the latter proved more obdurate. Fleetwood's account illustrates in an amusing manner the difficulty experienced by the city officials in disciplining noblemen's players, who, relying upon the protection of their patron, were apt to prove insolent and disobedient. "He sent me word," writes the Recorder, "that he was my Lord of Hunsdens man and that he wold not comme at me, but he wold in the mornyng ride to my Lord. Then I sent the under-shereff for hym, and he browght hym to me, and, at his commyng, he showtted me owt very justice; and in the end I shewed hym my Lord his masters hand, and then he was more quiet; but, to die for it, he wold not be bound. And then I mynding to send hym to prison, he made sute that he might be bounde to appere at the oier and determiner, the which is tomorowe, where he said that he was suer the court wold not bynd hym, being a counselers man; and so I have graunted his

[1] See Chambers, in *Modern Language Review*, II, 1 (October, 1906).

request, where he shal be sure to be bounde, or els lyke to do worse." [1]

The reasons for this action of the Lords in suppressing the theaters, and the results of it, are not clear. Apparently all performances in the City and the Liberties were stopped for a time; but the Theater and the Curtain survived unscathed this order for their destruction — if such it was — as they did subsequent similar edicts.

During this summer the players seem to have submitted to exclusion from London. But as the season for traveling and for performances in the outer suburbs ended and winter drew on, the Queen's company made another attempt to get admission into the City. With this object, they petitioned the Privy Council as follows, adducing the usual arguments to support their request:

"In most humble manner beseche yo[r] Lls. yo[r] dutifull and daylie Orators the Queenes Ma[ties] poore Players. Whereas the tyme of our service draweth verie neere, so that of necessitie wee must needes have exercise to enable us the better for the same, and also for our better helpe and relief in our poore lyvinge, the ceason of the yere beynge past to playe att anye of the houses w[th]out the Cittye of London as in our articles annexed to this our Supplicacion maye more att large appeere unto yo[r] Lls. Our most humble peticion ys, thatt yt maye please yo[r] Lls. to vowchsaffe the readinge of these few Articles, and in tender considerasion of the matters therein mentioned, contayninge the verie staye and good state of our lyvinge, to graunt vnto us the confirmacion of the same, or of as many, or as much of them as shalbe to yo[r] honors good lykinge. And therw[th]all yo[r] Lls. favorable letters unto the L. Mayor of London to p'mitt us to exercise w[th]in the Cittye, accordinge to the Articles; and also thatt the said l'res maye contayne some order to the Justices of Midd'x, as in the same ys mentioned, wherebie as wee shall cease the continewall troublinge of yo[r] Lls. for yo[r] often l'res in the p'misses, so shall wee daylie be bownden to praye for the prosperous preservation of yo[r] Lls. in honor, helth, and happines long to continew.

"Yo[r] Ll[s] most humblie bownden
and daylie Orators,
her Ma[ties] poor Players." [2]

---

[1] Halliwell-Phillipps, *Outlines*, 377–378. This letter is in part hard to understand. The text given by Collier, *English Dramatic Poetry*, I, 252–253, differs materially from that here quoted.

[2] From the text printed by Hazlitt, *English Drama*, 31–32, from Lansdowne MS. 20. It is also printed by Collier, *English Dramatic Poetry*, I, 212–213.

This petition, with the subsequent correspondence, has usually been dated 1575, on account of the careless indorsement of that date upon the manuscripts. But, as Mr. Chambers has suggested,[1] it must be at least as late as 1583. In the first place, the reply of the City to it contains a reference to the Paris Garden disaster of January 13, 1583. Most striking of all, the petitioners sign themselves the Queen's Majesty's Players, and the city authorities also refer to them by this title. Nc actors are thus designated in the other documents of this period except the Queen's company organized in March, 1583. The use of the title somewhat puzzled the historians who dated this correspondence in 1575. Collier suggested rather doubtfully that it referred to the Earl of Leicester's company;[2] but these players are nowhere so designated. The petition must, then, be later than March, 1583.

In their report on the request the municipal officials refer to this company as having performed in the city "last year."[3] Therefore the petition and the ensuing correspondence must be as late as 1584. The petition is obviously written in the autumn or the beginning of winter, and the players desire to prepare for their service at Court, — probably at the Christmas festivities, as in the winter of 1583. In view of all these facts, the most probable date for the occurrence is the latter part of November, 1584.[4]

The appeal of the Queen's players was evidently for permission to act again in the inn yards of the City, and also, as appears by their request for letters to the Middlesex Justices, at the Theater or the Curtain. The "Articles" which they say they have annexed to their petition have disappeared; but they evidently dealt with the regulations under which the players thought their performances should be allowed, — concerning hours,

---

[1] *Academy*, August 24, 1895.
[2] *English Dramatic Poetry*, I, 220.    [3] See below, pp. 173-174.
[4] Additional evidence in favor of the later date, as against 1575, may be adduced from the Council Register. No record of this petition, — though others are noted, — nor of any action on the request, appears in 1575. The Register is missing from June 26, 1582, to February 19, 1586. (*Acts*, XIII, xxxvi.) The affair therefore probably occurred within this period.

Strype, in his edition of Stow's *Survey*, rightly dates the petition after the Paris Garden disaster. See the passage quoted in *1821 Variorum*, III, 49-50, note.

days, plague time, etc., — and discussed the municipal ordinances affecting the stage. In harmony with the consideration shown to the City the preceding summer, the Privy Council, before granting the players' request, seems to have sent the petition and the articles to the London authorities, and to have asked for their opinion on the matter. In the same manuscript in the Lansdowne collection which contains the petition there are two documents which are evidently the reply of the City. The first is a letter disputing the players' assertions concerning the municipal ordinances regulating the drama, and stating that the writer is sending, for the better information of the Lords, copies of the two acts in question, — that of December, 1574,[1] and the order of expulsion which we have conjecturally dated 1582.[2] The letter also rehearses briefly the history of this legislation.

"It may please your good Lp.

" The orders in London whereunto the players referr them are misconceaued, as may appeare by the two actes of com'on Counsell which I send yow w'th note ☞ directing to the place.

"The first of these actes of Comon counsell was made in the maraltie of Hawes XVII° Regine, and sheweth a maner how plaies were to be tollerated and vsed, although it were rather wished that they were wholly discontinued for the causes appearing in the preamble; w'ch is for that reason somewhat the longer.

" Where the players reporte the order to be that they shold not playe till after seruice time: the boke is otherwise; for it is that they shal not onely not play in seruice time; but also shal not receue any in seruice time to se the same: for thoughe they did forbeare begining to play till seruice were done, yet all the time of seruice they did take in people, w'ch was the great mischef in withdrawing the people from seruice.

"Afterward when these orders were not obserued, and the lewd maters of playes encreasced and in the haunt vnto them were found many dangers, bothe for religion, state, honestie of manners, onthriftinesse of the poore, and danger of infection &c. and the preachers dayly cryeng against the L. Maior and his bretheren, in an Act of Com'on Counsel for releafe of the poore w'ch I send yow printed, in the Article 62 the last leafe; is enacted as there appeareth, by w'ch there are no enterludes allowed in London in open spectacle but in priuate howses onely at marriages or such like, w'ch may suffise, and sute is apointed to be made that they may be likewise banished in places adioyning.

[1] See above, p. 156.    [2] See above, p. 164.

"Since that time and namely vpon the ruine at Parise garden, sute was made to my S'rs to banishe playes wholly in the places nere London, according to the said lawe, letters were obtained from my S'rs to banishe them on the sabbat daies." [1]

The other document on the city side is a vigorous and interesting report which takes up point by point all the contentions and proposals made by the players in their petition and articles.[2] To the argument of the necessity of practice for the performances before the Queen, the municipal authorities retort that it is not fitting to present before her Majesty such plays as have been "commonly played in open stages before all the basest assemblies in London and Middlesex"; but that the players ought to "exercise" only in private houses. As for the actors' contention that they must play in order to earn their living, the City replies by asserting that no one should practise such a profession, but that plays should be presented by way of recreation by men with other means of subsistence, — an apparent reference to the custom of guild plays. The report of the municipal authorities on the regulations proposed by the actors is summed up in the "Remedies" quoted below. A few extracts, however, are interesting enough to be cited at length. The players had evidently suggested that performances should be allowed whenever the deaths from the plague were under fifty a week. To this the City retorts first, rather epigrammatically, that "to play in plagetime is to increase the plage by infection: to play out of plagetime is to draw the plage by offendinge of God vpon occasion of such playes." But if performances must be tollerrated in seasons of infection, the City thinks some better rule could be found than that proposed by the actors. "It is an vncharitable demaund against the safetie of the Quenes subiects, and per consequens of her person, for the gaine of a few, whoe if they were not her Ma^ties servaunts should by their profession be rogues, to esteme fefty a weke so small a number as to be cause of tolerating the adventure of infection." [3] The granting

---

[1] From a transcript of Lansdowne MS. 20, no. 11. The letter is not signed.

[2] Printed in full in Collier, *English Dramatic Poetry*, I, 214 ff. There is a summary in Fleay, *London Stage*, 46–47.

[3] Collier, *op. cit.*, 215. For a further account of the plague rule proposed by the City see below, p. 212.

of permission to the Queen's company only, they finally assert,
is "lesse evil than to graunt moe"; but they earnestly request
the Lords to specify, in their letters or warrants, the number
and the names of the Queen's players, since "last year, when
such toleration was of the Quenes players only, all the places of
playeng were filled with men calling themselves the Queenes
piayers." The company had evidently had no regular patent
or license.

As the players had proposed certain regulations, so the city
authorities, in their turn, apparently drew up the rules which
they thought should govern performances, — if plays must be
tolerated at all. These are entitled "The Remedies," and are
included in the same Lansdowne MS. with the other documents
just cited.

"That they hold them content with playeng in private houses at
weddings, &c. without publike assemblies.

"If more be thought good to be tolerated, that then they be restrained to the orders in the act of common Counsel, *tempore* Hawes.[1]

"That they play not openly till the whole death in London haue
ben by xx daies vnder 50 a weke, nor longer than it shal so continue.[2]

"That no playes be on the Sabbat.

"That no playeng be on holydaies, but after evening prayer, nor
any received into the auditorie till after evening prayer.

"That no playeng be in the dark, nor continue any such time but
as any of the auditorie may returne to their dwellings in London before
sonne set, or at least before it be dark.

"That the Quenes players only be tolerated, and of them their number, and certaine names, to be notified in your Ll[p] lettres to the L.
Maior and to the Justices of Midd'x and Surrey. And those her
players not to diuide themselves into several companies.

"That for breaking any of these orders their toleration cease."[3]

With this communication from the city authorities, our knowledge of the 1580–1584 controversy comes to an end. What
action the Privy Council took upon these "Remedies" does not
appear. But it is probable that some compromise measure

---

[1] That is, the act of December, 1574, considered above, pp. 156 ff.

[2] That is, the deaths from all causes, not from the plague alone, as the players
had apparently suggested.

[3] From the text given by Collier, *English Dramatic Poetry*, I, 217.

was adopted, including some of the municipal rules. Evidently the long struggle of the City did not avail to keep plays entirely out of London. Performances continued in the Liberties, and even—at least by the Queen's company, and later by others as well — in the inn yards of the City. The result must therefore have been bitterly unsatisfactory to the Puritans, who had pleaded so vigorously for the complete banishment of actors from all the neighborhood of London. But the earnest arguments of the municipal officials no doubt caused the enactment of restrictive measures more rigid than the Privy Council would otherwise have required.

The most bitter stage of the City's warfare on the drama was now over. Between 1584 and 1592 there seems to have been at least a partial cessation of the struggle. During the five years immediately following the dispute that we have just been tracing, there is little of importance to note in the regulation of the London stage, except a few orders issued by the Privy Council. These indicate that performances were continuing in and about London. In May, 1586, the danger from the plague grew serious enough to warrant the Lord Mayor in requesting the suppression of plays. The Lords accordingly prohibited performances in London, at the Theater, and at places about Newington.[1] A year later there seems to have been again danger of infection in the hot season. Because of this, and also of some "outrages and disorders" lately committed at playing places in London and the suburbs, the Privy Council, on May 7, 1587, ordered the Mayor, the Justices of Surrey, and the Master of the Rolls[2] to permit no more plays until after Bartholomew tide.[3] There had been for some time — at least since the Paris Garden disaster — a general rule against performances on Sunday; but it was irregularly enforced. On October 29, 1587, some inhabitants of Southwark complained to the Privy Council of the breach of this law, especially in the Liberty of the Clink, and the Lords ordered the Justices of the Peace to be more strict in preventing such offenses.[4]

For the next two years nothing of especial interest seems to

---

[1] *Acts*, XIV, 99, 102.  [2] See above, p. 54.
[3] *Acts*, XV, 70.  [4] *Ibid.*, 271.

have occurred in our department of stage history. Possibly the nation was too much absorbed in the conflict with the Armada to devote much attention to warfare over the theaters. In 1589 came the Martin Marprelate controversy, the trouble with the censorship and the temporary suppression of plays, which we have already discussed.[1] From the point of view of the London administration there are a few points to add to the history of this affair. It is noteworthy that the order for the suppression of plays was not sent to the Lord Mayor, as usual. In his letter to Lord Burghley, already quoted, he states, "Where by a l're of your Lordships, directed to Mr. Yonge, it appered unto me that it was your ho: pleasure that I sholde geve order for the staie of all playes within the cittie, in that Mr. Tilney did utterly mislike the same."[2] The Mr. Yonge here mentioned seems to have been the Richard Yonge who was one of the Middlesex Justices having authority over the Theater, the Curtain, and adjoining districts.[3] Why the Privy Council did not, as usual, communicate directly with the Mayor is not apparent. Perhaps they merely wished to stop the plays at the two theaters, and the Mayor, hearing of this, seized the opportunity to suppress all performances in the City as well.

The Mayor's account of the difficulty he had in stopping the plays in London is another illustration of the mutinous and disrespectful attitude towards the municipal authorities sometimes shown by the players, confident, as they seem to have been, of the powerful influence and protection of their patrons. Two companies were apparently performing in the inn yards of the City at the time, — the Lord Admiral's and Lord Strange's, — whom the Mayor summoned before him and, as he says, "to whome I speciallie gave in charge, and required them in her Majestys name, to forbere playinge untill further order might be geven for theire allowance in that respect: Whereupon the Lord Admeralls players very dutifullie obeyed; but the others, in very contemptuous manner departing from me, wente to the Crosse Keys, and played that afternoone to the greate offence

---

[1] See above, pp. 91–92.  [2] Hazlitt, *English Drama*, 34.
[3] See the order of June 23, 1592, addressed to him and to other Middlesex Justices. *Acts*, XXII, 549.

of the better sorte, that knew they were prohibited by order from your Lordship. Which as I might not suffer, so I sent for the said contemptuous persons, who haveing no reason to alleadge for theire contempte, I could do no less but this eveninge committ tow of them to one of the Compters." [1]

The agitation of the Martinist controversy resulted, as we have seen, in the appointment of a censorship commission on which the City was represented; but really marked the end of municipal licensing and the rise of the Master of the Revels to censoring power.

A rather quaint order was issued by the Lords on July 25, 1591, showing them as apparently for once more zealous against Sabbath breaking than the Lord Mayor himself, and coupling two somewhat incongruous requests. They have noticed, they inform the Mayor, some neglect of the order against playing on the Sabbath Day; and have also observed that performances on Thursdays are a "greate hurte and destruction of the game of beare baytinge and lyke pastymes, which are mayntayned for her Majestys pleasure yf occacion require." On these two days, therefore, they direct that no plays be allowed, for the greater reverence of God and the encouragement of the Queen's bear baiters. [2]

---

[1] Hazlitt, *English Drama*, 34–35.　　　[2] *Acts*, XXI, 324–325.

# CHAPTER V

## LOCAL REGULATIONS IN LONDON

### 1592–1642

THE last decade of the sixteenth century, the years during which Shakspere was rising to preëminence, is of much interest in the history of stage regulations. As viewed through the official documents, it presents a course of events somewhat different from the decade of the eighties. One is impressed particularly by the great disorders at the theaters. London during these years was apparently especially overrun by tramps and riotous persons. In 1595 and again in 1598, because of the large number of rogues and vagabonds in the City and the suburbs, the Privy Council found it necessary to appoint a Provost Marshal with power over London and the adjoining counties.[1] During the period the theaters seem to have been undoubtedly one of the chief gathering points for these vagabonds, for various sorts of cutpurses and rascals, and for the reckless apprentices who were thus lured from their work into evil ways. The city authorities realized vividly all these troubles. It is notable that throughout the decade this is the argument against plays which the municipality chiefly emphasizes, — that they serve as the rendezvous for rascals, nests of crime, and places of demoralization for the apprentices. The Puritan contention that theatrical performances are in themselves sinful, and draw down the wrath of God, is scarcely brought forward, — in contrast to the course of the argument during the years 1580–1584. The Privy Council, on its side, seems at times to have acquired something of the Puritan attitude. In 1593, for instance, it forbids plays at the

[1] *Acts*, XXIX, 132–133, 140, 206.

universities, because they may corrupt the students and allure them to "lewdness and vicious manners." [1] The danger of fomenting crime and disorder that arose from the London theaters, the Lords frankly recognized and tried to guard against. Though they continued to grant privileges to the few favored companies needed for the Queen's amusement, they passed at times extremely severe orders against the other theaters, — measures severe in their conception, at least, but never rigorously carried out.

As we have seen in a preceding chapter, by the year 1592 the Master of the Revels had to a considerable extent established his licensing power, and had authorized playing places in and about the City. In despair of securing from the Privy Council protection against this crown officer, the Aldermen appealed for aid to the Archbishop of Canterbury, and, though Whitgift was by no means of Puritan leanings, were successful in obtaining his intercession. [2] Their appeal, written on February 25, 1592, contains a vigorous recital of the dangers of the theaters, — informing the Archbishop of "the daily disorderly exercise of a number of players and playing houses erected within the City, whereby the youths of the City were greatly corrupted, and their manners infected with many evils and ungodly qualities, by reason of the wanton and profane devices represented on the stages. The apprentices and servants were withdrawn from their work, to the great hindrance of the trades and traders of the City, and the propagation of religion. Besides, to these places resorted the light and lewd disposed persons, as harlots, cutpurses, cozeners, pilferers, etc., who, under colour of hearing plays, devised divers evil and ungodly matches, confederacies and conspiracies, which could not be prevented." [3]

In the following summer danger of serious riots drove the Privy Council to recognize the justice of some of the Aldermen's accusations against the theaters. On May 30, 1592, the Lord Mayor reported to the Lord Treasurer a serious tumult and disorder in Southwark. [4] Fearing similar and graver rioting on Midsummer Night, the Lords issued, on June 23, an edict pro-

---

[1] *Acts*, XXIV, 427-428.　　[2] See above, p. 55-56.
[3] *Remembrancia*, 352.　　[4] *Athenæum*, January 23, 1869.

viding for rigid precautions against disorder in and about London on that occasion. The glimpse of armed householders on watch against mutinous apprentices which this affords, is an interesting illustration of the rather primitive methods of keeping order practised in Elizabethan London; and the command for the closing of the playing places shows a clear recognition by the Privy Council of the danger to which these resorts gave rise. The following extract is from the form of order sent to the Middlesex Justices.

"Whereas her Majestie is informed that certaine apprentyces and other idle people theire adherentes that were authors and partakers of the late mutynous and foule disorder in Southwarke in moste outrageous and tumultuous sorte, have a further purpose and meaninge on Midsommer eveninge or Midsommer nighte or about that tyme to renewe theire lewd assemblye togeather by cullour of the tyme for some bad and mischeivous intencion, to the disturbance and breache of her Majesty's Peace, and comyttinge some outrage. To prevente in tyme theis wicked and mischeivous purposes wee have given straighte order to the Maiour of London for the cittye and the liberties thereunto belonginge and to all other places neere to the same to have regarde hereunto, and so likewyse wee are in her Majesty's name straightlie to chardge and comaunde you presentlye upon sighte hereof to sende for the constables and some of the cheifest and discreetest inhabitauntes in Holborne, Clerkenwell, St. Giles in the Fieldes, &c. and other places neere thereaboutes, and to chardge and comaunde them to take order that there maye be a stronge and substancyall watch kept bothe on Midsommer eveninge, Midsommer night and Sondaye at nighte of housholders and masters of families, to contynue from the beginninge of the eveninge untill the morninge, and that all masters of servantes and of apprentices be straightlie chardged, as they will answere to the contrarye at theire perilles, to keepe theire servauntes in theire houses for those two nightes, so as they maie be within the dores before the eveninge and not suffered to come forthe, nor to have anye weapons yf they shoulde be so lewdlie disposed to execute any evill purpose. And yf notwithstandinge this straighte chardge and comaundement any servantes, apprentyces or other suspected persons shalbe founde in the streetes, to see them presentlie commytted to pryson. Especiallie you shall take order that theis watches of housholders maye be of that strength with theire weapons as they maie be hable yf there be anie uprore, tumult or unlawful assemblye to suppresse the same. Moreover for avoidinge of theis unlawfull assemblies in those quarters, yt is thoughte meete you shall take order that there be noe playes used in anye place neere thereaboutes, as the theator, curtayne or other usuall places where the same are comonly used, nor no other sorte of unlawfull or forbidden pastymes that draw togeather the baser sorte of people, from hence forth untill the feast of St. Michaell."[1]

By the orders sent out on this occasion, all plays were forbidden in and about London between June 23 and September 29, 1592. It seems probable that it was during this summer, and as a result of this restriction, that Lord Strange's company addressed to the Privy Council the undated petition preserved in the Dulwich MSS. This may, however, have been presented in 1593, though the very severe plague which lasted all that summer and autumn makes it seem improbable that the Lords would have granted in that season the permission to open the Rose which apparently resulted from the petition.[2] About August, 1592, then, — if we accept that year as the more probable, — Lord Strange's players petitioned the Lords for permission to reopen their playhouse on the Bankside, — that is, the Rose. Their company is large, they plead, and the cost of traveling the country intolerable. The opening of their theater will enable them to be ready to serve her Majesty, and it will also be a great help to the poor watermen, who earn their living largely by transporting the audiences to and from the Bankside.[3] This appeal was apparently seconded by a petition to the Lord High Admiral from the watermen, preserved among the same manuscripts. They beg for the opening of Henslowe's playhouse as a measure of relief for themselves and their families.[4] It was no doubt as a result of these appeals that the Lords issued the following undated order.

"To the Justices, Bayliffes, Constables and others to whome yt shall apperteyne. Whereas, not longe since, upon some considera-

[1] *Acts*, XXII, 549–551. And see above, pp. 145–146.
[2] Fleay (*London Stage*, 85–86) dates the petition 1592, as does Greg (*Henslowe Papers*, 42). Collier says 1593. (*Alleyn Memoirs*, 33.) There is no entry of the resulting Council Order in the Register for 1592. For the summer of 1593 the Register is lost. This perhaps points to the later date as the more probable one.
[3] Collier, *Alleyn Memoirs*, 33–34; *Henslowe Papers*, 42.
[4] Collier, *Alleyn Memoirs*, 34–35; *Henslowe Papers*, 42–43. Compare the suit of the watermen against the players' leaving the Bankside in 1613. *1821 Variorum*, III, 149 ff., note.

tions, we did restraine the Lorde Straunge his servauntes from play-inge at the Rose on the Banckside, and enjoyned them to plaie three daies at Newington Butts.[1]  Now, forasmuch as wee are satisfied that by reason of the tediousness of the waie, and that of longe tyme plaies have not there bene used on working daies, and for that a num-ber of poore watermen are therby releeved, yow shall permitt and suffer them, or any other there, to exercise themselves in suche sorte as they have don heretofore, and that the Rose maie be at libertie, without any restrainte, so longe as yt shalbe free from infection of sicknes.  Any commaundement from us heretofore to the contrye notwithstandinge." [2]

By January 28, 1593, the severe plague which raged during that year had already become so serious that the Privy Council ordered the prohibition of all plays, bear-baitings, and other like assemblages within the City or seven miles thereof.[3]  To assist the favored players during this hard season, the Lords issued, in the spring, to the companies of the Earl of Sussex and Lord Strange, traveling licenses authorizing them to perform anywhere outside the prohibited area.[4]

Another case illustrative of the interference of individual noble-men to secure for their players privileges within the City, such as we have already seen, is found on October 8, 1594, when the Lord Chamberlain, Lord Hunsdon, requested of the Lord Mayor permission for his company to perform at the inn yard of the Cross Keys.  As the document throws some interesting light on the conditions of the performances, it is worth quoting at length.

"Where my nowe company of players have byn accustomed for the better exercise of their qualitie and for the service of her Majestie if need soe requier, to plaie this winter time within the Citye at the Crosse Kayes in Gratious Street, these are to require and praye your Lordship to permitt and suffer them soe to doe, the which I praie you the rather to doe for that they have undertaken to me that where heretofore they began not their playes till towardes fower a clock, they will now begin at two and have don betwene fower and five, and will nott use anie drumes or trumpettes att all for the callinge of peopell

---

[1] This order to play at Newington is apparently not preserved, and its date and purpose are hard to establish.  The dating of all this series of documents is, in fact, decidedly unsatisfactory.

[2] Collier, *Alleyn Memoirs*, 36; *Henslowe Papers*, 43–44.

[3] *Acts*, XXIV, 31–32.     [4] See above, p. 34.

together, and shal be contributories to the poore of the parishe where they plaie accordinge to their habilities." [1]

Much as the London authorities disliked performances in the inn yards within the City, the Lord Mayor would hardly have dared to refuse the direct request of so powerful a nobleman and official; and we may probably assume that the Lord Chamberlain's company performed at the Cross Keys that winter, as they had been accustomed to do.[2]

But the new Mayor who took office on October 28 seems to have renewed with zeal the attack on the stage. On November 3, 1594, he wrote to the Lord Treasurer informing him of the intended erection of a new stage or theater on the Bankside — the Swan, no doubt — and praying that this might be prevented, on account of the evils arising therefrom.[3] This appeal seems to have been of no avail in stopping the building of the Swan; but the Mayor, not yet discouraged, made a far more sweeping demand in the following autumn, on September 13, 1595, — nothing less than the complete suppression of all plays about the City. Again he urges the disorder and crime hatched within the theaters.

"Among other inconvenyences it is not the least that the refuse sort of evill disposed and ungodly people about this Cytie have oportunitie hearby to assemble together and to make their matches for all their lewd and ungodly practizes, being also the ordinary places for all maisterles men and vagabond persons that haunt the high waies to meet together and to recreate themselfes, whearof wee begin to have experienc again within these fiew daies since it pleased her highnes to revoke her comission graunted forthe to the Provost Marshall, for fear of home they retired themselfes for the time into other partes out of his precinct, but ar now retorned to their old haunt, and frequent the plaies, as their manner is, that ar daily shewed at the Theator and Bankside, whearof will follow the same inconveniences, whearof wee have had to much experienc heartofore, for preventing

[1] Halliwell-Phillipps, *Illustrations*, 31–32; Maas, *Englische Theatertruppen*, 82.
[2] Fleay conjectures that the request was refused, but offers no proof. (*London Stage*, 134.) He is apt to underestimate the frequency of these inn-yard performances, falling into occasional errors in his stage history of this period because of his attempt to assign companies to fixed playhouses and not to inns.
[3] *Remembrancia*, 353.

whearof wee ar humble suters to your good Ll. and the rest to direct
your lettres to the Justics of Peac of Surrey and Middlesex for the
present stay and finall suppressing of the said plaies, as well at the
Theator and Bankside as in all other places about the Citie." [1]

But the Council apparently took no action. It would seem
that at this time the Mayor had succeeded, temporarily at least,
in stopping plays in the city inn yards. On July 22, 1596, the
plague again came to the aid of the Puritans, and the Lords
ordered the Justices of Middlesex and Surrey to suppress performances.[2] Another ally now seems to have helped the municipal authorities. Lord Hunsdon, the Lord Chamberlain, long
a warm friend to the players, died; and on August 8, 1596, Lord
Cobham was appointed in his place. Cobham apparently had
Puritan leanings, and the rigorous orders passed against the
players during the next couple of years have generally been
attributed to his influence. But as his short administration
was ended by his death on March 5, 1597, four months before
the order for the demolition of the theaters, it is difficult to be
sure how far he was responsible for the severity.

There is evidence, however, that in the summer of 1596 the
players felt the hardship of having a puritanical nobleman in
the position of Lord Chamberlain, — hitherto generally one of
the chief protectors of the drama. In a letter written by Nash
to William Cotton some time between June 29 and October 10 —
and apparently after August 8, when Cobham became Chamberlain — the dramatist complains that "the players are piteously
persecuted by the Lord Mayor and the Aldermen; and, however
in their old Lord's time they thought their state settled, it is now
so uncertain they cannot build upon it." The "old Lord"
seems to refer to Hunsdon, the late Chamberlain and friend to
the actors.[3]

The attack on the theaters was now continued vigorously.
In November, 1596, the inhabitants of Blackfriars petitioned the
Privy Council against the "common playhouse" which, they

[1] Halliwell-Phillipps, *Outlines*, 349–350. There is a brief summary in *Remembrancia*, 354.
[2] *Acts*, XXVI, 38.
[3] See Collier, *English Dramatic Poetry*, I, 292; Fleay, *London Stage*, 157.

informed the Lords, Burbage was about to construct in that Liberty.  In this appeal they emphasize the annoyance and danger that the playhouse will cause to the noblemen and other residents of the precinct "both by reason of the great resort and gathering togeather of all manner of vagrant and lewde persons that, under cullor of resorting to the playes, will come thither and worke all manner of mischeefe, and also the greate pestring and filling up of the same precinct, yf it should please God to send any visitation of sicknesse as heretofore hath been, for that the same precinct is allready growne very populous, and besides that the same playhouse is so neere the Church that the noyse of the drummes and trumpetts will greatly disturbe and hinder both the ministers and parishioners in tyme of devine service and sermons."  For these reasons, and also because "there hath not at any tyme heretofore been used any comon playhouse within the same precinct, but that now all players being banished by the Lord Mayor from playing within the Cittie by reason of the great inconveniences and ill rule that followeth them, they now thincke to plant them selves in liberties," the petitioners beg the Lords to forbid the use of this building as a playhouse.  The name of Lord Cobham, the Lord Chamberlain, a resident of the precinct, does not appear among the signers of the petition, but we find there that of George, Lord Hunsdon, son of the former Chamberlain, and about to succeed Cobham in that office. This seems to reverse the attitude towards players usually attributed to these two noblemen.[1]

The question of the Blackfriars theater presents many puzzling features.  It is now well known that the petition purporting to come from Burbage, Shakspere and others, immediately after the appeal from the Blackfriars residents, and stating that the playhouse has already been in use for years, is a forgery.[2] Though Burbage's theater did not come into existence until 1596, there had been, however, plays in Blackfriars for many years before this; and the statement of the inhabitants that there had never been any "common playhouse" in the precinct is

[1] The petition is printed at length in Halliwell-Phillipps, *Outlines*, 461–462.

[2] See its condemnation in *State Papers, Dom.*, 1595–1597, 310.  Hazlitt printed the document in good faith in *English Drama*, 35–37.

therefore at first a trifle puzzling. We must infer that they did not apply this term to the inn yard, priory hall, Revels Office building, or wherever the performances had hitherto taken place.[1] But they do call Burbage's proposed theater a "common playhouse," as does the order of the city authorities suppressing it in 1619. The players, however, and their patrons, seem to have been careful to call it a "private house," and this is the term applied to it in the royal patents of 1619 and 1625. By representing it as a "private house," the players apparently expected to escape the laws directed against "common playhouses," — a result that they seem to have achieved in part. It is difficult to see on what grounds they based their contention. Though the construction of this theater within doors was very different from that of the "common playhouses," the price of admission higher, and the audience apparently of a better class, the mere fact that money was charged for admission would seem to have stamped it as a public theater and subjected it to the usual laws. Such, at least, would have been the case under the regulations laid down by the London ordinance of 1574.[2] As a matter of fact, the status of the theater seems to have remained ill defined.

What action the Privy Council took on the petition from the inhabitants of Blackfriars does not clearly appear. According to the municipal order of 1619, which recites the history of this theater, after the appeal the Lords "then forbad the use of the said howse for playes, and in June, 1600, made certaine orders by which, for many weightie reasons therein expressed, it is limitted there should be only two playhowses tolerated, whereof the one to be on the Banckside, and the other in or neare Golding Lane, exempting thereby the Blackfryers." But in defiance of this law the owner of the theater "under the name of a private howse hath converted the same to a publique playhowse."[3] It seems at least fairly clear that, whether or no the Lords did accede to the request of the residents of the precinct, and whether or no they intended the order of 1600 to suppress the Blackfriars theater, — as the city authorities always insist they did, — that

<hr />

[1] See Bond's Lyly, I, 24–25, note; Chambers, *Tudor Revels*, 18.
[2] See above, p. 158.    [3] Halliwell-Phillipps, *Outlines*, 474–475.

playhouse, as a matter of fact, was completed according to Burbage's plan, and flourished practically undisturbed until 1619. It is possible that its apparent immunity during the earlier part of the period was partially due to the fact that it was occupied by the Chapel Children, — a company which, as we shall presently see, was probably exempt from many of the restrictions applying to common players. A playhouse of uncertain status, in a precinct of uncertain status, occupied by actors of uncertain status, its legal position is indeed hard to define.

In the following summer, the Lord Mayor made another attack on the theaters, — a move which seemed at first triumphantly successful. On July 28, 1597, in a letter to the Privy Council, he presented the following appeal: —

"Wee have fownd by th' examination of divers apprentices and other servantes, whoe have confessed unto us that the saide staige playes were the very places of theire randevous appoynted by them to meete with such otheir as wear to joigne with them in theire designes and mutinus attemptes, beeinge allso the ordinarye places for maisterles men to come together to recreate themselves, for avoydinge wheareof wee are nowe againe most humble and earnest suitors to your honors to dirrect your lettres as well to ourselves as to the Justices of Peace of Surrey and Midlesex for the present staie and fynall suppressinge of the saide stage playes as well at the Theatre, Curten and Banckside, as in all other places in and abowt the Citie."[1]

On the same day, in prompt response to this appeal, the Lords issued an order in the name of the Queen, for the prohibition of all plays within three miles of the City during the summer, until after November 1, and also for the demolition of all theaters within the same area. "Her Majestie being informed," they wrote to the Middlesex Justices, "that there are verie greate disorders committed in the common playhouses both by lewd matters that are handled on the stages, and by resorte and confluence of bad people," she has given order that there be no more plays during the summer, and also that "those playhouses that are erected and built only for suche purposes shalbe plucked downe, namelie the Curtayne and the Theatre nere to Shorditch, or any other within that county." The Justices are directed

[1] Halliwell-Phillipps, *Outlines*, 351.

to send for the owners of the playhouses and order them to "plucke downe quite the stages, gallories and roomes that are made for people to stand in, and so to deface the same as they maie not be ymploied agayne to suche use." If they do not speedily do this, the magistrates must inform the Council, which will take order to enforce this command. A similar communication, we find from the Council Register, was sent to the Justices of Surrey, "requiring them to take the like order for the playhouses in the Banckside, in Southwarke or elswhere in the said county within iij° miles of London." [1] As the new Blackfriars theater was not under the jurisdiction of either the Middlesex or the Surrey magistrates, it seems to have been excluded from these orders for demolition.

Assuredly the Mayor could hardly have desired a more sweeping and rigorous edict. Even now, as one reads its stern commands, it is difficult to realize that it had scarcely the slightest effect upon the theaters. Probably plays ceased for a time, but the order for the destruction of the playhouses apparently no one even tried to enforce. [2] Again we appreciate what powerful influence the players must have been able to command, what friendship on the part of their patrons or of the Queen must have been brought into play, to cause this nullification of the Council's orders at this time.

Just what it was that caused even a temporary desire, on the part of the Lords, to take such severe measures against the theaters, does not appear. Mr. Fleay suggests that the suppression of plays was due to the trouble over the representation of Sir John Oldcastle in *Henry IV;* [3] but there seems to be no evidence for this, and one would certainly not expect such a severe punishment for a comparatively slight offense, — one which was, moreover, apparently so promptly atoned for. [4] As I have al-

---

[1] *Acts*, XXVII, 313–314. Printed in part in Halliwell-Phillipps, *Outlines*, 350–351.

[2] The Theater, it is true, was torn down in the winter of 1598–1599, and its materials used in the construction of the Globe, on the Bankside. This, however, was not in consequence of the Council Order, but chiefly because of the expiration of Burbage's lease of the Holywell land. See Halliwell-Phillipps, *Outlines*, 354 ff.

[3] *London Stage*, 158.          [4] See above, pp. 96–97.

ready mentioned, William Brooke, Lord Cobham, the puritanical Lord Chamberlain to whose influence the order is often
attributed, had died four months before, and George, Lord
Hunsdon, admittedly the friend of the players, had been Chamberlain for about three months.

In spite of the stern attitude towards the drama taken temporarily by the Privy Council, we find, a few months later, that the Lords
had granted special privileges to the two companies accustomed
to perform before the Queen. On February 19, 1598, as we have
already seen, the Council mentioned the special license, the monopoly of playing, which they had given to the Lord Admiral's
and the Lord Chamberlain's companies; and ordered Tilney
to suppress the intruding third company, and any others who
might presume to play.[1]

That the Bankside theaters, at least, were flourishing in
the following summer, appears from an entry in the Parish
Register of St. Saviour's, on July 19, 1598. The vestry determined to appeal to the Privy Council for the suppression of the
playhouses in that vicinity, and to show "the enormities that
come thereby to the parish."[2] That the suffering of the residents from the gathering of disorderly persons at the theaters
may well have been exceptionally great during this summer, is
shown by the appointment of a Provost Marshal by the Privy
Council on September 6, to deal with the unusual number of
rogues and vagabonds in and about London.[3] Though the
parish did not succeed in getting the Bankside theaters suppressed, its feelings were doubtless somewhat mollified by the
arrangements later made, in March, 1600, for the players' contributions of money for the poor.[4]

The final notable stage in the history of theatrical regulations
under Elizabeth opens with the erection of the Fortune theater
about January, 1600, and includes the order for the restriction
of playhouses which followed upon this event and gave rise to
considerable governmental correspondence during the next few
years. The Middlesex Justices apparently opposed in some

---

[1] See above, p. 58.
[2] Chalmers, *Apology*, 404; *1821 Variorum*, III, 452, note.
[3] See above, p. 178.    [4] See above, p. 60.

way the erection of Alleyn and Henslowe's new theater. On
January 12, 1600, the Earl of Nottingham, Lord Admiral, came
to the aid of his company by sending to the Middlesex magistrates a letter "praying and requiring" them to permit his servant, Edward Alleyn, to proceed in "theffectinge and finisheing"
of the new playhouse. The site is very convenient, he urges, and
the house the actors have hitherto occupied, the Rose, in so
dangerous a state of decay that it is no longer fit for use. These
players, moreover, have acted before the Queen and are favored
by her.[1] In spite of this urgent appeal there seems to have been
further opposition to the theater. But the company now succeeded in getting support from the residents of the locality where
they wished to settle. "The Inhabitants of the Lordship of
Finsbury" sent to the Privy Council a "Certificate of their
Consent to the Tolleration of the Erection of the new Playhouse
there." As reasons for their approval, they stated that the place
chosen for the theater was a remote one, and that the erectors
of the house were to contribute a liberal sum weekly towards the
relief of the poor, — a duty which the parish itself was not
wealthy enough to perform adequately.[2] Perhaps impressed
by the unusual welcome accorded by the neighbors of the proposed playhouse, but more probably at the instigation of the
Lord Admiral, the Queen now seems to have intervened. On
April 8, 1600, the Privy Council sent to the Middlesex Justices
a warrant requiring them, by order of the Queen, to permit
Edward Alleyn to complete his theater in the "verie remote
and exempt place neare Gouldinge Lane." This new house, the
Lords write, is to take the place of the Rose, which is to be pulled
down,[3] — an arrangement later altered, as we shall see.

The erection of the new theater, coupled, apparently, with
continued disorders at the other playhouses, aroused renewed
opposition to theatrical performances. Impressed by the protests, the Privy Council, on June 22, 1600, issued an order "for
the restrainte of the imoderate use and Companye of Playe-
howses and Players." "Whereas divers complaintes," the act

[1] Collier, *Alleyn Memoirs*, 55–56; *Henslowe Papers*, 49–50.
[2] Collier, *Alleyn Memoirs*, 58; *Henslowe Papers*, 50–51.
[3] Collier, *Alleyn Memoirs*, 57; *Henslowe Papers*, 51–52.

recites, "have bin heretofore made unto the Lordes and others of her Majesties Privye Counsell of the manyfolde abuses and disorders that have growen and do contynue by occasion of many houses erected and employed in and about the cittie of London for common stage-playes, and now verie latelie by reason of some complainte exhibited by sundry persons againste the buyldinge of the like house in or near Golding-lane by one Edward Allen, a servant of the right honorable the Lord Admyrall," the whole question of theaters has again been taken up by the Lords. The purpose of the act and the attitude of the Council towards plays are now clearly expressed.

"Forasmuch as it is manifestly knowen and graunted that the multitude of the saide houses and the mys-government of them hath bin and is dayly occasion of the ydle, ryotous and dissolute living of great nombers of people, that, leavinge all such honest and painefull course of life as they should follow, doe meete and assemble there, and of many particular abuses and disorders that doe thereupon ensue; and yet, nevertheless, it is considered that the use and exercise of such playes, not beinge evill in ytself, may with a good order and moderacion be suffered in a well-governed state, and that her Majestie, beinge pleased at somtymes to take delight and recreation in the sight and hearinge of them, some order is fitt to be taken for the allowance and mayntenaunce of such persons as are thought meetest in that kinde to yealde her Majestie recreation and delighte, and consequently of the houses that must serve for publike playinge to keepe them in exercise. To the ende, therefore, that both the greate abuses of the playes and playinge-houses may be redressed, and yet the aforesaide use and moderation of them retayned, the Lordes and the rest of her Majesties Privie Counsell, with one and full consent, have ordered in manner and forme as followeth."

The rules laid down are very definite. First, as to the number of playhouses, — there shall be only two "to serve for the use of the common stage-playes," one to be on the Bankside, the other in Middlesex. Since the Fortune, as Tilney has informed the Lords, is to take the place of the Curtain — not of the Rose, as was first announced — Alleyn's new theater is the one authorized in Middlesex, and is to be occupied by the Lord Admiral's company. The Curtain is to be destroyed. On the Surrey side, the Council has permitted the Lord Chamberlain's company to choose a playhouse, and it has selected the Globe.

Apart from these two no theaters are to be allowed; nor shall there be any more performances in "any common inne for publique assembly in or neare aboute the Cittie."

Secondly, "forasmuch as these stage-plaies, by the multitude of houses and the company of players, have bin so frequent, not servinge for recreation but invitinge and callinge the people dayly from their trade and worke to myspend their tyme," it is ordered that these two privileged companies shall perform only twice each week, never on the Sabbath, or in Lent, or in time of "extraordinary sickness" in or about the city.

Thirdly, to secure the strict enforcement of these rules, it is ordered that copies be sent to the Lord Mayor and to the Justices of the Peace of Middlesex and Surrey, together with letters urging them to carry out the laws, imprison any who violate them, and report their proceedings to the Privy Council from time to time.[1] A copy of this urgent request follows in the Council Register.[2]

It seems almost useless to rehearse these orders here at such length, for their enforcement was evidently lax and irregular in the extreme, — if indeed they were ever enforced at all. The Lords themselves seem to have had little desire for the rigorous carrying out of these commands. Indeed, they apparently soon forgot all about them; for when, in May, 1601, complaints were made of the offensive play at the Curtain, and the Privy Council ordered the Middlesex Justices to censor it, the existence and activity of this theater seems not to have disturbed them in the least, and they made no allusion to the fact that some ten months before they had directed that it be demolished.[3]

But the existence of the regulations was soon recalled to their minds. The municipal and shire officials had apparently been as forgetful as the Lords, and the continued abuses gave rise to fresh complaints. In December, 1601, the Lord Mayor again protested to the Privy Council against the playhouses.

---

[1] The order is printed at length in Halliwell-Phillipps, *Outlines*, 466–468, and in *Acts*, XXX, 395–398.

[2] Halliwell-Phillipps, *Outlines*, 468–469; *Acts*, XXX, 411.

[3] See above, p. 100.

Thus reminded that the fault was not theirs, the Lords, in a burst of righteous indignation, replied sternly to the Mayor. The sarcasm of the opening sentence suggests that the writer felt satisfaction in being able to retort in such wise to the Puritan City.

"Wee have receaved a letter from you renewing a complaint of the great abuse and disorder within and about the cittie of London by reason of the multitude of play-howses and the inordinate resort and concourse of dissolute and idle people daielie unto publique stage plaies, for the which information as wee do commende your Lordship because it betokeneth your care and desire to reforme the disorders of the cittie, so wee must lett you know that wee did muche rather expect to understand that our order (sett downe and prescribed about a yeare and a half since for the reformation of the said disorders upon the like complaint at that tyme) had bin duelie executed, then to finde the same disorders and abuses so muche encreased as they are, the blame whereof, as we cannot but impute in great part to the Justices of the Peace of Middlesex and Surrey . . . so wee do wishe that it might appeare unto us that anythinge hath bin endeavoured by the predecessours of you, the Lord Maiour, and by you, the Aldermen, for the redresse of the said enormities and for observation and execution of our said order within the cittie."

The enforcement of the rule is again urged. Violators are to be put on bond or imprisoned. "And so praying yow," conclude the Lords, "as yourself do make the complaint and finde the enormitie, so to applie your best endeavour to the remedie of the abuse." [1]

On the same day, December 31, 1601, the Council sent a letter to the Justices of Middlesex and Surrey, severely censuring them for their negligence. "It is in vaine for us to take knowledg of great abuses and disorders complayned of and to give order for redresse, if our directions finde no better execution and observation than it seemeth they do, and wee must needes impute the fault and blame thereof to you or some of you, the Justices of the Peace." They summarize their order of a year and a half since, and vigorously describe the lack of enforcement. "Wee do now understande that our said order hath bin so farr from takinge dew effect, as, in steede of restrainte and redresse

[1] *Acts*, XXXII, 468–469; Halliwell-Phillipps, *Outlines*, 469–470.

o

of the former disorders, the multitude of play howses is much encreased, and that no daie passeth over without many stage plaies in one place or other within and about the cittie publiquelie made." The Justices, the Lords assert, have not reported on this matter, as they were ordered to do. They are now commanded to mend their ways.[1]

Apparently the exhortations of the Lords had little or no effect. That the Privy Council itself felt by no means bound to observe its own rules, and soon relapsed from its stern attitude, is shown — if proof be needed — by a letter which it sent to the Lord Mayor a few months later. On March 31, 1602, in violation of its own rule against performances in inn yards, the Council bade the Mayor allow the servants of the Earl of Worcester and the Earl of Oxford to play at the Boar's Head in Eastcheap.[2] According to Mr. Fleay's estimate, in spite of the restrictive measures eight playing places were open in and about London in 1602.[3]

The almost absurd laxness in carrying out these restrictions of 1600 is puzzling in part. From the Council's letter it would appear that even the city authorities had not endeavored to suppress unlawful plays. Why the Puritan opposition was thus relaxed — if it was — is not clear. Mr. Fleay's comment on the affair is that the ruling motive was not Puritan on the city side, but an "obstinate determination to assert their privileges," — leading the municipal authorities to suppress playing places whenever the Court wanted them open, and to allow freedom to them all when the Court wished to give a monopoly to the favored companies.[4] This is not convincing. Of course, the opposition on the city side was, as we have observed, not exclusively and merely Puritan in motive; but an "obstinate determination to assert their privileges" does not seem to describe their attitude. By this time they must have been pretty well hardened to the interference and encroachments of the royal government, which, as we have seen, had been almost continual for a quarter of a century. Their communications to the Privy Council seem to admit freely the right of the Lords to regulate

[1] *Acts*, XXXII, 466–468; Halliwell-Phillipps, *Outlines*, 470–471.
[2] *Remembrancia*, 355.  [3] *London Stage*, 161.  [4] *Ibid.*

the drama in and about London, and to entreat merely that these regulations may be restrictive enough to protect the City from the abuses of the theaters. The laxness of the municipality at this particular time — if indeed it was lenient to the playing places within London — may have been due to a variety of causes. Perhaps the Lord Mayor in office for the year 1600–1601 was not of Puritan inclinations, but personally in favor of the stage. Or he may have been merely lax and careless. Or the players may have brought all sorts of powerful influences to bear. Probably the immense public demand for plays at this time, forcibly described in the Council Order of 1600, was so intense that the general public opinion tended to prevent the enforcement of the restrictions. Moreover and finally, there seems to have been at this period, one might almost say, a presumption in favor of the non-enforcement of any given regulation.

There is another puzzling question in connection with the restrictive order of 1600. Was it intended to apply to the children's companies, or were they, as well as the two privileged men's companies, expected to perform? Were their playing places not considered as serving "for the use of the common stage-playes"? The Paul's Boys in their singing-school, and the Children of the Chapel in the new Blackfriars theater, seem to have acted undisturbed during this period of agitation; but whether this was due to their special exemption, or merely to the general non-enforcement of the law, is not clear. They are not mentioned in the orders and complaints which we have been considering. On March 11, 1601, however, when the Privy Council wrote to the Lord Mayor requiring him not to fail in suppressing plays during Lent within the City and the liberties thereof, they added "especyally at Powles and in the Blackfriars." [1] This indicates that the children's companies were performing as usual, and that the regulation of them was attended to at times. We know, indeed, from other sources, that they were especially successful during these years. The whole question of the status of these companies, which this brings up, is decidedly puzzling, and there seems to be, as yet,

[1] *Acts*, XXXI, 218.

very little available material throwing light on it. I would conjecture that these two companies were, in the eyes of the law, on a footing considerably different from that of the other players. Probably they were not technically regarded as professional actors, since their real profession was supposed to be choral singing. By virtue of their connection with the church, as choristers of St. Paul's and of the Royal Chapel; or because of their inclusion in the royal service; or on the strength of the royal patents authorizing the Masters to take up boys for choral purposes; or for all these reasons, — they were probably tacitly allowed special privileges and a status peculiarly their own. The laws restricting the number of "common players" and common playing places would therefore probably not apply to them. But the Lenten and Sunday regulations would be especially appropriate in their case, and the plague restriction, so essential for the welfare of the community, was probably also expected to be obeyed by them. Under James, as we have seen, the children were given regular patents for playing, and seem to have been placed on much the same footing as the other actors. Finally, in 1626, the patent to Giles forbade the use of the Chapel Children for dramatic purposes.[1]

On March 19, 1603, five days before the death of Elizabeth, the Privy Council ordered the Mayor and the Justices of Middlesex and Surrey to suppress all plays until further notice.[2] Whether this was because of Lent, of the plague, or of the Queen's illness does not appear. But plays evidently began again within less than six weeks after Elizabeth's death. We learn from Henslowe's Diary that the performances were stopped on May 5, "at the King's coming," two days before James' arrival in London, and resumed "by the King's license" on May 9.[3]

With the end of Elizabeth's reign we have reached the practical conclusion of the struggle between the municipal and the royal governments over plays. On the whole, the City met defeat. Though performances in the inn yards within the municipal jurisdiction seem now to have ceased, the obnoxious theaters in the Liberties continued to flourish undisturbed. All

[1] See above, pp. 37–38.
[2] *Acts*, XXXII, 492.
[3] *Henslowe's Diary*, 174, 190.

regulation of the drama was now organized under the system of royal patents and the administration of the Master of the Revels, — both of which we have already considered. The monopoly of playing in and about London granted by the royal patents had grown naturally out of the exclusive privileges awarded to the favored companies under Elizabeth. But whereas, during the later years of the Queen's reign, there had been some attempt to restrict the number of the men's companies to two, under James and Charles at least four or five were generally privileged to perform. The playing places authorized for the favored actors were specified in the patents; the Master of the Revels was intrusted with the regulation of performances; and there resulted at least the appearance, and to a considerable extent the practice, of greater regularity and consistency in the enforcement of the rules.

In the face of this system of royal regulation and authorization, the city government subsided.[1] It was, indeed, practically helpless. The fixed theaters were, until 1608, all outside the Mayor's jurisdiction,[2] and for the most part specially licensed by the Crown. Even when Blackfriars and Whitefriars came under the municipal authority, the players were effectually sheltered by the royal protection. But, on the whole, the state of the City was not so bad as it might have been. The obnoxious performances in inn yards were apparently now given up, and, with the improvement which seems to have taken place in the class of spectators who attended the theaters, disorders resulted much less frequently. There are, indeed, indications that the hostility towards plays hitherto felt by the municipal officials and the upper classes of the citizens had now somewhat diminished, and that the city government was no longer so intensely eager to banish all actors. But the Puritan antipathy to the drama, though it found for the time no expression in municipal

---

[1] In December, 1625, there was a slight recurrence of the old dispute. The Mayor and the Aldermen imputed the recent plague to the assemblages at the theaters, and requested the entire suppression of such performances, — apparently without result. See Collier, *English Dramatic Poetry*, I, 438.

[2] The later playhouses, the Cockpit, in Drury Lane, and the Red Bull, in Clerkenwell, were also beyond reach of the city officials.

legislation, remained deep and bitter, spreading through many classes of society and awaiting its chance for a decisive blow.

Though the victory of the City in the long controversy that we have been tracing would have seriously hindered the development of the drama, it is impossible to follow the dispute in detail without sympathizing with the municipality. There seems to have been much justification for their complaints against the theaters, which certainly in many cases fomented disorder and crime. And the invasion by the Crown of their rights of local self-government must sometimes have been exasperating in the extreme. That they should have been forced, merely in order to give the court players a chance to practise for the better diversion of the Queen, to tolerate performances which they sincerely regarded as highly dangerous in spreading the plague and gravely injurious to the morals and good order of the community, seems an act of tyranny which might well arouse a spirit of rebellion. But we must be careful not to read into their age the feelings of our own. With rare exceptions, at the mention of the Queen's name they seem to have bowed in loyal submission.

The chapters on the Master of the Revels and the censorship have covered most of the history of theatrical regulation in London during the years 1603-1642, when the crown officials were in charge. There remain to be considered only a few cases of royal and municipal legislation affecting the London stage. Most of these center about the famous precinct of Blackfriars, which, as we have seen, came under the municipal jurisdiction in 1608. The City made no move, for the present, against the King's company, which now began to occupy Burbage's playhouse; but in 1615, when the construction of a second theater in that precinct was begun, the municipality protested.

The case is a puzzling one. On May 31, 1615, a Privy Seal was apparently issued, directing a patent under the Great Seal to Philip Rosseter and others. This recites the grant of Rosseter's patent of January 4, 1610, for the Children of the Queen's Revels, who have been performing in Whitefriars, and it authorizes him to construct a new playhouse in Blackfriars, on land which he has leased for that purpose, — "all w<sup>ch</sup> premisses are scittuat and being w^th in the precinct of the Blackfryers neere Puddlewharfe, in the Subburbes of London, called by the name of the Ladie Saunders house, or otherwise Porters Hall, and nowe in the occupac'on of the said Robert Jones." The Revels Children, the Prince's company, and the Lady Elizabeth's are authorized to perform in this theater.[1]

Upon the grant of this patent Rosseter began to construct his playhouse. Whereupon the Mayor and the Aldermen, as we learn from an order of the Privy Council, complained to the Lords that he had pulled down "Lady Sanclers" house, at Puddle-wharf, in the precinct of Blackfriars, and was building a theater there, to the great prejudice and inconvenience of the governm^ent of the City. The Privy Council sent for Rosseter, and had his letters patent inspected by the Lord Chief Justice. As a result of their deliberations, because of the inconveniences urged by the Mayor, and especially the fact that the nearness of the proposed playhouse to a church would cause interruption of Divine Service on week-days, "and that the Lord Chief Justice did deliver to their Lordships that the license granted to the said Rosseter, did extend to the building of a playhouse without the liberties of London and not within the City," the Council ordered, on September 26, 1615, that there should be no theater constructed in that place. They bade the Mayor stop Rosseter and his workmen, and imprison them should they prove disobedient.[2]

Since Rosseter's patent, as we have it, expressly authorizes him, in the passage that I have quoted, to construct the theater on the very plot where he was building, the decision of the Chief Justice and of the Council is puzzling. Mr. Fleay suggests that the existing patent is a Collier forgery.[3] This may possibly be the case, though no motive for a forgery is here evident. But the apparent contradiction can, I think, be explained in another way. The Lord Chief Justice who rendered the decision was the famous Coke, removed from office about a year afterwards

---

[1] The patent is printed in Hazlitt, *English Drama*, 46–48, and in Collier, *English Dramatic Poetry*, I, 381–382.

[2] The order is printed in full in *1821 Variorum*, III, 493–494, note.

[3] *London Stage*, 263–264.

for opposing the royal and ecclesiastical prerogatives, and later a leader of the popular party in Parliament, where he vigorously fought against monopolies and other royal tyrannies. It may be that on this occasion he sympathized with the protest of the City against the invasion of their jurisdiction, and took advantage of a technical flaw in the phrasing of the patent, to decide against Rosseter. The authorization, as I have quoted it, specifies Lady Saunder's house in Blackfriars, but mentions it as situated "*in the Subburbes of London*," whereas Blackfriars was now actually within the City. This irregularity might justify Coke in saying that the license authorized a playhouse "without the liberties of London and not within the City." It will be noticed that the patent granted four years later to the King's company is careful to specify Blackfriars as "within our City of London."

Moreover, there is evidence that the King himself regretted the issue of the patent, and was not unwilling to have the Privy Council declare it void. For when Rosseter obstinately persisted in completing the theater, the Lords, on January 26, 1616 or 1617,[1] sent the following order to the Mayor.

"Whereas his Majesty is informed that notwithstanding divers commandments and prohibitions to the contrary, there be certain persons that go about to set up a playhouse in the Blackfryars, near unto his Majesty's Wardrobe, and for that purpose have lately erected and made fit a building which is almost if not fully finished: You shall understand that his Majesty hath this day expressly signified his pleasure, that the same shall be pulled down; so as it be made unfit for any such use. Whereof we require your Lordship to take notice, and to cause it to be performed with all speed, and thereupon to certify us of your proceedings." [2]

This seems to refer to Rosseter's house. Perhaps it had been decided that a theater so "near unto his Majesty's Wardrobe" would be inconvenient. Or influence of some other kind may have been brought to bear upon the King to make him practically annul his grant.

---

[1] Chalmers dates it 1616–1617. (*1821 Variorum*, III, 494, note.) Fleay thinks it was probably 1616. (*London Stage*, 264.) The later date certainly makes a very long interval elapse.

[2] *1821 Variorum*, III, 494, note.

In spite of all the opposition, Rosseter's theater seems to have been open for a few performances at least. The title-page of Field's *Amends for Ladies*, printed in 1618, states that it was "acted at the Blacke-Fryers, both by the Princes Servants, and the Lady Elizabeths." [1] As these were two of the companies for which the new playhouse was intended, it seems likely that the comedy was performed there.

A few years later the inhabitants of Blackfriars, perhaps encouraged by the fate of Rosseter's theater, determined to make an effort to free themselves from the inconveniences caused by Burbage's playhouse, long established in their precinct and now occupied by the King's company. The royal patent held by these players specified only the Globe as their authorized theater and gave them no explicit right to perform in Blackfriars. Their position therefore seemed open to attack. As the precinct was now within the jurisdiction of the City, the residents appealed, not to the Privy Council, as in 1596, but to the Mayor and the Aldermen. About January, 1619, the minister, the church-wardens, the sidesmen, the constables, the collectors, and the scavengers of the precinct addressed a petition to the municipal authorities, begging for the suppression of Burbage's playhouse and rehearsing the inconveniences caused thereby. [2] A letter supporting this petition was also submitted to the Mayor and the Aldermen signed by "divers honorable persons, inhabiting the precinct of Blackfriars." [3]

As a result, the city authorities issued, on January 21, 1619, an order for the suppression of the theater. This recites part of the history of the playhouse, as I have quoted above, and endeavors to make it appear that the performances there are in defiance of the orders of the Privy Council. [4] It also summarizes the complaints of the petitioners. This passage gives an interesting glimpse of conditions surrounding performances in the famous theater. It should be compared with the petition of 1596, setting forth the evils which the residents feared would result from the establishment of the playhouse, — especially the

---

[1] Hazlitt's Dodsley, XI, 88.　　[2] *Remembrancia*, 355.
[3] *Ibid.*, 356.　　[4] See above, p. 186.

influx of tramps and rascals.[1]   In contrast to this, it is now the
great press of coaches from which they suffer.   Apparently the
Blackfriars theater was attracting an audience greatly superior
in social status to what the precinct had anticipated.

"There is daily," the order recites, "so great resort of people, and soe
great multitude of coaches, whereof many are hackney coaches bringing
people of all sortes that sometimes all their streetes cannot conteyne
them, that they endanger one the other, breake downe stalles, throw
downe mens goodes from their shopps, hinder the passage of the in-
habitantes there to and from their howses, lett the bringing in of their
necessary provisions, that the tradesmen and shoppkeepers cannot
utter their wares, nor the passengers goe to the common water staires
without danger of their lives and lyms, whereby manye times quar-
rells and effusion of blood hath followed, and the minister and people
disturbed at the administracion of the Sacrament of Baptimse and
publique prayers in the afternoones."

The Corporation of London therefore orders that the theater
shall be suppressed and "the players shall from henceforth forbear and desist from playing in that house." [2]

But the King's company was too powerful to be in danger
from the municipal authorities.   Some effort to enforce the
order of suppression was probably made; and the King came to
the rescue of his servants.   On March 27, about two months
after the passage of the ordinance, a new royal patent was issued
to these players, expressly authorizing them to perform, not only
at the Globe, but also — without any flaw in the phrasing —
in "their private House scituate in the precincts of the Black-
friers within our Citty of London." [3]   In the face of such royal
authorization the precinct and the municipal government were
helpless.   The opposition to the playhouse subsided for a time.

In later years there were revivals of the Blackfriars agitation,
interesting chiefly as showing the necessity, even at this early
day, of traffic regulations in London.   During 1631 the church-
wardens and the constables of the precinct petitioned Laud,

[1] See above, p. 185.
[2] The order is printed at length in Halliwell-Phillipps, *Outlines*, 474–475.
[3] See above, p. 38, and Appendix.

then Bishop of London, for a revival of previous orders made for the removal of the playhouse.[1] They repeat the same complaints about the great numbers of coaches which were advanced in 1619. This appeal through ecclesiastical channels was apparently unsuccessful. Bishop Laud indorsed the petition "To the Council Table"; but the Privy Council seems to have taken no action on it. The agitation was resumed two years later with slightly more effect. The Lords appointed a Commission, including some of the Justices of Middlesex and the Alderman of the Ward, to investigate the question of the removal of the Blackfriars theater and decide on what recompense should be made to the players.[2] On November 20, 1633, the Commission reported that no agreement could be reached on the amount of the indemnity. The players demanded £21,000, the Commissioners valued it at near £3000, and the parishioners offered towards the removal of the theater £100.[3]

Apparently giving up this plan in despair, and endeavoring to remedy the evil in another way, the Privy Council, two days later, issued orders stringently regulating traffic to and from the Blackfriars playhouse. No coaches were to be allowed to come nearer the theater than "the farther side of St. Paul's Churchyard on the one side, and Fleet Conduit on the other." The Mayor was directed to enforce this regulation.[4] Apparently the new rule was distasteful to the players and their audiences, and at a council meeting on December 29 it was materially modified. "As many coaches as may stand within the Blackfriars gate" were now to be allowed to enter and stay there, or return thither at the end of the play.[5] As the King was present at this council meeting, it has been conjectured that he interceded on behalf of his players.[6] A letter from Garrard to Lord Deputy Wentworth, written on January 9, 1634, remarks on the new regulation and the audience's having to "trot afoot to find their

[1] The petition is printed at length in Collier, *English Dramatic Poetry*, I, 455–457. There is an abstract in *State Papers, Dom.*, 1631–1633, 219–221.

[2] Collier, *op. cit.*, I, 476–477, note; *State Papers, Dom.*, 1633–1634, 266.

[3] *State Papers, Dom.*, 1633–1634, 293.

[4] Collier, *op. cit.*, I, 478–479; *Remembrancia*, 356, 357; *State Papers, Dom.*, 1633–1634, 293.

[5] Collier, *op. cit.*, I, 479.     [6] *Ibid.*

coaches." "'Twas kept very strictly for two or three weeks," he writes, "but now I think it is disordered again." [1]

All audiences were not of such dignity as those that attended the Blackfriars theater, and at times the authorities still had to be on their guard against disorder. On May 25, 1626, for example, the Privy Council directed the Justices of Surrey to take precautions against riot at the Globe. "We are informed," write the Lords, "that on Thursday next divers loose and idle persons, some sailors and others, have appointed to meete at the Play-house called the Globe, to see a play (as is pretended), but their end is thereby to disguise some routous and riotous action." The Justices are therefore commanded to permit no performance on that day, and also to "have that strength about you as you shall think sufficient for the suppressing of any insolencies, or other mutinous intentions." [2]

In the stage history of the period there are a few other cases to be considered, connected with the authorization, or proposed authorization, of playhouses about London. There were several ineffectual attempts to secure permission for a theater in Lincoln's Inn Fields. Some time in James' reign the Prince's company sought a license for such a playhouse; but eleven Justices of the Peace certified that the place was inconvenient. [3] In 1620 John Cotton, John Williams, and Thomas Dixon were slightly more successful. King James issued orders for a patent granting them permission to erect an amphitheater in Lincoln's Inn Fields; but finding that some of the clauses seemed to give them greater liberty, "both in the point of building and using of exercises," than was intended, he stayed the grant at the Privy Seal, and ordered its terms modified. [4] Apparently in consequence of this difficulty, the writ was never issued. In Charles' reign Williams and Cotton again sought a patent. After some

---

[1] Strafford Letters, I, 175, quoted in Wheatley and Cunningham, *London Past and Present*, I, 200.

[2] Extract from the Council Register, printed in Collier, *English Dramatic Poetry*, I, 445-446, note.

[3] See the Lord Chancellor's letter of September 28, 1626, printed in Collier, *op. cit.*, I, 414-445.

[4] See James' letter to the Privy Council, September 29, 1620, printed in Collier, *op. cit.*, I, 407-408, and Hazlitt, *English Drama*, 56-57.

consideration the Lord Chancellor, on September 28, 1626, reported against the proposed grant. It was, he declared, different from that suggested in 1620, which provided for a theater that was to be principally for martial exercises and "extraordinary shows and solemnities," whereas this proposed house would probably be devoted only to common plays and sports. Moreover, the monopoly awarded in the power to restrain all other shows on one day in the week was much more extensive than that formerly suggested. In view of these arguments and of the fact that there were already too many buildings in Lincoln's Inn Fields, the Lord Chancellor advised against the patent, which was evidently never issued.[1]

The French comedians who visited London in 1635 were apparently more successful in carrying out plans for a theater. They performed for some time at the Cockpit, in Drury Lane, and then secured a royal warrant authorizing them to construct another theater in the same street, — or rather to adapt for that purpose an existing building. The following note in a manuscript book in the Lord Chamberlain's records informs us of this.

"18 April 1635: His Majesty hath commanded me to signify his royal pleasure, that the French comedians (having agreed with Monsieur le Febure) may erect a stage, scaffolds, and seats, and all other accommodations, which shall be convenient, and act and present interludes and stage plays, at his house, in Drury Lane, during his Majesty's pleasure, without any disturbance, hindrance, or interruption. And this shall be to them, and M. le Febure, and to all others, a sufficient discharge, &c."[2]

Sir Henry Herbert's Office Book gives us further information on the subject. On May 5, 1635, he records the grant of the foregoing warrant to Josias d'Aunay, Hurfries de Lau, and others, to "builde a playhouse in the manage-house." This, says Herbert, "was done accordinglye by my advise and allowance."[3]

One other authorization of a proposed theater remains to be noted. On March 26, 1639, D'Avenant obtained a patent under

---

[1] See the Chancellor's letter, printed in Collier, *op. cit.*, I, 444–445.
[2] Chalmers, *Apology*, 506–507, note.     [3] *1821 Variorum*, III, 122, note.

the Great Seal, permitting him to construct a theater within the City of London, upon a plot of ground adjoining the Three Kings Ordinary in Fleet Street, already allotted to him, or upon any other which may be assigned by the Commissioners for Building; and on certain conditions to give performances therein.[1] In an indenture dated October 2, 1639, D'Avenant declares that the site in Fleet Street has been found inconvenient and unfit, and pledges himself not to build on any other plot without further authorization.[2] Just why the plan for this theater was given up is not apparent. D'Avenant's appointment, on June 27, 1640, to take charge of the Cockpit, perhaps prevented his further search for a site for a new playhouse.[3]

In concluding this account of governmental regulations dealing with the London stage, it seems useful to summarize some of the chief lines of legislation, — apart from the main system of licensing and censorship which we have considered in previous chapters. These minor features have been touched on from time to time in the course of the present section and the preceding one, but may now be assembled in clearer order.

A notable custom prevailing to a considerable extent during Elizabeth's reign was the taxation of the players for the benefit of the sick and the poor. Probably such contributions were first offered by the actors, as an inducement to the local officials to permit them to perform. In the letter written by the London government to the Lord Chamberlain on March 2, 1574, disapproving of the proposal of a licensing patent empowering the patentee to authorize playing places in the City, the municipal officials remark that similar requests have been made before, and that the petitioners have offered in return large contributions "for the relief of the poor in hospitals."[4] Probably the players had already made such payments; for in the city ordinance of December 6, 1574, provision is made that all owners of licensed playing places shall contribute regularly for the use of the poor in

---

[1] *1821 Variorum*, III, 93–95. See above, p. 43.
[2] *Ibid.*, 520–522, note; Collier, *op. cit.*, II, 28–29.
[3] Chalmers, *Apology*, 519, note.
[4] Hazlitt, *English Drama*, 23–24. See above, p. 154.

hospitals, or of the poor of the City visited with sickness, such sums as may be agreed upon by the Mayor and the Aldermen on the one part, and the licensed householder on the other. All fines and forfeitures collected for offenses against this act are to be devoted to the same purpose.[1]

The practice seems to have continued to some extent throughout the sixteenth century. In 1594 the Lord Chamberlain's company, seeking permission to play at the Cross Keys, offered to contribute to the parish poor.[2] In 1600 such payments from the Bankside theaters were ordered by the Archbishop of Canterbury, the Bishop of London, and the Master of the Revels, as we learn from the entry in the Parish Register of St. Saviour's referring to the "tithes of the playhouses" to be paid by the players and "money for the poor."[3] Finally, in the same year, when seeking the approval of the residents of Finsbury for the erection of the new Fortune theater, the managers offered to contribute liberally to the parish poor.[4] I have found no further references to this practice in and about London. Probably when the players and the playing places were authorized by royal warrant, and there was no longer any necessity of placating the local officials and residents, the custom died out.[5]

There is visible during this period only a slight germ of the modern building and fire laws which apply particularly to theaters. The municipal authorities frequently refer to the danger to the audience caused by weak buildings and scaffolds. In the city ordinance of December 6, 1574, there is a provision requiring that the playing places must be approved and licensed by the Mayor and the Aldermen, and the owner put on bond.[6] It was perhaps intended that the construction of the temporary scaffoldings and stages should be inspected and passed upon. But there is no indication that such supervision was regularly exercised.

There was some attempt to regulate the hours of performances.

---

[1] Hazlitt, *English Drama*, 30. See above, p. 158.　[2] See above, p. 182–183.
[3] Chalmers, *Apology*, 405. See above, p. 60.
[4] *Henslowe Papers*, 50–51. See above, p. 190.
[5] The Long Parliament adopted a modification of it. See below, p. 226.
[6] Hazlitt, *English Drama*, 29. See above, pp. 157–158.

In the earliest enactments of this kind the players were forbidden to act during the time of Divine Service on Sundays and Holy Days, — as in the royal patent to Leicester's company in 1574 and the municipal ordinance of December in the same year.[1] In 1582, when the Privy Council suggested that performances should be allowed after Evening Prayer on Holy Days, the Mayor objected to the rule, protesting that it would delay the action of the plays to a very inconvenient time of night, especially for servants and children.[2]  The regulation seems to have been established, nevertheless; but the dangers involved in the audience's returning to their homes after dark continued to disturb the municipal authorities.  In the "Remedies" which they proposed in 1584, they included the rule, "That no playeng be on holydaies, but after evening prayer, nor any received into the auditorie till after evening prayer"; and they added, "That no playeng be in the dark, nor continue any such time but as any of the auditorie may returne to their dwellings in London before sonne set, or at least before it be dark."[3]  To avoid the danger involved in such late performances, the Lord Chamberlain's company offered as an inducement to the City, in the autumn of 1594, that they would begin at two o'clock and finish between four and five, instead of commencing at four, as heretofore.[4]

In the traveling license issued to Lord Strange's company in 1593, they are forbidden to act during the "accustomed times of Divine Prayers";[5] but this provision was not included in the royal patents issued by the Stuarts.  To what extent, if at all, the regulation continued, I have not been able to ascertain. There were certainly performances during Divine Service on some occasions.  Among the objections against Rosseter's Blackfriars theater, in 1615, is included the fact that it would disturb the congregation in the adjoining church during Divine Service upon week-days.[6]  And in the order of 1619, suppressing Burbage's Blackfriars playhouse, mention is made of the disturbance caused by the coaches to the minister and people at

---

[1] Hazlitt, *English Drama*, 26, 29–30.  See above, pp. 34, 158.
[2] *Remembrancia*, 351.  See above, p. 165.        [3] See above, p. 174.
[4] See above, p. 182.        [5] *Acts*, XXIV, 212.  See above, p. 34.
[6] *1821 Variorum*, III, 493–494, note.  See above, p. 199.

public prayers in the afternoon.[1] The inhabitants of the precinct, in their petition for relief, had complained that the crush of vehicles inconvenienced them almost daily in winter time, not excepting Lent, from one or two o'clock till five at night.[2] What further attempt, if any, was made to regulate the hours of performances does not appear.

Throughout our period there was almost continual agitation about performances on Sunday. As early as 1543 we have observed an apparent objection to some sorts of shows on that day;[3] but in general Sunday was, during the earlier part of Elizabeth's reign, the day especially selected for performances. The municipal ordinance of December, 1574, remarks that plays are "chiefly used" on Sundays and Holy Days,[4] and merely forbids their presentation during the time of Divine Service. Gosson, in his *Schoole of Abuse*, published in 1579, notes that the players, because they are allowed to act every Sunday, "make four or five Sundays, at least, every week";[5] and the Puritan denunciations of the usual Sunday performances are frequent at this early period.[6] The rise of this strong disapproval soon produced orders forbidding plays on Sunday. On December 3, 1581, when the Privy Council asked the Mayor to admit certain companies to the City, they required that the players be not allowed to perform on the "Sabbath Day," — a term which shows the spread of Puritan ideas.[7] Some time during this same year or earlier, the Lord Mayor had evidently issued orders against Sunday performances, as we find from a letter written by one Henry Berkley "respecting some of his men committed to prison for playing on the Sabbath Day, contrary to the Lord Mayor's orders, which were unknown to them."[8] In 1582, again, the Lords suggest that the privileged companies be restrained from playing on Sunday.[9] Of course the rule was not rigidly and

[1] Halliwell-Phillipps, *Outlines*, 475. See above, p. 202.

[2] *Remembrancia*, 355. [3] See above, p. 151–152.

[4] Hazlitt, *English Drama*, 27. See above, p. 157.

[5] Published by the Shakspere Society, II, 31.

[6] See, for example, the title-page of Northbrooke's *Treatise* (1577); Stockwood's Sermon of 1578, cited in Halliwell-Phillipps, *Outlines*, 348; and the citations in *1821 Variorum*, III, 145–146, note.

[7] *Acts*, XIII, 269. [8] Abstract in *Athenæum*, January 23, 1869.

[9] *Acts*, XIII, 404. See above, p. 164.

P

consistently enforced. The Paris Garden disaster, in January, 1583, occurred at a Sunday performance, and led to renewed edicts from Privy Council and Mayor against such profanation of the Sabbath.[1] Even the favored Queen's company, according to the Lords' order of December 1, 1583, was not to be allowed to perform on that day.[2] The "Remedies" proposed by the city in 1584 of course included a law against acting on Sunday.[3] Complaints of the non-enforcement of the rule are rather frequent. The inhabitants of Southwark protested in 1587 against the Sabbath performances in the Liberty of the Clink, and the Privy Council exhorted the Justices of Middlesex and Surrey to prevent such occurrences.[4] In 1591 the Lords called the attention of the Mayor to the neglect of their order against "plays on the Sabbath Day."[5] Their restrictive regulations of 1600 included the same rule.[6]

In reviewing the history of national regulation under the Stuarts, we have already considered the royal proclamations and the statutes which from 1603 on forbade Sunday plays.[7] The law was not rigidly enforced, any more than the others that we have investigated; and the Puritan complaints of its violation, from Pyrnne and others, are fairly frequent.[8] The royal patents apparently contain no provision about Sunday performances. It is notable that the "Letters of Assistance" granted in 1618 by the Privy Council to John Daniel for his provincial children's company provides that they may play, "the tymes of Devine Service on the Saboth daies only excepted,"[9] — seeming to imply that they may perform at the other hours on Sunday.

The rule against performances in Lent was apparently enacted rather early. It is not included in the London ordinance of 1574. But on March 13, 1579, the Privy Council ordered the Mayor and the Middlesex Justices to stop all plays "during this time of Lent," and to notify the Lords what players had been performing since the beginning of the Lenten season. This

---

[1] See above, pp. 165–166.   [2] See above, p. 168.   [3] See above, p. 174.
[4] *Acts*, XV, 271.  See above, p. 175.
[5] *Acts*, XXI, 324–325.  See above, p. 177.   [6] See above, p. 192.
[7] See above, pp. 20–21.   [8] See Thompson, *Puritans and Stage*, 188.
[9] Hazlitt, *English Drama*, 50.

would seem to imply that the actors had been violating an already existing law. The Council commanded also that this order "be observed hereafter yearly in the Lent time." [1] The rule was supposed to be in force, I imagine, during all the rest of the period. It was included in the restrictive regulations of June 22, 1600.[2] Occasionally we find in the Council Register entries of orders to the magistrates to stop plays in the Lenten season, or to permit them, "Lent being past." [3] The players' breach of the law in 1615 has already been noticed, and the practice inaugurated by the Master of the Revels, at least as early as 1617, of selling dispensations for performances during the prohibited period.[4] The Lenten plays complained of by the inhabitants of Blackfriars in 1619,[5] were probably a result of the licenses purchased from Buc by the King's company.

One of the most important series of regulations affecting the London stage dealt with performances in time of plague. The danger of infection caused by assemblages at plays was early recognized by the City and by the royal government. Bishop Grindal, in 1563, as we have seen, requested the suppression of the players for a year on this account.[6] In subsequent years we have observed frequent complaints of this danger and frequent prohibition of plays because of the great prevalence of the disease or the fear of its development in the hot season. There seems to have been at first no definite rule about the time of such suppression. When the plague increased to a considerable degree, or the summer promised to be a dangerous one, performances were sometimes ordered stopped entirely until autumn. Just when the first attempt was made to regulate this matter according to a definite system, to provide that plays should stop when the death-rate rose to a certain figure, does not clearly appear. The first suggestion of this sort that I have noted is the proposal apparently made by the Queen's company in 1584, — that plays in London should be allowed whenever the total number of deaths from the plague should fall as low as fifty a week. In their reply to this the city authorities discuss the "permission of plays

---

[1] *Acts*, XI, 73–74.  [2] See above, p. 192.
[3] *Acts*, XXXI, 218; XXXII, 511.  [4] See above, p. 75.
[5] See above, p. 209.  [6] See above, p. 152.

upon the fewness of those that die in any week" in a manner which seems to imply that the idea is a new one. On the whole they do not approve of it, and they point out that the report of deaths from the plague is not a reliable indication of the prevalence of the disease. If any such regulation must be adopted, they advocate a much more stringent one. The ordinary deaths in London, when there is no plague, amount weekly to "between forty and fifty and commonly under forty." Now the city officials propose that when the total deaths in London from all diseases shall for two or three weeks together be under fifty per week, plays may be performed, and may continue so long as the mortality remains under that figure.[1] In the "Remedies" which they drew up at this time, they embodied this rule.[2] What specific regulation, if any, the Privy Council adopted as a result of this discussion, we do not know. Probably it was a compromise one.

In 1593 a change was made in the plague reports. It had become apparent that the weekly certificate of the deaths from the disease within the City did not give sufficient information as to the progress of the infection, and it was therefore ordered, on August 4, that Westminster, St. Catherine's, St. Giles, Southwark, and Shoreditch should be included in the bills of mortality.[3] This increase of the area covered in the weekly certificate should be borne in mind when one compares the regulation later adopted with the very liberal one suggested by the players in 1584.

The royal patent to the King's company in 1603 — one of the worst plague years — provides merely that they may perform "when the infection of the plague shall decrease."[4] But the Queen's company patent, probably granted in the same year, and the Privy Council order of April 9, 1604,[5] lay down an explicit rule, — that plays may be given except when the deaths from the plague amount to more than *thirty* weekly "within the City of London and the Liberties thereof." This may have been the law for some years before James' accession, and it was certainly

[1] Collier, *English Dramatic Poetry*, I, 215–216. See above, p. 173.
[2] See above, p. 174.   [3] *Acts*, XXIV, 442, 443.
[4] See above, p. 37.   [5] Printed in full in *Henslowe Papers*, 61–62.

the law for some time thereafter. Mr. Fleay's assumption that forty was the specified number invalidates his proof of the exactness with which the rule was enforced in 1593.[1]

There is no provision concerning the plague in the royal patents of 1606, 1609, 1610, and 1613. The King's company patent of 1619 contains the first mention of *forty* as the legal number. The players may perform "when the infection of the plague shall not weekly exceed the number of forty by the certificate of the Lord Mayor of London."[2] The same provision is contained in the patent granted to this company in 1625.[3] Possibly this number remained the legal one throughout the period; or it may have been changed to fifty. Two entries in Herbert's Office Book for the years 1636–1637 point to the latter as the fixed figure. "At the increase of the plague to 4 within the citty and 54 in all. — This day the 12 May, 1636, I received a warrant from my lord Chamberlen for the suppressing of playes and shews." And he later notes that on February 23, 1637, "the bill of the plague made the number at forty foure, upon which decrease the king gave the players their liberty, and they began the 24 Feb."[4] On March 1, according to Collier's extracts from the Council Register, on the increase of the infection, plays were suppressed again, and were not permitted until October 2 following.[5] This does not harmonize with Mr. Fleay's theory of the number specified and the exactness with which the law was enforced, for his tables show that the plague deaths were over forty from the beginning of 1637 until August 17, when they fell below that number and remained there until the next summer.[6]

Judging from the extreme laxness with which most laws seem to have been enforced, we should indeed be chary of believing that the plague rule was followed with precision. Probably the players often disobeyed it, as did the Cockpit company in May,

---

[1] He has compared, he says, the dates of the performances in Henslowe's Diary with the plague tables for that year. There are no other tables extant for Elizabeth's reign. (*London Stage*, 162.) For a statement of Fleay's error, and references to mentions of the rule of thirty in the literature of the period, see Thorndike, *Influence of Beaumont and Fletcher on Shakspere*, 14–15.

[2] Hazlitt, *English Drama*, 51.    [3] *Ibid.*, 58.    [4] *1821 Variorum*, III, 239.
[5] Collier, *English Dramatic Poetry*, II, 15–16.    [6] *London Stage*, 162.

1637.[1] And apparently the Master of the Revels sometimes secured for them some relaxation of it.[2] That it was by no means a regulation operating with mechanical exactness, but was subject to variation according to different influences and personalities, and the will of various high officials, appears from an interesting account, given in a letter from Garrard to Wentworth, of a meeting of the Privy Council. It deals with the suppression of plays in the year we have just been considering, — 1637. And with this illustration of the conflict of jurisdictions and the way in which the enforcement of the laws was sometimes determined, we may conclude our account of the London regulations.

"Upon a little abatement of the plague, even in the first week of Lent, the players set up their bills, and began to play in the Black-fryars and other houses. But my Lord of Canterbury quickly reduced them to a better order; for at the next meeting of the Council his Grace complained of it to the King, declared the solemnity of Lent, the unfitness of that liberty to be given, both in respect to the time and the sickness, which was not extinguished in the City, concluding that if his Majesty did not command him to the contrary he would lay them by the heels if they played again. My Lord Chamberlain [Pembroke and Montgomery] stood up and said that my Lord's Grace and he served one God and one King; that he hoped his Grace would not meddle in his place no more than he did in his; that the players were under his command. My Lord's Grace replied that what he had spoken in no way touched upon his place, etc., still concluding as he had done before, which he did with some solemnity reiterate once or twice. So the King put an end to the business by commanding my Lord Chamberlain that they should play no more."[3]

[1] Collier, *English Dramatic Poetry*, II, 15–16.    [2] See above, p. 76.
[3] Strafford Letters, II, 56; quoted in Wheatley and Cunningham, *London Past and Present*, I, 200–201. This letter is dated March 23, 1637.

# CHAPTER VI

## THE PURITAN VICTORY

THE day of triumph had now come for the party at whom
the players had so long gibed and scoffed. The term "Puritan"
is, of course, a very broad and vague one. Coined about 1564,
the word was applied at first to the men who sought the purest
form of worship — *religio purissima* — by reform from within
the Church of England, — at first chiefly in matters of form and
ceremony, and later in some points of Calvinistic doctrine. As
the extension of the term broadened, it acquired a political significance, denoting those who were contending for the principles
of civil liberty and who, from the latter part of Elizabeth's reign,
controlled the House of Commons, — the opponents of the court
party. It was even loosely applied to all men who protested
against the immorality and corruption in church and state, the
"life of practical heathenism," as Gardiner calls it, which they
saw around them, and who sought religious reform and the political rights of the people. It came, moreover, to denote the somewhat ascetic type of mind, intensely concerned with things moral
and religious, with which we now most often associate the word.[1]

In the early years of its development Puritanism had among
its representatives men of high rank in church and state, such
as Archbishop Grindal and the Earl of Leicester. But as it
intensified to a rather extreme type, and the line between the
Court and the popular party became more sharply drawn, its
adherents were found chiefly among the middle class and the
poor, — the tradesmen in the towns and the small proprietors in
the country. In these sections of society it spread with rapidity
and strength, so that early in James' reign it was probably the
temper of the majority of Englishmen.

---

[1] See Campbell, *The Puritan*, I, xxvii; II, 237 ff.; Gardiner, *History of
England*, III, 241–242.

The great political party loosely called Puritan, or Parliamentary, or Roundhead, of course included "Puritans" of all degrees and types. Their attitude towards the drama, as towards other questions, varied considerably; but on the whole they were opposed to it. Some were opposed merely to its abuses, as exemplified on the contemporary stage; some were opposed to it altogether and absolutely, as essentially sinful and irreligious; all were inclined to discipline it with a strong hand, when opportunity should arise.

The City of London was one of the great centers of Puritanism. The attitude towards plays taken by the municipal government during the last quarter of the sixteenth century was largely caused, as we have seen, by various economic and social considerations. But it also shows strongly at times the moral and religious view of the stage characteristic of the extreme Puritan, and seems to indicate that the wealthier burgess class was during these years decidedly Puritan in its convictions. The new party must, of course, have increased pretty steadily throughout the period, for at the opening of the Civil War the capital was practically solid for the Parliamentary side.[1] But there are signs that Puritanism in respect to the drama did not spread with steady regularity or remain firm in the influential burgess class; that, on the contrary, the antipathy to plays grew less violent among the ruling citizens in London. As the playhouses became less disorderly resorts, and were frequented by a better class, the opposition of the municipal officials, we have seen, largely died out. Under James and Charles it is evident that the theaters appealed rather less to the populace and became to a greater extent the resort of fashionable court society. The wealthier citizens, and especially their wives, when inspired by any desire to ape the manners of the court set, would therefore acquire a taste for the drama. In the plays of the period there are frequent hits at the eagerness of the city dames to get admission to the court masques. Their desire to participate in the amusements of the upper class could be more easily gratified at the theaters of the better sort.

A striking indication that the relation between the City and

[1] See Sharpe, *London*, II, 173.

the stage at this period was not always one of open warfare, and the attitude of the municipal officials not extremely Puritanic, may be found in the dramatic character of many of the Lord Mayor's shows, and the fact that prominent playwrights were hired to devise them. During the first half of the seventeenth century, Munday, Dekker, Middleton, Webster, and Heywood were the composers of these pageants that ushered in the new chief magistrate of the City,[1] — until the austere Puritan régime put a stop to the shows for sixteen years.[2] Moreover, the dramatist Middleton, in 1620, was even appointed Chronologer of London,[3] and was succeeded ih that office by Jonson.[4]

The decline in the puritanical zeal of the city officials was noted and lamented in Rawlidge's *Monster Lately Found Out*, published in 1628. The author named plays among other disgraces of London, and commended the earlier "pious magistrates" and "religious senators" for their zeal in urging Elizabeth and her Council to suppress the stage. Had their successors followed their worthy example, he believed sin would not have been so rampant in the city.[5]

Though the more prominent and influential citizens became in many cases thus lenient towards the drama, there are indications of the spread of Puritan ideas among the populace. An interesting event in 1617 seems to show that even the apprentices, formerly, as we have seen, among the chief frequenters of performances, were beginning to turn against the theater. The London prentices had long practised the curious custom of attacking and demolishing houses of ill fame on Shrove Tuesday, — a habit to which the drama of the period contains many allusions. On Shrove Tuesday of 1617, during some especially active rioting, the apprentices extended the range of their moral crusading and attempted to pull down the Cockpit theater, which they succeeded in damaging to a considerable extent.

[1] See Fleay, *London Stage*, 422; and Fairholt, *Lord Mayors' Pageants.* At the end of the sixteenth century, also, from at least 1586 on, such pageants were devised at times by prominent playwrights. The incompleteness of the records of the shows for these years, however, makes it impossible to get much light on the relations between dramatists and officials at this time.

[2] Fairholt, *op. cit.*, 62.       [3] Bullen's Middleton, I, l–lii.

[4] Castelain, *Ben Jonson*, 63, 65, 67.     [5] Thompson, *Puritans and Stage*, 144.

The disorder was evidently serious, for on the following day the Privy Council wrote urgently to the Lord Mayor, ordering rigorous measures against the offenders.[1] And a year later, learning of the apprentices' plan to renew their attack on the same occasion, and pull down the Red Bull as well as the Cockpit, the Lords commanded the Mayor and the Justices to set strong watches to keep the peace.[2]

An odd ballad on the Cockpit attack of 1617, printed by Collier as contemporary with this affair, but perhaps of doubtful authenticity, praises the moral zeal of the apprentices.[3] One should certainly be cautious in attributing any such serious motive to the rioting. It does seem to show, however, that it had now become usual, in some sections of the prentice body at least, to class theaters with the most disreputable resorts, as fit game for attack; and it perhaps indicates some spread of opposition to the playhouses among the populace. That such opposition must have been growing, as the city developed the adherence to the Puritan or Parliamentary party which it showed at the outbreak of the Civil War, seems fairly obvious.

It remains to summarize very briefly the Puritan attack on the stage that culminated in the Ordinances of the Long Parliament. Developing from the essentially moral tendency of the typical Puritan attitude of mind, — at the opposite pole from the typical tone of the drama of the period, — and based largely on the patristic writings, in which the Church Fathers violently denounced the degenerate Roman stage, the opposition to the Elizabethan drama early found definite expression. From 1576 on, and perhaps before, a succession of vigorous sermons by non-conforming clergymen, at Paul's Cross and elsewhere, bitterly assailed the evils of the London stage.[4] Formal literary attacks also began early. The period during which these

---

[1] The order is printed in Chalmers, *Apology*, 466, note; and in *1821 Variorum*, III, 495–496, note.

[2] The order is printed in Collier, *English Dramatic Poetry*, I, 394, note.

[3] Collier, *op. cit.*, I, 386 ff. See also Mackay, *Songs and Ballads of the London Prentices*, 94–97.

[4] For example, White in 1576, Stockwood in 1578, Spark in 1579, Field in 1583, etc. See Thompson, *Puritans and Stage, passim*, and Halliwell-Phillipps, *Outlines*, 368.

chiefly flourished was the decade from 1577 to 1587, — including those years in which the opposition of the city government to plays was especially intense.[1] Northbrooke's *Treatise* in 1577, Gosson's *Schoole of Abuse* in 1579, *A Second and Third Blast of Retrait* in 1580, Gosson's *Playes Confuted* in 1582, Stubbes' *Anatomie of Abuses* in 1583, and Rankins' *Mirrour of Monsters* in 1587 — to name only the most prominent — reflect the bitter opposition to plays felt at this time. During the next quarter of a century the only notable contribution to the controversy was Rainolde's *Overthrow of Stage-Playes*, published in 1599. In the second decade of the seventeenth century, however, literary attacks again became frequent. Wither's *Abuses Stript and Whipt* in 1613, the *Refutation* of Heywood's *Apology for Actors* in 1615, the *Shorte Treatise Against Stage-Playes* in 1625, Rawlidge's *Monster Lately Found Out* in 1628, — all these renewed the literary onslaught which culminated in Prynne's *Histrio-Mastix*, published in 1632, a summary and amplification of all previous attacks.

The general line of argument followed is much the same in all these writings. The authors rely to a great extent on authority. They quote texts from the Bible which they interpret as condemning plays. They bring to bear a perfect battery of quotations from the Church Fathers denouncing the stage. They cite the classics, — chiefly Plato's banishing of poets from his ideal commonwealth, and strangely distorted interpretations of Cicero and others. They bring forward the Roman laws against actors and the legislation of Church Councils. They condemn the sinfulness of appareling boys in women's clothes, and other features of the contemporary drama. Most convincingly of all, they portray the evil associations of the theaters, the demoralizing companions whom the London youth there meets, the indecency and immorality presented upon the stage, with examples of the dire effects they have wrought. Some of the writers — notably Northbrooke, the earliest — do not condemn plays altogether, but think that under certain circumstances some of them, such as academic plays, are permissible. But the general tendency is to forbid them utterly, as snares of the Devil, irreligious

[1] See above, p. 160.

and sinful abominations, — in the words of the municipal edict of banishment, "great provoking of the wrath of God, the ground of all plagues." [1]

A characteristic summary of the Puritan line of argument may be found on the very elaborate title-page of Prynne's *Histrio-Mastix*.[2] "Histrio-Mastix. The Players Scourge, or Actors Tragædie, Divided into Two Parts. Wherein it is largely evidenced, by divers Arguments, by the concurring Authorities and Resolutions of sundry texts of Scripture; of the whole Primitive Church, both under the Law and Gospell; of 55 Synodes and Councels; of 71 Fathers and Christian Writers, before the yeare of our Lord 1200; of above 150 foraigne and domestique Protestant and Popish Authors, since; of 40 Heathen Philosophers, Historians, Poets; of many Heathen, many Christian Nations, Republiques, Emperors, Princes, Magistrates; of sundry Apostolicall, Canonicall, Imperiall Constitutions; and of our owne English Statutes, Magistrates, Universities, Writers, Preachers. That popular Stage-playes (the very Pompes of the Divell which we renounce in Baptisme, if we beleeve the Fathers) are sinfull, heathenish, lewde, ungodly Spectacles, and most pernicious Corruptions; condemned in all ages, as intolerable Mischiefes to Churches, to Republickes, to the manners, mindes and soules of men. And that the Profession of Play-poets, of Stage players; together with the penning, acting and frequenting of Stage-playes, are unlawfull, infamous and misbeseeming Christians. All pretences to the contrary are here likewise fully answered; and the unlawfulness of acting, of beholding Academicall Enterludes, briefly discussed; besides sundry other particulars concerning Dancing, Dicing, Health-drinking, &c. of which the Table will informe you. By William Prynne, an Vtter-Barrester of Lincolnes Inne."

The attitude taken by the Puritans towards the statutes regulating players is from our point of view especially important. Inspired by the Roman and the Canonical laws against actors,[3]

---

[1] See above, p. 164.
[2] Dated 1633, but published 1632. For an account of the book, see Thompson, *Puritans and Stage*, chap. 15, and Ward, *English Dramatic Literature*, III, 240 ff.    [3] See above, p. 21.

the Puritans from the first seem to have seized eagerly upon the
mention of players in the statutory definition of rogues and vagabonds, and to have assumed that this branded them all as of
that outcast status.   Referring to the Queen's company in 1584,
the pick of the "quality," the London officials, as we have seen,
remarked that "if they were not her Majesty's servants," they
would "by their profession be rogues." [1]   An excellent summary
of this view may be found in Prynne.   He cites the mention
of players in the Statutes 14 Elizabeth, cap. 5, and 39 Elizabeth,
cap. 4, and the provision for licensing them,[2] — "which license," he asserts, "exempted them onely from the punishment,
*not from the infamy*, or stile of *Rogues and Vacabonds*."   Since
these laws did not prove effectual in suppressing plays, Prynne
goes on to say, the Statute 1 James I, cap. 7, enacted that no
license from any baron or other honorable personage of greater
degree should free wandering players from the penalties of
vagabondage.[3]   "So that now," writes Prynne, "by these several
acts of Parliament . . . all common Stage-playes *are solemnely
adiudged to be unlawfull and pernicious Exercises, not sufferable
in our State: and all common Stage-players, by whomsoever
licensed; to be but Vacabonds, Rogues, and Sturdy Beggars*." [4]
"So that all Magistrates," he continues, "may now justly punish
them as Rogues and Vacabonds, where-ever they goe, (yea they
ought both in law and conscience for to doe it, since these severall
Statutes thus inforce them to it) notwithstanding any License
which they can procure, since the expresse words of the Statute of
*I. Iacobi. cap. 7. hath made all Licenses unavaylable to free them
from such punishments*." [5]   The system of royal patents for
players which had grown up Prynne thus denounces, indirectly
if not explicitly, as unconstitutional.   The Master of the Revels
he has less scruple in attacking openly.   "Magistrates in sundry
Citties and Counties of our Realme, have from time to time, punished all wandring Stage-players *as Rogues*, notwithstanding
the *Master of the Revels, or other mens allowance, who have no
legall authority to license vagrant Players*."[6]

[1] See above, p. 173.   [2] See above, pp. 27 ff.   [3] See above, p. 28.
[4] *Histrio-Mastix*, 496; the italics are Prynne's.   [5] *Ibid.*, 497.
[6] *Ibid.*, 492.

It is possible that the Puritan majority in Parliament, when passing the Statute 1 James I, cap. 7, had indeed intended, or at least desired, to abolish all licenses for wandering players, though they must have realized that the system of royal patents which had already developed would probably continue.[1] But, as we have seen, the government certainly adopted no such interpretation of the law. By the patents that the King granted to the royal companies, authorizing their performances and requesting that, as his servants, they might be shown favor for his sake, and by the elaborate licensing system developed under the crown official, the Master of the Revels, the government provided adequately for the license of worthy players, and gave them a legal status amply sufficient to protect them from being classed as vagabonds.

Not all Puritans, indeed, interpreted the statutes as rigorously as did Prynne. The *Shorte Treatise against Stage-Playes*, printed in 1625, evidently did not regard plays as already entirely forbidden by law, for it besought Parliament "by some few Words added to the former Statutes, to restreyne them for euer hereafter."[2] But throughout the period Puritan writers taunted the players with their classification as vagabonds, and the attitude of the whole party made sufficiently evident what policy they would pursue when the governmental authority should be in their hands. The actors realized the fate that was impending. In the *Stage-Players Complaint*, printed in 1641, which laments the sad state of the profession caused by the serious plague in London, a player prophecies worse times to come. "Monopolers are downe, Projectors are downe, the High Commission Court is downe, the Starre-Chamber is down, & (some think) Bishops will downe, and why should we then that are farre inferior to any of those not justly feare, least we should be downe too?"[3]

The misgivings of the players were soon proved only too well founded. The Long Parliament now took the reins of government, and on September 2, 1642, issued the following solemn Ordinance of the Lords and Commons.

"Whereas the distressed estate of Ireland, steeped in her own blood, and the distracted estate of England, threatened with a cloud of blood

[1] See above, pp. 35–38.　　[2] Hazlitt, *English Drama*, 232.　　[3] *Ibid.*, 256.

by a civil war, call for all possible means to appease and avert the wrath of God appearing in these judgments: amongst which fasting and prayer, having been often tried to be very effectual, have been lately and are still enjoined: and whereas public sports do not well agree with public calamities, nor public stage-plays with the seasons of humiliation, this being an exercise of sad and pious solemnity, and the other being spectacles of pleasure, too commonly expressing lascivious mirth and levity: it is therefore thought fit and ordained by the Lords and Commons in this Parliament assembled, that while these sad causes and set-times of humiliation do continue, public stage-plays shall cease and be forborne. Instead of which are recommended to the people of this land the profitable and seasonable considerations of repentance, reconciliation and peace with God, which probably will produce outward peace and prosperity, and bring again times of joy and gladness to these nations." [1]

This edict, it will be noticed, does not express the extreme Puritan view. It forbids only public performances, and these but temporarily. Besides religious antipathy to plays, motives of political caution probably caused the suppression, as in early Tudor days. The party in power must have realized the hostility felt towards them by the players, the adherents of the Court, and feared lest the performances should be used to foment rebellion against the Parliamentary rule.

When the Puritans passed a law suppressing plays, plays were really suppressed. Though sporadic attempts to revive performances were made during the next decade, this edict practically closed the theaters, and certainly marked the end of the Elizabethan drama. Most of the actors seem to have accepted the pronouncement as final. Some addressed mocking petitions to Parliament *via* "the great god Phœbus Apollo and the nine Heliconian Sisters," begging for the relaxation of the law.[2] But the majority of the prominent players entered the King's army, and there, as the *Historia Histrionica* tells us, "like good men and true, served their old master, though in a different, yet more honourable capacity." Only one of any note, Swanston, sided with the Parliamentary party.[3]

---

[1] Collier, *English Dramatic Poetry*, II, 36; Hazlitt, *English Drama*, 63. See also Gardiner, *Great Civil War*, I, 14–15.

[2] See Hazlitt, *English Drama*, 259 ff.; and Thompson, *Puritans and Stage*, 184.

[3] Wright, *Historia Histrionica*, 409.

The suppression of plays was to last, according to the edict, only during the troubled times of conflict. In 1647 the war was considered practically at an end; but the opposition to the stage continued and even grew more extreme. Apparently some players ventured to perform, for on July 16, 1647, the House of Commons ordered that the Lord Mayor and the Justices of the Peace in and about London "be required to take effectual Care speedily to suppress all publick Plays and Play-houses, and all Dancings on the Ropes," and desired the con-currence of the Lords in this edict.[1] The Upper House assented, but amended the order by adding bear-baitings to the list of shows to be suppressed, and providing that the edict should continue until January 1, 1648. Against this time limit some of the Lords protested, on the ground that it was the desire of Parliament that stage-plays should be forbidden forever. But the Commons apparently did not feel that the mention of a date for the expiration of this particular order implied that plays were to be allowed thereafter, and on July 17 they accepted without protest the bill as amended by the Lords.[2]

About this time or earlier there seems to have been, according to Collier, an attempt to perform Beaumont and Fletcher's *A King and No King*, — a production promptly stopped by the Sheriffs.[3] Even after the new order against plays, some actors continued to be rebellious. Complaints were made to the Com-mons of the "bold Attempt of Stage-Players playing at Publick Houses in the City, contrary to Ordinance of Parliament," and on October 18, 1647, a more severe edict "for the better suppression of Stage-plays, Interludes and Common Players" was passed by the House.[4] With the approval of the Lords this was issued on October 22.[5] It directs and empowers the Lord Mayor, the Sheriffs, and the Justices of the Peace to search all playing places in and about London, and arrest all persons who may be proved to have performed in plays. Definitely assuming the Puritan

---

[1] *Journals of the House of Commons*, V, 246.
[2] *Ibid.*, 248; *Journals of the House of Lords*, IX, 334–335.
[3] See Collier, *English Dramatic Poetry*, II, 37, 40; Fleay, *London Stage*, 365.
[4] Rushworth, *Collections*, pt. IV, vol. ii, 844.
[5] *Ibid.*, 847, 848; Collier, *op. cit.*, II, 110–111; Hazlitt, *English Drama*, 64–65.

view, the ordinance declares that all such actors are to be brought before the next General Sessions of the Peace, "there to be punished as Rogues, according to law."

Though Parliament evidently considered that the original edict of suppression passed in 1642 was still in force, and had no real intention of relaxing the prohibition, some of the players seized upon the time limit set for the expiration of the order of July 17, 1647, as an excuse for performing, and in January, 1648, ventured to open their theaters. The public seems to have responded with eagerness. On January 27 it was reckoned that no less than one hundred and twenty coaches set down spectators at one theater alone, — the Fortune. At the Red Bull Beaumont and Fletcher's *Wit Without Money* was performed.[1]

The Puritan spirit of Parliament was now aroused to extreme measures. On January 22, 1648, the Commons were "informed that many Stage-Plays were acted in the several parts of the City and County of Middlesex, notwithstanding the Ordinance of Parliament to the contrary. The House hereupon ordered, That an Ordinance should be drawn for suppressing all Stage-Plays, and taking down all their Boxes, Stages and Seats in the several Houses where the said Plays were usually Acted, and make it unserviceable for Acting any Plays in for the future; and for making a Penalty for such as shall disobey the said Ordinance: and this Ordinance to be brought in with all convenient speed. They further Ordered, That the Lord Mayor and Sheriffs, and Justices of the Peace of the City of London, and the several Militia's of the Cities of London and Westminster, and likewise of the Hamlets, should take care for the suppressing of all Stage-Plays for the time to come."[2] Apparently no less eager than the Commons to put down such performances, the Lords, on January 31, sent to the House an Ordinance for Suppressing Stage-Plays. But the Commons preferred the act that their own committee had drafted, which was accordingly passed by both Houses and issued on February 11.[3]

---

[1] Gardiner, *Great Civil War*, IV, 69, quoting contemporary newspapers.

[2] Rushworth, *Collections*, pt. IV, vol. ii, 972.

[3] *Ibid.*, 980, 991–992; Scobell, *Acts and Ordinances*, 143–144; Hazlitt, *English Drama*, 66 ff.; Collier, *op. cit.*, II, 44 ff., note.

This rigorous ordinance takes the extreme Puritan stand. "Whereas the Acts of Stage-Playes, Interludes, and common Playes, condemned by ancient Heathens, and much lesse to be tolerated amongst Professors of the Christian Religion, is the occasion of many and sundry great vices and disorders, tending to the high provocation of Gods wrath and displeasure, which lies heavy upon this Kingdome, and to the disturbance of the peace thereof; in regard whereof the same hath beene prohibited by Ordinance of this present Parliament, and yet is presumed to be practised by divers in contempt thereof." For the better suppression of such performances the Lords and Commons therefore declare that "all stage-players and players of interludes and common plays" shall be considered rogues in the eyes of the law, within the statutes of Elizabeth and James, and liable to the pains and penalties therein provided. They shall be proceeded against according to these statutes "whether they be wanderers or no, and notwithstanding any License whatsoever from the King or any person or persons to that purpose." The status of vagabond was thus imposed upon all players, — not merely unlicensed traveling ones, as in the laws heretofore. And the system of royal patents and licenses by the Master of the Revels was utterly abolished, leaving the actors with no possibility of legal protection. The extreme Puritan view advocated by Prynne thus became the law of the land.

The Ordinance further directs the Lord Mayor, the Sheriffs, and the Justices of the Peace to "pull down and demolish . . . all Stage-Galleries, Seats, and Boxes, erected and used for the acting or playing, or seeing acted or plaid, such Stage-Playes" in and about London. Any player proved to have acted in such performances shall be publicly whipped and bound by sureties never to act again, or in default of such security committed to jail. If he offend a second time, he shall be punished as an incorrigible rogue, according to the statutes. All money taken as admission fees shall be forfeited to the churchwardens of the parish, and devoted to the use of the poor. And every person present as a spectator shall be fined five shillings for each offense, — the money to be used for the same charitable purpose.

All Mayors, bailiffs, constables, and other officers, soldiers, and all persons were ordered to assist in the enforcement of this rigorous ordinance. And in September, 1648, when Captain Bethan was made Provost Marshal, he was directed to "seize upon all Ballad Singers, Sellers of Malignant Pamphlets, and to send them to the several Militias, and to suppress Stage-playes." [1]

In spite of all these severe measures some players still ventured to perform. According to the *Historia Histrionica*, "they made up one company out of all the scattered members of several; and in the winter before the King's murder, 1648, they ventured to act some plays, with as much caution and privacy as could be, at the Cockpit. They continued undisturbed for three or four days; but at last, as they were presenting the tragedy of the 'Bloody Brother' . . . a party of foot-soldiers beset the house, surprised 'em about the middle of the play, and carried 'em away in their habits, not admitting them to shift, to Hatton House, then a prison, where, having detained them some time, they plundered them of their clothes, and let 'em loose again." [2] But even such mishaps could not discourage them. "Afterwards, in Oliver's time," the *Historia* continues, "they used to act privately, three or four miles, or more, out of town, now here, now there: sometimes in noblemen's houses, in particular, Holland House at Kensington. . . . At Christmas and Bartholomew Fair, they used to bribe the officer who commanded the guard at Whitehall, and were thereupon connived at to act for a few days at the Red Bull, but were sometimes, notwithstanding, disturbed by soldiers." [3]

On one occasion at least the actors endeavored by humble submission and promises of good behavior to soften the rigor of the law. About 1650 "diverse poor and distressed men, heretofore the Actors of Black-Friers and the Cock-Pit," petitioned Parliament. They cannot support themselves and their families, they plead, and they beg that they may be allowed to play for a short time on trial, to demonstrate their inoffensiveness. They will produce "only moral and harmless representations."

[1] Whitelocke, *Memorials*, 332.    [2] Wright, *Historia Histrionica*, 409–410.
[3] *Ibid.*, 410–411. Concerning the "drolls" acted on these occasions, see the note, *ibid.*, and Ward, *English Dramatic Literature*, III, 280.

To any one appointed to oversee them they promise implicit obedience, and they assure Parliament that they are willing to contribute "for the service of Ireland or as the State shall think fitting." [1] Their appeal evidently had no effect.

Unable to secure any relaxation of the law, the players occasionally, as we have seen, dared to act in defiance of it. The troubles in which such venturesome performers involved themselves appear at times in the records of these years. On December 20, 1649, for example, some actors in St. John Street (where the Red Bull was situated) "were apprehended by Troupers, their Cloaths taken away, and themselves carried to prison." [2] Again, in December, 1654, at the same playhouse, the Red Bull, the players "being gotten into all their borrowed gallantry and ready to act, were by some of the souldiery despoiled of all their bravery, but the souldiery carried themselves very civilly towards the audience." [3] In September, 1655, the Red Bull players were once more in trouble and, as usual, lost some of their costumes. The soldiers, less civil on this occasion, put to rout the assemblage with many "broken crowns," seized some of the actors and confiscated their clothes, and made the spectators pay the fine of five shillings each or, in default of this, leave their cloaks behind them. [4] About January 1, 1656, seven players who dared to perform at Newcastle were arrested and publicly whipped as rogues and vagabonds. [5] And among the instructions issued to Major-General Desborow in this same month, he was ordered to suppress all horse-races, cock-fighting, bear-baiting, stage-plays, or other unlawful assemblies, by seizing the persons met on such occasions. [6] On the whole, in spite of the sporadic breaches of the law, it is evident that the ordinance of suppression was, especially with the aid of Crom-

[1] Petition printed in *Notes and Queries*, June 16, 1894, by C. H. Firth, from a volume of pamphlets of the year 1650.

[2] Whitelocke, *Memorials*, 419.

[3] *The Perfect Account*, December 27–January 3, 1654–1655, quoted by C. H. Firth in *Notes and Queries*, August 18, 1888.

[4] *State Papers, Dom.*, 1655, 336; *Weekly Intelligencer*, September 11–18, 1655, quoted by C. H. Firth in *Notes and Queries*, August 18, 1888.

[5] Whitelocke, *Memorials*, 619; *Public Intelligencer*, January 14–21, 1656, quoted by C. H. Firth in *Notes and Queries*, August 18, 1888.

[6] *State Papers, Dom.*, 1655–1656, 103.

well's soldiery, rather rigorously enforced, and that the English stage was during these years practically non-existent.

In 1656 the ingenious D'Avenant devised a form of entertainment which would not come under the ban of the law.   On May 21 of that year, by permission of the authorities, he presented, "at the back part of Rutland House, in Aldersgate Street," an entertainment of declamation and music "after the manner of the ancients."   And later in the same year he produced at the same place his *Siege of Rhodes*, "made a Representation by the Art of Prospective in Scenes, and the Story sung in Recitative Musick." [1]  Emboldened by his success, in 1658 D'Avenant ventured to produce a similar entertainment, *The Cruelty of the Spaniards in Peru*, at the old theater of the Cockpit in Drury Lane.   The new Protector, Richard, seems to have had his attention drawn to this enterprise.   On December 23, an investigation was ordered into the nature of this "Opera," and by what authority it was produced.   A general consideration of the acting of stage-plays was also directed, and a later report upon the question. [2]   The attitude of the government now seems to have become lenient, and D'Avenant's venture continued successfully until the Restoration and beyond.   But this work of his belongs to the new era.   The Elizabethan drama had passed forever.

It is customary in histories of the drama and the stage to express some judgment, generally severe, upon the Puritan suppression of the theaters.   But fair decisions on such actions in the past are not easy.   According to their own standards, the Puritan or Parliamentary party certainly did right in rigorously prohibiting the drama.   And it is not impossible for modern English and American minds, still so deeply impregnated by the spirit of the Puritan movement, to appreciate their point of view. To men who had already developed something of the modern sensibility in matters of decency and morality, most of the later Elizabethan drama must indeed have seemed hopelessly abhorrent.   Motives of political prudence, moreover, also urged

---

[1] See Ward, *English Dramatic Literature*, III, 281–282; Whitelocke, *Memorials*, 639.

[2] *1821 Variorum*, III, 93, note.

the dominant party to act against the stage. Their moral zeal, it is true, carried them to an extreme, — just as the lack of that quality had carried the playwrights to the opposite pole, whither again, in the perpetual swinging of the pendulum back and forth across and beyond the golden mean, the reaction against Puritanism was to carry the men of the Restoration. There was much to justify extreme measures at the time of the closing of the theaters. As one thinks of the stage of the period, no longer expressive of the best feelings of the nation, as one remembers the preposterous horrors into which tragedy had degenerated, and the inexpressibly offensive indecency of much of the comedy of the time, and with this picture of the drama in mind, reads the grave and dignified phrases of the edict of 1642, one feels that, for the moment at least, the Puritans had the better part.

# APPENDIX

## ROYAL PATENTS TO COMPANIES OF PLAYERS

FOR convenience of reference I have here tabulated all the royal patents to companies, so far as I know them, which have been preserved or which are specifically mentioned in documents of the period. There were certainly others of which we have as yet no definite notice. Several of the companies named below are known to have existed for some time before the date of their first extant patent.

### 1574, May 7.   The Earl of Leicester's company.
Privy Seal directing a Great Seal.
Printed above, pp. 33–34.   See also pp. 49–50, 155.

### 1603, May 19.   The King's company.
Globe theater.   Great Seal.
Printed above, pp. 36–37.   Transcripts of all the stages through which the warrant passed — the Docket, the Bill of Privy Signet, the Writ of Privy Seal, and the Patent under the Great Seal — are printed in Halliwell-Phillipps, *Outlines*, 595 ff.

### 1603, July (?).   The Queen's company.
Boar's Head and Curtain theater.
This exists only in a rough, undated draft.   In the *Calendar of State Papers* (*Dom.*, *Add.*, 1623–1625, 530), where a brief abstract is given, it is conjecturally dated July, 1603.
Printed in Collier, *English Dramatic Poetry*, I, 336–337.
Mr. Fleay doubts the authenticity of this document (*London Stage*, 190–191); but his reasons are not convincing.   (1) He objects that it licenses the company's playing within London, whereas no men players were allowed at this date within the City.   But it permits their performances there only on the cessation of the plague, and there is no proof that men players were not allowed in London at this time under such circumstances.   (2) He objects that it provides that deaths from the plague shall be under 30 a week, "whereas 40 is well known to be the correct number."   But the letter of the Privy Council to the Lord Mayor on April 9, 1604, specifies 30, and 40 is not mentioned until the King's company patent of 1619.   (See above, pp. 212–213.)   (3) He objects that it mentions the Boar's Head and the Curtain as the

231

usual playhouses of the company, whereas we know that Worcester's men — these same actors — played at the Rose in May, 1603, and at the Red Bull and Curtain in 1609, while of a Boar's Head playing house no other mention is found since Queen Mary's time. But a letter from the Privy Council to the Lord Mayor on March 31, 1602, grants permission to this same company to play "at the Boar's Head in Eastcheap." (*Remembrancia*, 355.)

### 1604, January 31.   The Children of the Queen's Revels.
Warrant to Edward Kirkham and others.   Blackfriars theater. Privy Seal directing a Great Seal.
Printed in Hazlitt, *English Drama*, 40–41; Collier, *English Dramatic Poetry*, I, 340.
See above, pp. 19, 61.

### 1606, April 30.   The Prince's company.
Fortune theater.   Privy Seal.
Printed in the *Shakspere Society Papers*, IV, 42–43.
See above, pp. 37, 63.

### 1609, April 15.   The Queen's company.
Red Bull and Curtain theaters.   Privy Seal.
Printed in the *Shakspere Society Papers*, IV, 45–46.

### 1610, January 4.   The Children of the Queen's Revels.
Warrant to Philip Rosseter and others.   Whitefriars theater. Great Seal.
Mentioned in Patent of May 31, 1615.   See below.

### 1610, March 30.   The Duke of York's company.
Authorization to perform in and about London, "in such usual houses as themselves shall provide."   Privy Seal.
Printed in the *Shakspere Society Papers*, IV, 47–48.

### 1613, January 4.   The Elector Palatine's company.
Fortune theater.   Privy Seal directing a Great Seal.   Issued on the Elector's taking over the company of the deceased Prince of Wales.
Printed in Hazlitt, *English Drama*, 44–46.   Order for Privy Seal in Collier, *English Dramatic Poetry*, I, 366–367.

### 1615, May 31.
Patent to Philip Rosseter and others granting permission to erect a theater in Blackfriars.   Privy Seal directing a Great Seal.
Printed in Hazlitt, *English Drama*, 46–48; Collier, *English Dramatic Poetry*, I, 380 ff.
This is not itself a company patent, but it mentions that of Janu-

ary 4, 1610, and it authorizes performances in the proposed theater by the Children of the Queen's Revels, the Prince's company, and the Lady Elizabeth's company.

See above, pp. 198 ff.

### 1615, July 17. Her Majesty's Servants of her Royal Chamber at Bristol.

A provincial traveling company. Great Seal. To John Daniel. Mentioned in the Letters of Assistance of April, 1618. See below.

Apparently it was first intended to grant this patent to Samuel Daniel, the poet, John Daniel's brother. See Sir George Buc's letter of July 10, 1615, consenting to its issue, in *State Papers, Dom.*, 1611–1618, 294. And see above, p. 64.

### 1618, April.

Letters of Assistance from the Privy Council to John Daniel, confirming the patent of July 17, 1615.

Printed in Hazlitt, *English Drama*, 49–50; Collier, *English Dramatic Poetry*, I, 395–396.

### 1619, March 27. The King's company.

Globe and Blackfriars theaters. Privy Seal (?).

Printed in Hazlitt, *English Drama*, 50–52; Collier, *English Dramatic Poetry*, I, 400–401.

See above, pp. 201–202.

This patent is often misdated 1620. Hazlitt labels it "March 27, 1619–1620"; but as the year began, according to the old style, on March 25, this is meaningless. The document is indorsed "vicesimo septimo die Martii Anno. R. Regis Jacobi decimo septimo," — *i.e.* March 27, 17 James I. Elizabeth died on March 24, 1603. March 27, 1 James I, was therefore in 1603, and March 27, 17 James I, in 1619. In the *State Papers, Dom.*, 1619–1623, 28, the patent is properly dated March 27, 1619, new style.

### 1620, February 24. Patent to Robert Lea and others.

Mentioned by Sir Henry Herbert after the Restoration. Halliwell-Phillipps, *Dramatic Records*, 93.

See above, p. 64.

### 1622, July 8. The Children of the Revels.

Warrant to Robert Lee, Richard Perkins, and others, "late comedians of Queen Anne deceased" No theater named. Order for a Privy Seal.

Printed in *1821 Variorum*, III, 62, note.

### 1625, June 24. The King's company.

Globe and Blackfriars theaters.   Privy Seal.

Printed in Hazlitt, *English Drama*, 57–59; Collier, *English Dramatic Poetry*, I, 435–436.

Issued by Charles I on his taking over his father's company, and in the same form as the patent of March 27, 1619, to the same players. See above, p. 38.

### 1628, December 9.   The Lady Elizabeth's company.

Privy Seal.

Abstract in *State Papers, Dom.*, 1628–1629, 406.

### 1630–1631.   Patent to Andrew Cave and others.

Mentioned by Sir Henry Herbert after the Restoration.   Halliwell-Phillipps, *Dramatic Records*, 93.

See above, p. 64.

# LIST OF BOOKS CITED

THE following list does not represent all the sources consulted in the preparation of this essay. Its purpose is merely to indicate the full title and the edition used in the case of each of the books cited in the foot-notes, in order to facilitate reference. Articles in journals, magazines, and such series of publications as those of the Shakspere Societies and the Modern Language Association are not included here, for in all such citations sufficient particulars are given in the foot-notes.

*Acts of the Privy Council of England.* New series, 1542–1604. Ed. J. R. Dasent. 32 vols. London, 1890–1907.

Agas, Radulph. *Civitas Londinum: A Survey of the Cities of London and Westminster, the Borough of Southwark and Parts Adjacent, in the Reign of Queen Elizabeth.* Ed. W. H. Overall. London, 1874.

*Alleyn Papers: A Collection of Original Documents Illustrative of the Life and Times of Edward Alleyn and of the Early English Stage and Drama.* Ed. J. P. Collier. Shakspere Society Publications, vol. XVIII. London, 1843.

Arber, Edward. *An Introductory Sketch to the Martin Marprelate Controversy.* English Scholar's Library, no. 8.

Arber, Edward. *Transcript of the Registers of the Stationers' Company, 1554–1640.* 5 vols. London, 1875–1894.

Ascham, Roger. *The Scholemaster.* Ed. Edward Arber. Westminster, 1903.

Baker, G. P. *The Development of Shakespeare as a Dramatist.* New York, 1907.

Beaumont and Fletcher. *Works.* Ed. Henry Weber. 14 vols. Edinburgh, 1812.

Beaumont and Fletcher. *Works.* Variorum Edition. 12 vols. London, 1904–.

Benham, William, and Welch, Charles. *Mediæval London.* London, 1901.

Besant, Sir Walter. *London in the Time of the Stuarts.* London, 1903.

Birch, W. de G. *Historical Charters and Constitutional Documents of the City of London.* London, 1887.

Brandl, Alois. *Quellen des weltlichen Dramas in England.* Quellen und Forschungen zur Sprach- und Culturgeschichte, no. 80. Strassburg, 1898.

Brome, Richard. *Dramatic Works.* 3 vols. London, 1873.

Bullen, A. H. *Collection of Old English Plays.* 4 vols. London, 1882–1885.

Campbell, Douglas. *The Puritan in Holland, England and America.* 2 vols. New York, 1892.

Castelain, Maurice. *Ben Jonson: L'Homme et l'Œuvre.* Paris, 1907.

Chalmers, George. *An Apology for the Believers in the Shakspeare-Papers which were Exhibited in Norfolk-Street.* London, 1797.

Chalmers, George. *A Supplemental Apology for the Believers in the Shakspeare-Papers.* London, 1799.

Chambers, E. K. *The Mediæval Stage.* 2 vols. Oxford, 1903.

Chambers, E. K. *Notes on the History of the Revels Office under the Tudors.* London, 1906.

Chapman, George. *Works: Plays.* Chatto and Windus Edition. London, 1874.

Chapman, George. *Works: Poems and Minor Translations.* Chatto and Windus Edition. London, 1875.

Cibber, Colley. *Apology for the Life of Mr. Colley Cibber, Written by Himself.* Ed. R. W. Lowe. 2 vols. London, 1889.

Collier, J. P. *History of English Dramatic Poetry to the Time of Shakespeare, and Annals of the Stage to the Restoration.* 3 vols. London, 1879.

Collier, J. P. *Memoirs of Edward Alleyn, Founder of Dulwich College.* Shakspere Society Publications, vol. I. London, 1841.

Cunningham, Peter. *Extracts from the Accounts of the Revels at Court, in the Reigns of Queen Elizabeth and King James I.* Shakspere Society Publications, vol. VII. London, 1842.

Dodsley, Robert. *Old Plays.* Ed. W. C. Hazlitt. 15 vols. London, 1874–1876.

*1821 Variorum.* See Shakspere.

Fairholt, F. W. *History of Lord Mayors' Pageants.* Percy Society Publications, vol. X. London, 1843.

Fleay, F. G. *A Biographical Chronicle of the English Drama, 1559–1642.* 2 vols. London, 1891.

Fleay, F. G. *A Chronicle History of the London Stage, 1559–1642.* London, 1890.

Fleay, F. G. *A Chronicle History of the Life and Work of William Shakespeare, Player, Poet and Playmaker.* New York, 1886.

Foxe, John. *Ecclesiastical History, conteyning the Actes and Monumentes of Martyrs.* 2 vols. London, 1576.

Gardiner, S. R. *History of England from the Accession of James I to the Outbreak of the Civil War, 1603–1642.* 10 vols. London, 1893–1895.

Gardiner, S. R. *History of the Great Civil War.* 4 vols. London, 1893–1897.

Gosson, Stephen. *The Schoole of Abuse, containing a Pleasant Invective against Poets, Pipers, Players, Jesters and such like Caterpillars of a Commonwealth.* Shakspere Society Publications, vol. II. London, 1841.

Halliwell-Phillipps, J. O. *A Collection of Ancient Documents respecting the Office of Master of the Revels, and Other Papers relating to the Early English Theatre, from the Original Manuscripts formerly in the Haslewood Collection.* London, 1870. Running title, *Dramatic Records.*

Halliwell-Phillipps, J. O. *Illustrations of the Life of Shakespeare.* London, 1874.

Halliwell-Phillipps, J. O. *Letters of the Kings of England.* 2 vols. London, 1846-1848.

Halliwell-Phillipps, J. O. *Outlines of the Life of Shakespeare.* London, 1882.

Halliwell-Phillipps, J. O. *Visits of Shakespeare's Company of Actors to the Provincial Cities and Towns of England.* Brighton, 1887.

Harrison, William. *Description of England in Shakspere's Youth.* Ed. F. J. Furnivall. New Shakspere Society Publications, series 6, no. 1, 5, and 8. London, 1877-1881.

Hazlitt, W. C. *The English Drama and Stage, under the Tudor and Stuart Princes, 1543-1664. Illustrated by a Series of Documents, Treatises and Poems.* Printed for the Roxburghe Library, 1869.

Hazlitt, W. C. *The Livery Companies of the City of London.* London, 1892.

Henslowe, Philip. *Diary.* Ed. W. W. Greg. Part I, Text. London, 1904.

*Henslowe Papers, being Documents Supplementary to his Diary.* Ed. W. W. Greg. London, 1907.

Herbert of Cherbury, Edward, Lord. *Autobiography.* Ed. S. L. Lee. London, 1886.

Heywood, Thomas. *An Apology for Actors.* Shakspere Society Publications, vol. III. London, 1841.

*Historical MSS. Commission Reports.* London, 1871-.

Holinshed, Raphael. *First, Second and Third Volumes of Chronicles.* 3 vols. in 2. London, 1586-1587.

Ingram, J. H. *Christopher Marlowe and his Associates.* London, 1904.

Jonson, Ben. *Works.* Ed. W. Gifford and F. Cunningham. 9 vols. London, 1875.

Jonson, Chapman, and Marston, *Eastward Hoe,* and Jonson, *Alchemist.* Ed. F. E. Schelling. Belles Lettres Series. Boston, n.d.

*Journals of the House of Commons,* 1547-.

*Journals of the House of Lords,* 1509-.

Kelly, William. *Notices Illustrative of the Drama and Other Popular Amusements, chiefly in the Sixteenth and Seventeenth Centuries, Extracted from MSS. of the Borough of Leicester.* London, 1865.

Koeppel, Emil. *Quellenstudien zu den Dramen Chapm.n's, Massinger's und Ford's.* Quellen und Forschungen zur Sprach- und Culturgeschichte, no. 82. Strassburg, 1897.

Kyd, Thomas. *Works.* Ed. F. S. Boas. Oxford, 1901.

Lang, Andrew. *Social England Illustrated; a Collection of Seventeenth Century Tracts.* In the English Garner. Westminster, 1903.

*Letters and Papers, Foreign and Domestic, of the Reign of Henry VIII, Calendar of.* Ed. J. S. Brewer, J. Gairdner, and R. H. Brodie. London, 1862–.

Lodge, Edmund. *Illustrations of British History.* 3 vols. London, 1791.

Loftie, W. J. *History of London.* 2 vols. London, 1884.

Lyly, John. *Complete Works.* Ed. R. W. Bond. 3 vols. Oxford, 1902.

Lyly, John. *Endymion.* Ed. G. P. Baker. New York, 1894.

Lysons, Daniel. *Environs of London.* 7 vols. London, 1800–1811.

Maas, Hermann. *Aussere Geschichte der englischen Theatertruppen in dem Zeitraum von 1559 bis 1642.* Materialen zur Kunde des älteren english. Dramas, XIX. Louvain, n.d.

Mackay, Charles. *A Collection of Songs and Ballads relative to the London Prentices.* Percy Society Publications, vol. I. London, 1841.

Massinger, Philip. *Believe As You List.* Ed. T. C. Croker. Percy Society Publications, vol. XXVII. London, 1849.

Merewether, H. A., and Stephens, A. J. *The History of the Boroughs and Municipal Corporations of the United Kingdom.* 3 vols. London, 1835.

Middleton, Thomas. *Works.* Ed. A. H. Bullen. 8 vols. London, 1885–1886.

Nash, Thomas. *Complete Works.* Ed. A. B. Grosart. 6 vols. London, 1883–1885.

Nicholls, Sir George. *A History of the English Poor Law.* 2 vols. New York, 1898.

Nichols, John. *Progresses and Public Processions of Queen Elizabeth.* 3 vols. London, 1823.

Northbrooke, John. *A Treatise against Dicing, Dancing, Plays and Interludes.* Ed. J. P. Collier. Shakspere Society Publications, vol. XIV. London, 1843.

*Old English Drama.* 2 vols. London, 1825.

Ordish, T. F. *Early London Theatres.* London, 1894.

Price, W. H. *The English Patents of Monopoly.* Harvard Economic Studies, vol. I. Boston and New York, 1906.

Prynne, William. *Histrio-Mastix: The Players Scourge or Actors Tragœdie.* London, 1633.

Raumer, F. L. G. von. *History of the Sixteenth and Seventeenth Centuries Illustrated by Original Documents.* Translated from the German. 2 vols. London, 1835.

*Remembrancia. Analytical Index to the Series of Records Known as the Remembrancia, Preserved among the Archives of the City of London.* A.D. 1579–1664. Ed. W. H. Overall and H. C. Overall. London, 1878.

Rendle, William. *Old Southwark and its People.* Southwark, 1878.

Rushworth, J. *Historical Collections, containing the Principal Matters from the Sixteenth Year of King James to the Death of King Charles I.* 4 parts in 7 vols. 1659–1701.

Rymer, Thomas, and Sanderson, Robert. *Fœdera, Conventiones, Literæ, et Cujuscunque Generis Acta Publica.* 20 vols. London, 1726–1735.

Schelling, F. E. *Elizabethan Drama,* 2 vols. Boston and New York, 1908.

Scobell, Henry. *A Collection of Acts and Ordinances of General Use, Made in the Parliament Begun and Held at Westminster the Third Day of November, Anno 1640.* London, 1658.

Shakspere, William. *1821 Variorum. The Plays and Poems of William Shakespeare, with the Corrections and Illustrations of Various Commentators: Comprehending a Life of the Poet and an Enlarged History of the Stage by the Late E. Malone.* Ed. J. Boswell. 21 vols. London, 1821.

Sharpe, R. R. *London and the Kingdom.* 3 vols. London, 1894–1895.

*Sir Thomas More.* Ed. A. Dyce. Shakspere Society Publications, vol. XXIII. London, 1844.

Small, R. A. *The Stage Quarrel between Ben Jonson and the So-called Poetasters.* Forschungen zur englischen Sprache und Litteratur, vol. I. Breslau, 1899.

*State Papers.*

Calendar of State Papers, Domestic Series, of Edward VI, Mary, Elizabeth and James I, 1547–1625. Ed. R. Lemon and M. A. E. Green. 12 vols. London, 1856–1872.

*Calendar of State Papers, Domestic Series, of the Reign of Charles I, 1625–1649.* Ed. J. Bruce and W. D. Hamilton. 23 vols. London, 1858–1897.

*Calendar of State Papers, Domestic Series, during the Commonwealth, 1649–1660.* Ed. M. A. E. Green. 13 vols. London, 1875–1886.

*State Trials. A Complete Collection of State Trials and Proceedings for High Treason and Other Crimes and Misdemeanors.* Ed. T. B. Howell and T. J. Howell. 33 vols. London, 1816–1826.

*Statutes of the Realm.* Record Commission. 9 vols. in 10. London, 1810–1828.

Stephen, J. F. *History of the Criminal Law of England.* 3 vols. London, 1883.

Stephenson, H. T. *Shakespeare's London.* New York, 1905.

Stow, John. *A Survey of London.* Ed. W. J. Thoms. London, 1842.

Strype, John. *The History of the Life and Acts of Edmund Grindal.* Oxford, 1821.

Stubbs, William. *Constitutional History of England.* 3 vols. Oxford, 1887–1891.

Thompson, E. N. S. *The Controversy between the Puritans and the Stage.* Yale Studies in English, vol. XX. New York, 1903.

Thorndike, A. H. *The Influence of Beaumont and Fletcher on Shakspere.* Worcester, 1901.

*Variorum of 1821.* See Shakspere.

Ward, A. W. *A History of English Dramatic Literature to the Death of Queen Anne.* 3 vols. London, 1899.

Warner, Rebecca. *Epistolary Curiosities, consisting of Unpublished Letters of the Seventeenth Century, Illustrative of the Herbert Family.* Bath, 1818.

Warton, Thomas. *History of English Poetry.* 4 vols. London, 1824.

Wheatley, H. B., and Cunningham, P. *London Past and Present.* 3 vols. London, 1891.

Whitelocke, Bulstrode. *Memorials of the English Affairs from Charles I to Charles II.* London, 1682.

Winwood's *Memorials. Memorials of Affairs of State in the Reigns of Queen Elizabeth and King James I, Collected (chiefly) from the Original Papers of the Right Honourable Sir Ralph Winwood, Kt. Sometime One of the Principal Secretaries of State.* London, 1725.

Wotton, Sir Henry. *Reliquiæ Wottonianæ; or A Collection of Lives, Letters, Poems.* London, 1672.

Wright, James. *Historia Histrionica.* In Hazlitt's edition of Dodsley's *Old Plays,* vol. XV, pp. 399-431.

# INDEX

Beggars, Definition of Sturdy, 14 Elizabeth, cap. 5, 29–30

*Believe as You List*, by Massinger, refused a license by Herbert, 81; licensed on revision, 123; Gardiner on, 123–24

Benger, Sir Thomas, a very inefficient Master, 48, 50; death of, 50

Berkeley, Henry, Letter of, on playing on Sunday, 209

Bethan, Captain, appointed Provost Marshal, 227

Bible, Tyndale's translation of, condemned, 7

Bills of mortality, Increase of area covered by, 212

*Biron's Conspiracy* and *Tragedy*, Trouble from, for Chapman, 105–7; Buc's refusal to license, for the press, 106; licensed after much mutilation, 107

Blackfriars district exempt from Lord Mayor's jurisdiction, 144; payments for repairs in, referred to a commission, 145; Lord Cobham named to preserve order in, 146; granted to the City, 146, 197, 200; rights of sanctuary in, 147; inhabited largely by Puritans, 147; plays in, 185; City protested against Rosseter's Theater in, 198–99

Blackfriars Theater, 38, 76; appeal of inhabitants against, to Privy Council, 144, 184–85, 201–2; question of, puzzling, 185–87; excluded from orders for demolition, 188; Children of the Chapel at, 187, 195; commission on removal of, 203; playing at, stopped, 214; authorized theater of the Children of the Queen's Revels, 232; of the King's Company, 198, 201, 233, 234

Blagrave, Thomas, Clerk of the Revels, served as Acting Master, 48, 50

Boar's Head in Eastcheap, Performances allowed at the, 194; authorized theater of Queen's Company, 231, 232

Boar's Head without Aldgate, Players at, arrested, 12

*Bondman, The*, by Massinger, Duke of Buckingham satirized in, 123

Bonner, Bishop, of London, prohibited plays in churches, 42

Book, the usual word for a play, 80 n

Book of Common Prayer, Interludes deriding the, forbidden, 9, 13–14

Book of Sports issued by James I, 20; ratified by Charles I, 20

Bourchier, Henry, *see* Essex, Earl of

Box at each theater furnished gratis to Herbert, 76

Boyle, R., on *Barnevelt*, 115

Boys with good voices taken from schools for the Chapel Royal, 32, 48, 51; forbidden to act in plays, 38

Braynes, John, Indictment of, 160

"Bridge Without," Ward of, 141

Bristol, Messenger from Master's Office sent to, 73; Her Majesty's Servants of her Royal Chambers at, 233

Brome's, Alexander, *English Moor*, played by the Queen's Company, 129

Brooke, William, *see* Cobham, Lord

Browne, Edward, in Earl of Worcester's company, 32

Browne, Robert, in Earl of Worcester's company, 32

Buc, Sir George, appointed Master of the Revels to succeed Tilney, 62; as an author, 63; extended the Master's jurisdiction, 63–64; licensed a playhouse in Whitefriars, 64, 73–74; censored and licensed plays, of, 66; censored the *Second Maiden's Tragedy*, 78; the first to license plays for printing. 64, 79, 84; letter from Chapman to, on his refusal to license *Biron* for the press, 106; grants the license, 107; expurgations from the *Second Maiden's Tragedy*, 109–12, 118, 134; his censorship of *Sir John Van Olden Barnevelt*, 114–18; not unreasonably severe, 117. *See also* Herbert; Master of the Revels; Tilney

Buc's Office Book, 46, 74, 75; burned, 66 n

Buckingham headed movement against Spain, 119, 122; portrayed in *Game at Chess*, 119; portrayed by Massinger, 123–24

Buggin, suggests that workmen be compelled to serve the Revels Office, 48

Building and fire laws, Germ of, 207

Bull, The, in Bishopsgate St., 165

Bullbaiting forbidden on the Sabbath, 20; power to license, 46

Bullen, A. H., on *Barnevelt*, 116

Burbage, James, in Earl of Leicester's company, 33; and others driven to the Liberties, 158; indictment of, 160

Burbage, Richard, in the King's Men, 36

Burbage's private theater, *see* Blackfriars Theater

Burgess class, The wealthier, decidedly Puritan, 216

Burghley, Lord, Three reports to, on reorganization of Revels Office, 48–49; letter of Lord Mayor to, 55, 176; letter from Fleetwood to, 94; Paris Garden disaster reported to, 165–66

Calvert, Samuel, Letter of, to Winwood, on the boldness of actors, 101

Cambridge, Scholars of, that go a-begging, 30

Canterbury, Archbishop of, 13; requested to appoint a member of commission on censoring, 18, 55; requested by Aldermen of London to influence Tilney to stop plays, 55–56, 179; arranged for players to contribute to parish poor, 60, 207; and Bishop of London sole censors and licensers of all printed books, 84; and Herbert, 126; stopped playing at Blackfriars in Lent, 214

Canterbury, Mayor of, arrested actors, 12

Cardinals, Comedy acted in defamation of, 6

Castelain, M., attributes troubles of Jonson and Chapman to *Sir Giles Goosecap*, 104

S

C. A. N.

# VITA

Virginia Crocheron Gildersleeve was born in New York City on October 3, 1877. She received her early education at private schools in her native city, especially at the Brearley School, where she was prepared for college. Entering Barnard College, Columbia University, in the autumn of 1895, she proceeded to the degree of A.B. in June, 1899. During the year 1899–1900, as Fiske Graduate Scholar in Political Science at Columbia University, she pursued courses in Medieval History under Professor James Harvey Robinson, in American History under Professor Herbert L. Osgood, and in Sociology under Professor Franklin H. Giddings. She received the degree of A.M. in June, 1900. For the next five years she taught in the Department of English in Barnard College, as Assistant and Tutor. From 1905 to 1908 she devoted herself to graduate study under the Faculty of Philosophy in Columbia University, pursuing courses in English under Professor William P. Trent, Professor Ashley H. Thorndike, Professor George P. Krapp, Professor William W. Lawrence, Professor William Allan Neilson, now of Harvard University, and Professor John W. Cunliffe, now of the University of Wisconsin; in Old French under Professor Henry A. Todd; and in Comparative Literature under Professor Jefferson B. Fletcher.